£12.99

DOORS OF V[

GW01337158

Doors of Valhalla
An Esoteric Interpretation of Norse Mythology

Vincent Ongkowidjojo

Copyright First Edition © 2016 VINCENT ONGKOWIDJOJO

All rights reserved. No part of this work may be reproduced or utilized in any form by any means, electronic or mechanical, including *xerography, photocopying, microfilm*, and *recording*, or by any information storage system without permission in writing from the publishers.

Published by
Mandrake of Oxford
PO Box 250
OXFORD
OX1 1AP (UK)

Printed on acid free paper certification from three leading environmental organizations: the Forest Stewardship Council™ (FSC®), the Sustainable Forestry Initiative® (SFI®) and the Programme for the Endorsement of Forestry Certification (PEFC™)

Acknowledgements

Chiëla Wellens for illustrations
Astrid Grunwald for author photograph

Also by Vincent Ongkowidjojo

Secrets of Asgard: An Instruction In Esoteric Rune Wisdom, Mandrake, 2011

Contents

PREFACE 7
INTRODUCTION 17
DOOR 1 THE SEVEN AND THE NINE 21
DOOR 2 ON THE SEAT OF THE WILL 41
DOOR 3 AN INTERPRETATION OF THE VISION 54
DOOR 4 THE EVOLUTION OF CONSCIOUSNESS 70
DOOR 5 A BEING OF TWO WORLDS 109
DOOR 6 THE GERMANIC TRINITY 123
DOOR 7 THE MEAD OF POETRY 145
DOOR 8 THE SAYINGS OF THE ODIN 176
DOOR 9 LORD OF LOVE AND WISDOM 186
DOOR 10 THE LABOURS OF THOR 214
DOOR 11 GODS AND GODDESSES 242
DOOR 12 THE SAYINGS OF LOKI 256
DOOR 13 BEYOND THE MYTHS 296
BIBLIOGRAPHY 301
AFTERWORD BY DAVID PARRY 305

APPENDICES
VOLUSPA 309
LOKASENNA 324
CABINET DE CURIOSITÉS 339

INDEX 345

```
      E
  E   H   E
      E
```

FIMBULGALDR

From the Rune of Light within the mind of Odin
Let Light stream forth into the minds of all human beings
May Light descend on Midgard

From the Rune of Love within the heart of Odin
Let Love stream forth into the hearts of all human beings
May Balder return to Midgard

From the Well of Urd where the Will of Odin is known
Let Orlog guide the little will of every human being
The Orlog which the Aesir know and serve

From the Hall which we call Humanity
Let the Plan of Love and Light work through
And may it bind the Wolf for good

May Light and Love and Might unfold the Plan on Midgard

Preface
by Maria Kvilhaug

The "Worlds" of
Old Norse Mythology

An introduction

Few subjects are more confusing than the subject of the various *heimir* – "worlds" –in Old Norse, pre-Christian cosmology. During the decades of studying the subject, I have seen countless charts and maps attempting to make sense out of the incomprehensible, attempting to fit the Norse "worlds" into an understandable geography–and none of these attempts have been very convincing.

Nine Worlds Beneath Niflhel

If we go to the oldest primary sources, the Edda poems, we first hear of nine worlds (*níu heimir*) in the *Voluspá* poem (st.2), and these nine worlds are promptly identified as nine *iviði*–"within woods"–a feminine term that elsewhere in Norse sources describes sorceresses or giantesses. According to another Edda poem, *Hrafnagaldr Oðins*, the *iviðja* (the "within wood" sorceress) "brings forth the ages".

The nine worlds, that are also nine "within wood" sorceresses, are worlds that existed before the present world tree "sprouted from the sea below", or else nine feminine cosmic beings that came together to create the present, masculine world, which is often also described as a personified, cosmic being. We are reminded of another myth in which the god Heimdallr ("Great World") was born from nine mothers (*Heimdalargaldr*, known from the Prose Edda, and *Hyndluljóð*, Poetic Edda).

There are many references to nine such female beings in the Edda poetry, whether they are giantesses, valkyriur, norns or goddesses, and they are often identified with waves, rivers or the lights that illuminate dark space. The number nine is also associated with the number of nights that Hermóðr has to travel to reach Níflheimr, the number of nights that Óðinn has to suffer before being able to "pick up the runes", and the number of nights that Freyr has to yearn before he can reach the "breezeless grove of the pine conifer" in which he will be united with the love of his life.

Apart from that reference to nine ancient worlds somehow involved in the very creation of the present world, like nine mothers giving birth to one son, the concept of "nine worlds" is only referred to twice: By Snorri Sturluson in his Prose Edda, when he lets slip that "Hel rules nine worlds," and in the Edda poem *Vafthrúðnismál*, where the giant *Vafthrúðnir* (Powerful Head Veil) reveals that he knows the secrets of the giants and of all the gods because he has been to "all the worlds" *(hvern hefi ec heim vm komit)*, and these are elaborated in the following sentence as "nine worlds beneath Níflhel" *(nio kom ec heima, fyr niflhel neðan)*.

The Early Cosmos

"Gáp var, Ginnunga." (Voluspá, st.2)

In the Edda poem *Voluspá*, the description of the nine mother worlds to the present world tree is followed by a reference to the giant Ymir building his "settlement" at a time when there was no growth, no life, no Earth, no sea, and no sky. Only an "open mouth" *(gáp)* existed, belonging to the "sacred descendants" *(ginn-unga)*.

In the Prose Edda, Snorri tries to explain this scenario. There was this great abyss of nothingness, the *Ginnungagáp*, and in the northern end of that abyss, there was a realm of frost and ice, the *Níflheimr* (Mist World), which is the same as the *Níflhel* (Mist Hidden) beneath which the nine worlds are situated, and, ultimately, *Hel* (Hidden, the world of the dead). This primordial realm contained a well, the *Hvergelmir* (Bellowing Mill) which is the source of all the rivers that run through the cosmos, rivers that are later identified as nine giantesses.

In the southern end of that abyss, there was a realm of poisonous gases and fire, the *Muspellheimr* (Spark World), and is ruled by *Surtr* (Sooted One, Sour One), and this "heavenly lineage" is flaming and burning, and impossible to inhabit unless one is born from it. This is the realm from which the Sun is later hurled out into cosmos on her search for her "heavenly steeds" and her "halls".

Creation began when the *Élivágar*–the "ancient waves" begin to move like streams of water from the southern realm of heat and gases towards the northern realm of ice and mist. When the southern streams hardened because of the frost from the north, a being was created, or built, namely Ymir, the world giant, or primordial Sound (from *ýmr* – "sound", "murmur", "voice").

Ymir, is furthermore, nurtured by the four streams of milk that ran from the great cow, *Auðhumbla* (Abundant Brew Ingredient), who nurtured herself from the frost of Níflheimr. As her hot southern tongue swept over the frosty realm, another being slowly emerged, *Búri* (Encaged), and from this being emerged the three Aesir who gave shape to the present universe by parting the body of *Ymir* (Sound) into countless parts (tunes?). Only then could Sun claim her "halls" and shine her heating light upon the rocks of the hall Earth, which began to produce the green growth.

The Worlds of Earth, and Around

As soon as the Earth is fertile, Snorri moves onto describing her. In the Norse language, the Earth is constantly referred to as "she" and "her". In his introduction, Snorri explained that the Heathen ancestors, after observing the likenesses between Earth and all the living beings that dwell on her, concluded that the Earth has a life and mind of her own, that she is wonderful of nature, incredibly mighty and tremendously ancient, that she raises all life and takes all life back into herself, and thus they considered her the ultimate ancestral mother, and traced their lineages back to her.

She is round on the outside, Snorri now explains. This was written back in 1225AD, on Iceland. Indeed, the concept of a round Earth was well known to 13th century Norsemen, at least. In the Norwegian 1250AD document *Konungs Skuggsjá*, she is said to be *bólottr* (ball-like), and is also called *Iarðarbollr* (The Earth Ball). Outside of her lies the deep ocean (cosmos). Along the shores of this cosmic ocean do we find the land of the giants, which is later referred to as either *Iotunheimr* (Giant World) or *Utgarðr* (Outer World/Settlement). Inside the sphere of Earth, there is a wall that marks the known world, namely *Miðgarðr* (Middle Settlement), in which the first man and woman are given breath, vitality and mind by the gods. After the gods made humans, they built a place for themselves in the middle of the Middle Settlement.

The place is known as *Ásgarðr*, (God World), and here is a seat, the *Hliðskiolf* (Opening View Seat), from which Óðinn may look into all the worlds. Here also lies the *Iðavellir*, "Fields of Streams Returning to Source", *Hörg* (Sanctuary–the splendid hall of the goddesses, also known as *Vingolv*– the Floor of Friends), as well as the high seat of the All-Father and twelve other seats belonging to the other gods, and this was called *Gladsheimr* (Joy World).

If we were to make a geographical map of the worlds now presented, based on what we now know of the universe and the Earth, Snorri's description can only mean that the Giant World is the cosmic sphere that surrounds Earth, literary the Outer World (or outer space), outside of the atmosphere, because the sky is clearly described as a part of the Earth sphere. The Middle Settlement is the realm on the inside of the Earth's sky, the world in which we may walk and live and breathe. And the central realm of the gods in this round Earth, situated in the middle of the Middle World, can only be within the core of Earth herself.

That the divine realm is an underworld realm may sound weird to modern people who are used to consider the underworld or Earthly realm as lower than the heavenly ones, but this is not the case if you take the perspective of ancient Heathens. We may recall that creation and the birth of the gods began in the realm of Hel/Niflheimr. And it is the outside of the Earth's sphere that is the dark and dangerous realm in Heathen cosmology.

Snorri moves on to describe the Earth's neighborhood. To the east of *Miðgarðr,* that is, in the Outer World of the giants, there is a forest called *Jarnviðr* (Iron Wood), and there live the sorceresses known as the *jarnviði*, like the *iviði* before, ruled by the great *iviðja* who gives birth to the dangerous wolf-like sons of *Fenrir* (Greed) who devour the flesh of dead corpses, and who constantly threaten to dim out all the heavenly bodies. This is why Thor often is said to "go east" in order to slay trolls, the frosty rock giants that wage perpetual war against his mother Earth and her children.

The World Tree

From describing a cosmology that is almost scientific in its approach, albeit described in poetical terms, Snorri suddenly moves onto a description that appears far less so. Snorri claims that the gods keep their main sanctuary by the ever green ash called Yggdrasill (Old Steed), with branches that reach across the entire universe and above the heaven. He has three roots that keep him standing and that spread particularly widely.

The first root is situated in the middle of where Ginnungagáp was before, among the "frosty thurses". This used to be the place of nothingness, in which the streams first met to create the first being of sound which became the source of matter in the early universe. Now, it is ruled by frost giants. Here also lies a well, the *Mímisbrunnr* (Well of Memory), in which all the experience of the world is stored and remembered, and this well is drunk from daily by the giant *Mímir* (Memory).

The second root is situated in *Niflheimr* (Mist World) that other primordial cosmic world from which the gods emerged, and which is now ruled by Hel, the goddess of the dead. Here lies the third well, the Bellowing Mill from which all rivers run, and besides is the place where the souls of dead people are ground into flour and brought back to the world by way of the cosmic rivers. Inside this well are many serpents that suck the life out of the dead, and particularly one large serpent called Níðhoggr (Waning/Shame/Below Biter), which feeds from the world tree.

The third root is in heaven, and beneath this root lies the realm of the norns. Here, the goddesses of fate decide the laws of cosmos and the destinies of all mortals. From this realm emerge the norns that become followers to human beings, like guardian angels. This root is watered every day by the norn (fate goddess) Urðr (Origin) who takes the water with aurr (mud) from the Well of Origin. The gods from Ásgarðr, which we now know is situated in the middle of the Middle World, or within the core of Earth, ride to this root to hold parliament by way of the *Bifrost* (Shivering Voice), also known as the rainbow bridge.

The Heavenly Worlds

Snorri moves on to describe the various forces that live in this tree, but since we are about worlds, we shall move directly to his description of the heavens. We are now up by the third root, the heavenly root where the norns dwell and where the gods gather to hold parliament.

Apart from the Well of Origin, where all fate begins, there are many other realms. Snorri lists them:

1. *Alfheimr* (Elf World), where the *liósalfar* (light elves) dwell (but the *dokkalfar* – "dark elves" live beneath the Earth).
2. *Breidablik* (Broad View), the most beautiful place in Heaven, with that place called Glitnir (Shiny), home to Balder and Nanna.
3. *Himinbjorgr* (Heavenly Mountain), by the end of Heaven, where the Shivering Voice rainbow bridge ends, and where Heimdallr blows his horn.

4. *Valaskialf* (The Shelf of Choice), where Óðinn keeps his Hlíðskiolf (Opening Seat) just as he was said to keep it in Ásgarðr, and from which he may look into all the worlds.
5. *Gimlé* (Shielded from Fire) In the southern end of Heaven lies the place that is fairest of all and brighter than the Sun, where the souls of righteous and "treason-free" people are entitled to dwell.
6. *Andlangr* (Long Breath) – home of light elves. To the south of Gimlé.
7. *Víðbláinn* (The Wide Blue – or the Wide Death, since "the blue", *bláinn*, is a metaphor for a corpse or death) – home of light elves. Beyond Andlangr.

The Twelve Worlds

In one of the Edda poems that Snorri based his description on, the Grímnismál, twelve divine worlds are listed and numbered as first world, second world and so on, in the following order:

1. *Þrúðheimr* (Power World) – realm of Thor, with the *Þrúðvangar* (Power Fields), from where the thunder god protects the Earth against assaults from the Outer World.
2. *Ýdalir* (Yew Valleys) – which is also described as *Alfheimr* (Elf World), and which was once ruled by the god Ullr, but was given to the god Freyr as a tooth-gift.
3. *Valaskialf* (Shelf of the Chosen) – inhabited by the unnamed "god"
4. *Sokkvabekkr* (Sunken River) – inhabited by Óðinn and *Saga* (History – a name for Frigg) as a happy couple drinking together from golden goblets every day while cool waves resound above, and thus perhaps associated also with Frigg's realm, *Fensalar* (The Moist Halls)
5. *Gladsheimr* (Joy World) – where the Hall of the Chosen, our famous "Valhalla", may be perceived from afar. Snorri said this realm was in Ásgarðr.
6. *Þrymheimr* (Drum World) – where Skaði now dwells after the death

of her father.
7. *Breidablik* (Broad View) – Baldr's realm.
8. *Himinbjorgr* (Heaven Fortress/Mountain) – Heimdall's realm
9. *Folkvangr* (People Field) – where Freyia rules the "seating of the hall" in the People Field, choosing the chosen like a valkyria, deciding on the fates of the souls of the dead.
10. *Glitnir* (The Glittering) – where *Forseti* (Front Seated) gives just verdicts, and where all quarrels are put to sleep, and the fires of passion are quenched.
11. *Noatún* (Ships' Harbor) – where Njorðr dwells, steering the winds and the waves and the rivers of the world – the place the ships of life return.
12. *Víðarr's Land Víði* (The Wide Land of the Expanding One) – The mentioning of this twelfth world is the beginning of a series of stanzas that describe the realm of Valhalla in a way that appears to be poetical riddles attempting to describe a higher state of being.

My Thoughts on the Twelve Worlds

Even though there are some aspects to the Old Norse descriptions that appear more like natural philosophy well on its way towards a scientific understanding of the cosmos, delving deeper only makes them more confusing, because the worlds seem to fluidly overlap one another, and the descriptions of their whereabouts often seem contradictory. This could be because we are dealing with many different traditions and sources, and the fact that no Heathen ever wrote down a dogmatic text that put the "one truth" down once and forever.

But we could also be dealing with metaphorical descriptions. Old Norse myths and poetry are characterized exactly by their way of describing a few things in countless different poetical terms. It is very possible that the worlds could, on some level, for example be describing inner states of being or perception just as much as they are attempting to describe the world and the dimensions of reality around us.

In my book, *The Seed of Yggdrasill*, I suggested that we could perhaps reach a better understanding if we looked at the myths from the perspective of Indian yogis who understand the gods and their realms as realms within ourselves, or at least corresponding with realms within our own beings, each "chakra" in the energetic body being perceived as the abode of particular gods and goddesses. I also suggested that if we look at how the twelve worlds are being described and the associations to the gods that inhabit them, we could be looking at levels of perception or being. The twelve worlds could correspond to forces within ourselves:

1. Electromagnetism (Thor's realm), Thought, Mind
2. Passion, Hunger, Life Force, Growth, Vitality (Freyr the god of growth/Ullr the hunter)
3. Spirit, breath, awareness
4. Subconscious, the silent knowledge of everything, not spoken (Frigg knows all destiny but speaks not)
5. Joyful state of hope where Valhalla (salvation) may be seen from afar and the dead may be chosen
6. Desire, Hunger, Danger, Vibration (Drum World)
7. Objective and just perception, harmonious, mutual love, wisdom, compassion, completion, broadness of mind (Balder's Broad View)
8. The highest perception, ability to hear, see and remember everything (Heimdallr, Mímir)
9. Here, the fate of people in life and death is ruled by Freyia.

It was earlier said that Hel rules in nine worlds, and since Hel is equal to death, we could perhaps suggest that the first nine worlds are the worlds of mortals, the worlds in which people can still die – indeed, "the nine worlds beneath Níflhel".

In the Edda poem *Vafthrúdnismál*, the giant brags that he knows so much because he has been to all the worlds – all the nine worlds beneath Níflhel. And yet he is beaten by Óðinn because Óðinn knows the secret he whispered into the ears of his dead son's corpse: the secret to immortality, the worlds beyond the mortal realms.

It is in the ninth world that Freyia decides whether a soul should stay with her (in her nine worlds of mortality), or be sent on its way to Valhalla. Thus the next three worlds could very well correspond to the three worlds mentioned by Snorri as being the home of light elves and immortals.

10. *Glitnir* – The Glittering: Justice, calm, inner peace, home of righteous souls, survivors of Ragnarok, and the children of the gods who survived also. Could correspond to Snorri's Gimlé (Shielded from Fire). This is the place where passion is quenched and all quarrels end.
11. *Noatún* - Movement, vibration, returning to the origin (ships symbolize life). Could correspond to Snorri's *Andlangr* (Long Breath) where the immortal Light Elves live.
12. The Wide Land of the Expanding One - "The Wolf of Greed" is conquered and the soul is expanded. Could correspond to Snorri's *Viðbláinn*, the "Wide Death".

I have left further speculations about the various "worlds" to others to contemplate, hoping to be of assistance in the gathering of "facts" – that is, the facts of what the Edda poets and Snorri Sturluson said about cosmos. In his *Doors of Valhalla*, Vincent Ongkowidjojo makes an honest attempt to consider the worlds of Norse mythology as various planes of consciousness on the path towards spiritual enlightenment in the light of Theosophy and Vedic traditions.

Maria Kvilhaug (MA), author of *The Seed of Yggdrasill*

INTRODUCTION

What is consciousness? Consciousness is the light by which the human being sees. What he sees, he records in the archives of his mind. Information is gathered by the five external senses, their internal correspondences and their subtle correspondences.

By the light of the mind, the individual sees himself as separate of what surrounds him. Realization of the separation of the external world and the internal world generates a sense of self-consciousness. A standpoint is taken. A personality is born.

The person makes of his personality what he thinks he is, either in accordance with the Law of Evolution or in conflict. If in conflict, the Law of Karma binds him, but by the light of the mind, the individual sees the relation between cause and effect and understands the responsibility he has over his own life.

The individual understands that he has a choice and can make a difference amongst his peers. Slowly but surely he exerts his right to Free Will. The individual learns to master his own destiny. And by the light of the mind, the individual sees ahead and builds towards an ideal future.

The whole story of evolution is an alternation of action and reaction. Consciousness is the capacity to aptly respond to change by exploiting memory. The aptness of responding improves through experimentation. The choice to act in any given situation teaches the individual the relation between cause and effect, between the application of will and the consequent result. Any conscious act of intention refines the personality. The long process of experimentation slowly but surely develops the individual's intelligence.

All reaction to action is recorded in memory and after the initial chain of action and reaction, the cut of the reaction remains. This generates memory. Water from a source eventually reaches the sea, but the river remains in existence.

Awareness is a type of reaction, registering the impact of change upon the mind. The person can either be conscious of it or not. Even if you are unaware of the drop of water flowing in the river, it is still there and moving.

Every decision is the product of what has been learned in the past and what is aimed at in the future. The conscious application of these aspects defines the evolution of mankind.

Intention is the capacity to create change. If the human being was comprised of memory and awareness only, he would be a slave of his world. Through intention, he is able to become a master. He grasps toward what he cannot yet know. The power of Free Will forces the mind of the individual to act in the present. The person is then faced with the aspects of his being with which he daily works.

Memory	Past	Passive passive
Awareness	Past-Present	Active passive
Decision	Present-Future	Active active
Intention	Future	Passive active

Because these aspects of the mind are related to aspects of time, their functions correspond to the Norns of Norse mythology; the decision-making ability to Verdandi. Her name means Who is Becoming. The aspect of intention corresponds to Skuld, the young Norn of the future, who is also a Valkyrie. Her role on the battlefield exemplifies the need to act. Her name can be interpreted as Promise. Urd is the awareness of what has happened, a resource of knowledge and experience. The fourth aspect, memory, can be equated with Mimir.

The role of these mental aspects resounds in the myths. And as the story of the gods unfolds, so does the evolution of consciousness.

The Ageless Wisdom

Esoteric philosophy promulgates that a human being has not only a body but also a soul. Throughout history, this has been the natural viewpoint regardless of culture or nation. World religions are based on the premise; priesthood and witch doctor exist because of this. Even if today's ideas about the invisible side of nature are confused, we can still allow for the hypothesis of an immanent spiritual aspect.

Today's confusion arises from the inability of the exact sciences to explain two of the most basic phenomena that we experience. What is life? What is consciousness? Esoteric science provides an answer to these questions. What is more, it explains the relationship between things. One of the main principles to acquire is the Law of Cause and Effect. This goes beyond the mechanic laws of nature. It deals primarily with energies and forces.

Esoteric science speaks plainly about the things you cannot see but are always there. The modern Western tendency towards rational thinking focuses the mind on concrete things and ends in materialism. Yet, the body of lore that esoteric science teaches has always been available to one and all. It has been given out publicly by prophets. Privately it was taught in the mystery schools of old. We believe that the early Germanic peoples and later their Northern European descendants had exactly such schools in which students were trained in the Ageless Wisdom.

The principles and laws of esoteric science were associated with deities and natural phenomena. Relations between man and his soul were visualized in myth and ritual. The body of lore was specific for each school, area and epoch, but its underlying truths were always universal. Indeed, it is my earnest viewpoint that initiates of Germanic mystery schools were in contact with Celtic schools and maybe even with those of Ancient Greece.

There is no isolation when one embarks on a spiritual Path. No.

Instead, it opens the mind, and energy flows from one particular path into the universal one.

Throughout the ages myths have been the main instrument to lead people unto the spiritual path. The images of myth and story create a response in the mental and astral vehicles of the individual, and they sink deeply into the subconscious. But behind the symbols and images lie real energies and entities. And thus the common man and woman are gently seduced to partake of the deep current of the world of ideas, ideals, truth, vision and Light.

Mythological cycles around the world are specifically connected to certain group minds and folk minds, but are nothing less than a different clothing of one and the same truth. Today, however, humanity is moving towards a more universal approach. Universal truth can and must be expressed individually, but it will always be rooted in a common source. It is therefore necessary to open the ways of our forebears to the current of a universal teaching.

In modern days, the Ageless Wisdom was first given out by Helena Petrovna Blavatsky and later by different writers such as Dion Fortune, Annie Besant, and Alice Bailey. They all use a very specific terminology inspired by Hindu mythology. Much of these concepts have found their way into the modern mind. It therefore makes sense to relate what they have to say about the world of the soul to the myth and mystery of Ancient Scandinavia. It is my intention to translate Norse mythology into the common language of esoteric philosophy.

DOOR 1
THE SEVEN AND THE NINE

According to a person's development, consciousness tends to centre on either ideas or feelings. In esoteric teaching, these two fields of experience relate to two different planes of reality. Ideas are the objects of the mental plane whereas feelings relate to the emotional plane. Although thoughts and feelings are intangible, people experience them as real. And still the average human being only sees and recognizes the plane of tangible matter; on this plane, the physical body is found.

Contemporary exoteric science starts from the bottom up. It explores physical reality and tries to explain subtler experiences such as feeling and thinking as products of physical phenomena. Esoteric science explains things from the top down. It starts with a concept of the absolute and states that a higher plane of existence influences a lower plane. From this perspective, brain activity and hormonal secretion are effects caused by mental and emotional changes.

A layered reality explains why we are able to raise consciousness; in meditation, it expands when it reaches a higher plane. The efforts of attaining a higher state result in initiation which is the method to stabilize the mind on a higher plane.

The ever-growing inclusiveness of human consciousness is symbolized by Yggdrasil. The tree grows ever larger and more perfect. It is rooted in nine worlds signifying the different states of attainment.

The Layers of Reality

Esoteric literature usually lists seven distinct planes. We have already encountered the physical plane, the astral or emotional plane, and the mental plane. Beyond that there is a causal plane on which the soul is found. Even higher states exist above that.

The lower planes are easier to define because they are more familiar to us. The nature of the higher planes remains a little vague. It follows that the many authors on esoteric matters have slightly differing interpretations of the seven planes, although the same names always return.

The three lowest planes are never disagreed upon. They are the physical, emotional and mental. But Dion Fortune, for example, divides most of her planes into two sublayers. She has a lower emotional and an upper emotional, and a lower mental and an upper mental realm. In this way, she arrives at seven planes much quicker than most other writers.

Alice Bailey has the most elaborate system. In her work, it is explained that every plane contains seven subplanes. This makes up 49 planes. The lowest plane is the physical plane, of which the three lowest subplanes coincide with the three states of aggregation, namely solid, liquid and gaseous. The upper four subplanes form the etheric layer of reality. All this subdividing easily makes room for discerning nine distinct planes associated with the Nine Worlds of Norse mythology.

Many of the planes are associated with concepts from the Sanskrit language due to the influence of Blavatsky's work. The emotional world is termed Kama. The mental world is Manas. The word is cognate with the English 'mind' and the Rune name Mannaz. The next two levels are usually associated with the soul although Blavatsky originally intended them to also pertain to the Monad. They are labelled Buddhi and Atma. Buddhi corresponds to the Gnostic term Nous. The Sanskrit word is related to the English verb 'to bud'. Atma is cognate with Old Norse *önd*. Respectively, they correspond to intuition and spirit. The Buddhic Plane is that of the intuition. It symbolizes to the seat of the soul. The levels above that are too abstract to describe, but the first is the world of the human Monads. The other has no name in the English language.

	Blavatsky	Leadbeater	Fortune	Bailey	Powell	Steiner
7.		Adi	Unmanifest	Logoic	Adi	
6.	Atma	Anupadaka	Upper Spiritual	Monadic	Anupadaka	
5.	Buddhi	Atma	Lower Spiritual	Spiritual	Spiritual	Spirit-Man
4.		Buddhi	Higher Mental	Intuitional	Intuitional	Life-Spirit
3.	Higher Manas	Mental		Abstract Mental	Mental	Conscious Soul
	Lower Manas		Lower Mental	Concrete Mental		Intellectual Soul
2.		Astral	Upper Astral	Emotional	Emotional	Sentient Soul
			Lower Astral			
1.	Prana	Physical	Etheric	Etheric	Physical Activity	Etheric Body
	Astral					
	Physical			Physical		Physical Body

The table shows the input of some influential writers on the subject. Blavatsky, Leadbeater, Bailey and Powell all use the Sanskrit words, which are not displayed in the table unless no other concept is associated with the plane. The tabulation reflects my understanding of their respective terminology.

In Blavatsky's work, the concept Atma refers to the human Monad and Buddhi refers to the soul. The latter is sometimes called the Causal Body. Her Lower Manas includes the concept of Kama, associated with the animal body. Consciousness is called Kama-Manas if referring to the lower mind and Buddhi-Manas if to the higher. Prana is the life principle on the physical plane. Her concept of astral body is misleading in modern writing because the etheric body is intended.

The term Kama-Manas is also used in Bailey's writings. In my understanding, it refers to an individual's psyche, because the activity of the lower mental and the emotional nature are sometimes hard to discriminate. Bailey calls the lower mind the Concrete Mental and the higher mind the Abstract Mental. The latter is also termed the Causal Plane. Powell's terminology largely coincides with that of Bailey. The seventh plane is also called Divine in Bailey's writings.

Steiner's concepts refer particularly to the states of human consciousness and not to the planes on which they operate. Hence his ninefold terminology. The Sentient Soul (*Empfindungsseele*) coincides with the lower Soul Body (*Seelenleib*). His Conscious Soul (*Bewusstseinsseele*) coincides with the higher Spirit-Self (*Geistselbst*).

The Lower Spiritual of Dion Fortune is the plane on which the human Monads differentiate according to the seven Rays. It therefore corresponds to the Atmic Plane. On the Upper Spiritual Plane, the Monads reside. Her Higher Mental Plane seems to correspond to the quality of intuition, but her correlations are not clear.

The Logoic Plane refers to the plane of manifestation on which the consciousness of the Planetary Logos resides. The concept of Logos refers to either planetary or solar entities.

Man on the Planes

Since the human being is a being on almost all those levels, ranging from the Monadic down to the physical, he experiences the forces of each in one way or another. On each plane, the Self appropriates the substance of the plane to interact with that plane. These are the selves or vehicles that comprise the human being. That is why we speak of the physical, etheric, emotional, mental, causal body, or vehicle.

Most teachings and ancient traditions agree on a layered reality including the physical, emotional and mental in our direct experience of perception, but always include higher states of consciousness relating to soul and spirit. These concepts have names in Egyptian, Greek, Gnostic, Chinese tradition, and in many others. Naturally, the same applies to the

Northern tradition. Concepts such as *geð*, Hugr and Hamr are intrinsically linked with the layers of reality on which the individual functions.

Most advanced systems of teaching divide the human self into triads. The concepts of soul and spirit are each subdivided into three aspects. Similarly, the physical, emotional and mental levels comprise one triad. In the works of Alice Bailey, this latter triad encompasses the personality. The complete human being is a triad of personality, soul and Monad. The soul includes the Higher Manas, Atma and Buddhi. The Monad has three aspects, relating to the three Rays of Aspect, namely Power, Love/Wisdom and Intelligence.

Rudolf Steiner, too, discerns nine selves. These nine are subdivisions of a greater triad, namely body, soul and spirit. His concept of body contains the same aspects as in other esoteric traditions. Yet, he relates only the physical, etheric, and astral vehicles to the body proper. His concept of soul is divided into a Sentient Soul, an Intellectual Soul, and a Consciousness Soul. The spirit subdivides into spirit-self, life-spirit, and spirit-man. These correspond to Manas, Buddhi, and Atma respectively.

The ninefold system is also found in Gurdjieff's teachings. One of his main ideas is the Law of Three, meaning that every phenomenon is the result of three forces. He furthermore states that a process happens in seven steps, which he calls the Law of Seven. The combination results in his Enneagram diagram.

So, the seven are really nine.

The idea of a triad of triads seems universal. The Kabbalistic Tree of Life consists essentially of three triads. In the Northern tradition, we have Nine Worlds, rooted in three wells. It seems reasonable to associate the Nine Worlds with the nine selves.

The different worlds of perception are areas of consciousness ranging from the very dense to the very subtle. That is what it means to ascend or descend Yggdrasil. The individual is able to raise his awareness

7.	Adi	Logoic		Ginnungagap	0.
6.	Anupadaka	Monadic	Monad	Muspelheim	1.
5.	Atma	Spiritual	Soul	Alfheim	2.
4.	Buddhi	Intuitional		Vanaheim	3.
3.	Manas	Causal		Asgard	4.
		Mental	Personality	Midgard	5.
2.	Kama	Emotional		Jotunheim	6.
1.		Etheric		Svartalfheim	7.
				Niflheim	8.
		Physical		Helheim	9.

up and down the World Tree through an act of effort. According to Norse mythology, the Nine Worlds are extensions of the Tree.

The consciousness of most people today is either centred on the emotional or on the mental plane. Through meditation, the mind deepens and becomes aware of the body and its etheric counterpart. These correspond to Niflheim and Svartalfheim. From that deeper state of mind, consciousness can be raised to the deep emotional and the deep mental, corresponding to Jotunheim, Midgard, Asgard and Vanaheim.

Let us discuss each of the Worlds from this perspective.

HELHEIM

The densest realm is Helheim, the world of the dead. It is called the Plane of Effects because nothing can be caused upon this plane. What happens on one plane is always caused by the plane above it and what is caused by that plane will produce an effect on a lower plane. There is no plane lower than the dense physical plane. It therefore curiously relates to death.

Death symbolizes the transmutation of energy from any plane to the plane below it. That is why the realm of Hel or Hella is the symbol of the dense physical plane. Helheim is the only world where no creation is possible. It is an archive. On this plane, the physical body is found.

It is said that the physical plane is not a principle. For example, we can imagine how the weak and strong forces as well as electro-magnetism and gravity cause what we perceive as the material world. The material world cannot cause something itself. It can only appear, behaving according to laws governed by a layer of reality deeper than itself.

NIFLHEIM

Helheim is a place in Niflheim. We therefore surmise that Niflheim belongs to the physical plane as well. The difference between the two is the following. Helheim is the world we perceive through the five external senses, such a sight, hearing, and touch. Niflheim is what we perceive when we lock down input from the external senses and bring awareness back to what happens inside the body. We suddenly become aware of the breathing, the heartbeat, warmth in the body, and so on. These sensations are registered with the five internal senses, such as pressure sensors and heat sensors. Through those sensors, a person is able to detect the etheric or energy body.

In order to shift awareness from the external world to the physical internal world the superficial mind must be shut off. It takes a slightly deeper state of mind to become aware of the body's internal sensations. This is always the first step in meditation. As Helheim is associated with the superficial waking consciousness, Niflheim is associated with the so-called body mind. We can possibly consider Niflheim and Helheim to be one realm.

SVARTALFHEIM

Snorri Sturluson compares the dwarves with maggots. They crawl like larvae in the flesh of Ymir. The giant was killed by the gods and his corpse was used to shape the Earth. From its body, the dwarven race emerged. At some point, the gods decided that these creatures could become useful and gave them intelligence.

The dwarven realm is situated very close to the body. It comprises the living, and even intelligent, counterpart of the physical vehicle. Therefore Svartalfheim represents the etheric body.

Dwarves are associated with the earth, with stone and rock. They live in the earth and underneath it, but never on it. Their life permeates the physical body. Many legends picture their zeal and activity. They represent vitality or Prana.

JOTUNHEIM

The giant kind is associated with the world of emotions. There are a handful of reasons for this. First of all, the giants are older than the gods which means that they represent a more primitive state of consciousness. Secondly, they are masters of illusion and magic. Their magical abilities are mentioned everywhere in the myths, but the story of Thor travelling to Utgard is a typical example. Utgard is a different name for Jotunheim. Thirdly, they are associated with water a number of times. The alchemical element of Water is a universal symbol of the emotions and the astral world. The first habitat of the giants is Niflheim, which is a world of water. In the creation story, they also drown in water. Their second habitat is by the sea. They are pushed to Midgard's shores because the gods would like to settle on the land. Moreover, Utgard is depicted as an island in the sea. Kvilhaug particularly associates the giantesses with the sea, the gods of the sea and islands in the sea. And last but not least, their names and actions evoke strong emotions. Anger and passion are the two emotions displayed most.

The gods, as exponents of the rational mind, try to manage the giants and their activities.

MIDGARD

Midgard represents the energy with which humanity is mostly working today. This world stands for the concrete mental realm. This means that mankind is constantly looking for ways to express ideas, ideals and visions in a physical way.

Midgard coincides with the human psyche. It represents that typical modern aspect of the human being which constantly thinks, ponders and worries. Being centred in this world explains why people think in words, while the members of the animal world think in pictures and feelings. In the human world, we always feel the need to verbalize what we think and feel.

Midgard represents a necessary stage in the evolution of consciousness. It centres the mind of the individual on the mental plane. From the concrete mental, he will readily discover the world of the abstract mental. And the latter will become his ticket into the kingdom of the soul. Being mentally centred is a prerequisite to soul contact. In this way, Yggdrasil becomes the alignment of the threefold personality with the soul and beyond.

ASGARD

The world of the gods represents the ideal of humanity. Asgard symbolizes the world of the soul. From their own plane, the Aesir are Lords of Inspiration, moving the minds of men and women into right action, right speech and right thought.

The Aesir are creator gods. They create thought-forms, causing effects on the lower planes. The Aesir are also gods of order and organization. They differentiate between one thing and another. And everything they do has been well thought through. Every day they hold counsel and discuss the affairs of the world. All this is typical of the mental world. The heavenly Asgard represents the alchemical element of Air, which has always been the symbol of the mental world. This world stands for such abstract fields of study as mathematics, metaphysics and gnosis.

In particular, Asgard represents the causal plane.

VANAHEIM

The next world, which the individual contacts, is the Buddhic Plane. While the Aesir represent the rational and the mental, the Vanir are the complete opposite. They embody the feeling world, they communicate through empathy, and they sense things before they happen. They represent intuition. The Vanir, in particular the goddesses, are famous for knowing the future. Frigg knows the fate of every being.

Living in this world will result in a more peaceful existence. It is the world of "perfect trust and perfect love". The currents from this world make a person understand why people do what they do.

ALFHEIM

Frey of the Vanir is the Lord of the Light Beings of Alfheim. The elven race is usually described as being beautiful, light, and pure. Their realm lies to the south, close to the Source of all material existence, symbolized by Muspelheim. As such, the elves represent the Masters of the Wisdom. In Norse myth and poetry, the Aesir and Alfar are often mentioned together. They comprise one group of souls, namely the Spiritual Hierarchy.

Alfheim is characterized by a sense of freedom and a sense of bliss.

MUSPELHEIM

In relation to the other worlds, Muspelheim is an ancient world beyond reach. It existed before anything else and caused creation to develop. Snorri identifies this world with 'light'. Sparks (*gneisti*) and particles (*sía*) were flung from the Fire World into the wide Unmanifest of Ginnungagap. These sparks represent the human Monads preparing for appropriating the different selves down to the etheric layer.

According to *Gylfaginning* 8, *gneistar* and *síur* were taken from Muspelheim and the stars were made from them. The symbolism is clear if we remember Crowley's adage "Every man and every woman is a star". Muspelheim correlates to the Monadic plane.

GINNUNGAGAP

Ginnungagap is not really a world. Rather it is a condition of potential in which the Nine Worlds are embedded. It is itself the product of higher forces, symbolized by Muspelheim and Niflheim, but on a higher arc. This condition corresponds to Fortune's concept of the Unmanifest. It is only unmanifest in relation to the seven planes of perception with which we deal here. On its own level, it will be subdivided again in seven times seven planes. Therefore, if the seven planes discussed above represent the 'physical' plane from a cosmic point of view, than the Unmanifest of Ginnungagap equates more or less with the cosmic astral plane.

The Seven Rays

Another grand septenary wielded in esoteric literature is that of the seven Rays. These currents of energy are associated with particular colours and qualities.

Dion Fortune correlates the seven Rays with the seven planes. When she names the Rays she calls them by the name of the planes. From the writings of Alice Bailey, a similar correlation seems true. Nonetheless, the Rays must be seen as seven objective energies manifesting in every aspect of life and on every plane of existence.

The seven Rays are divided into three primary Rays of Aspect and four subsidiary Rays of Attribute. The seven are the Ray of Power, the Ray of Love and Wisdom, the Ray of Active Intelligence, the Ray of Harmony, the Ray of Science, the Ray of Devotion, and the Ray of Ceremonial Order.

Let us discuss them from the perspective of the Northern tradition.

FIRST RAY

The First Ray is called the Ray of Power or the Ray of Will. In the mind, it is expressed as intention. In magic, it is known as Thelema, the Higher Will. It expresses itself as destruction. Everything it touches shatters. Its power is likened to lightning that strikes. But the destruction of the form liberates the content. It releases energy and manifests power. This is how creation and destruction are linked.

Qualities associated with this Ray are strength, perseverance and open-mindedness. In the personality this power manifests as ambition, pride, willfulness and the desire to control others.

The energy of this Ray is nicely embodied in the Hindu god Shiva. He is a god of both creation and destruction. In the Norse myths, the Great Architect behind the destruction of the world is identified as Surt. This fire giant of Muspelheim represents pure power. Nothing can withstand it. In a contained form we encounter its power as Thor.

Aphorisms taken from *Esoteric Psychology* associated with this Ray are "dynamic power, solitariness, detachment and singleness of purpose". These qualities suit Surt and Thor. As pure Will, the Ray manifests through Odin's aspect as Vili. The fiery aspect of this energy is especially found in myths about the Norse solar goddess. According to Norse legend, the heat of the Sun destroys.

The magical weapons Gungnir and Mjolnir wield First Ray energy. Its power is also felt in the great event of Ragnarok.

SECOND RAY

The Second Ray is the Ray of Love/Wisdom. The concepts of Love and Wisdom are so intimately connected that they are one and the same thing in relation to this energy current. The virtues of this Ray are love, empathy and the ability to see the other's point of view. Its vices are suspicion, selfishness and indifference.

An abstract concept related to this Ray is the Word. Wisdom, Love and the Word are all attributes of Odin. Moreover, he is the Cosmic Christ, who is the state of consciousness associated with this Ray. According to Dion Fortune, love is the great quality of this Ray. She calls it the Christian Ray, after Jesus of Nazareth, and associates it with the Concrete Spiritual Plane. The Second Ray manifests as intuition.

Other epithets of the Lord of this Ray are Giver of Wisdom and Conferrer of Names. The epithets suit Odin. Odrerir is the vessel in which all the Second Ray qualities are gathered.

THIRD RAY

The Third Ray is the Ray of Active Intelligence. Sometimes, it is called the Ray of Adaptability or the Ray of the Higher Mind. Abstract thinking, such as higher mathematics and philosophy are associated with this Ray. Some of its qualities are sincerity, clear intellect, caution and patience. Wrongly expressed it manifests as criticism.

The concepts of adaptability and pragmatism suit the shapeshifting abilities of Loki. He is a problem-solving god. The same concepts apply to Kvasir, who is viewed as a god of wisdom. In Odin, the energy expresses itself as common sense.

Some of the aphorisms of this Ray are "the power to produce synthesis on the physical plane, the power to evolve, the power to manifest, and balance". The story of the Vanic War and the subsequent creation of Kvasir are linked with these phrases. Kvasir is known for his good counsel. He is The One Who Produces Alliance, which is one of the names for the Lord of this Ray. Incidentally, many of Kvasir's traits are shared with Heimdal.

Titles for this Lord's Ray include Keeper of Records and Lord of Memory. These epithets suit Mimir and the Norns.

FOURTH RAY

The Fourth Ray is that of Harmony, Beauty, Art, and Unity. It is often called the Ray of Harmony through Conflict because its energy usually produces conflict. A state of balance and harmony is achieved through the friction of opposing energies. This is experienced as struggle or suffering, but in the long run it always yields personal growth. Again, it reminds us of the story of the truce between the Aesir and Vanir. Powell names this Ray the Ray of Activity.

The keywords of this Ray apply to Freyja. She embodies the dual aspects of desire; the one tends to the body, the other to the spirit. Her magnetism expresses the dynamics of any pair of opposites. The Vanir in general embody Fourth Ray qualities, such as strong affections, sympathy, generosity, and, for Njord in particular, worrying.

In Egyptian myth, the Ray is associated with the birth of Horus. The story corresponds to the birth of Balder. As a son of Frigg and Odin, he symbolizes the synthesis of the Aesir and Vanir, of the male and female, of heaven and earth. The archetypal Son may as well be Thor.

The Ray explains the need for involution and incarnation in order to evolve and aspire. Balder may be associated with this Ray, because he "penetrates the depths of matter" as the words from *Esoteric Psychology* put it. Balder is also known as the most beautiful god. The ring Draupnir is associated with this Ray. Njord, too, is associated with this Ray. He has an aspect of beauty, in particular his feet, referring to the plane of matter. After the Vanic War, he integrates his own family into the bigger family of the Aesir.

The Fourth Ray governs humanity as a whole. The conflict of the human being is that of standing midway between two worlds. The human being is a being of light in incarnation, and for the most part not conscious of it. That makes the gods Mannaz, Heimdal and Thor guardians of this Ray. Odin and his self-sacrifice on the Tree of Death also relate to this Ray.

FIFTH RAY

The Fifth Ray is the Ray of Concrete Knowledge and Science. It relates to information. This Ray primarily reflects the qualities of the Third Ray. As the Third Ray corresponds to the higher mind, the Fifth is called the

Ray of the Lower Mind. Keywords are accuracy, justice, common sense, but also arrogance and prejudice.

The quality of this Ray is associated with the work of the dwarves. The Brisingamen necklace is the associated object.

Names for the Lord of this Ray include the Divine Intermediary, Heavenly One, the Guardian of the Door, the Connector, the Door into the Mind Divine, the Dispenser of Knowledge. All of these epithets suit Heimdal rather well. He guards the Aesic heaven and connects it with humankind through the Bridge of Fire. In *Rigsthula*, he travels among mankind in order to dispense good advice for the profane and esoteric knowledge for the occult. The god is likened to the Cherubim guarding the Gates of Eden with their flaming sword.

Some of the aphorisms of this Ray also point to Heimdal. Such a one as "the manifestation of the great white light" refers to him as the White God; and "purification with fire" relates to Bifrost. The bridge connects heaven and earth in two ways. It functions as a means of incarnation on the one hand and as a way of initiation on the other. The Fifth Ray supposedly carries the initiatic energy. This associates with Bifrost/Heimdal and Gungnir/Odin.

SIXTH RAY

The Sixth Ray is the Ray of Devotion, Idealism. It is expressed in all those who fight for what they believe in. In a most extreme form, it creates fanatics. The quality of this Ray reminds us of the Second Ray.

The energy of this Ray implies the effort to achieve. One of the weapons to accomplish this is the sword. Frey was willing to give away his sword in exchange for the object of his devotion represented by Lady Gerd. The fact that Gerd is threatened with a curse to coax her into a marriage with Frey suits this Ray. The end justifies the means.

Another sword is wielded by Vidar, who devotes his life to one significant moment. His final act liberates man and god from the wolf

Fenrir. Before that time, Vidar is the Silent God. He has the "power to detach oneself". His purpose borders on "self-immolation". The developing qualities of this Ray, such as strength, self-sacrifice, purity, truth and serenity, relate to Vidar.

The Ray is associated with the red of desire and blood. The magic that this results in might be associated with Odin. One particular epithet of this Lord's Ray is the One Who leads the Twelve. Some of the same qualities are found in Thor and Tyr. Both gods team up in *Hymiskvida* in order to obtain a certain object. The qualities of single-mindedness, loyalty, reverence, over-rapid conclusions and fiery anger suit Thor well. Typical vices are jealousy, superstition and self-deception.

SEVENTH RAY

The Seventh Ray is the Ray of Ceremonial Order, or Magic, sometimes called Ceremonial Organization. The Ray has a close connection with the First Ray. Qualities include perseverance and self-reliance, but also routine, formalism and narrow-mindedness.

As the names of this Ray reveal, its energy is expressed through creation and organization. The elemental forces are closely associated with this energy. This Ray consequently possesses "the power to create, the power to vivify and the purpose of revealing the divine beauty". The power to vivify relates to the vitality of the physical body. All these associations point to the race of dwarves. The rhythms of law and order associated with this Ray connect with Tyr.

In a symbolic sense, the power to create includes the building of thought-forms, which are tangible forms of thought on the mental and astral plane. This connects the Ray with Odin as a Magician and a Demiurge.

In *Esoteric Psychology*, it is said of this Ray Lord that his brothers whispered the qualities of his existence into his ear when he "left the most high place and descended into the seventh sphere to carry out the work". The phrase reminds us of Balder, who is shipped to Helheim after his death. Odin whispered secrets into his ears before he sailed off. In the myth, death symbolizes the transition from a higher to a lower plane.

Ray I	Thor
Ray II	Odin
Ray III	Mimir
Ray IV	Freyja
Ray V	Heimdal
Ray VI	Vidar
Ray VII	Balder

The first three Rays form a triad which is found in basically every other triad. In the Northern tradition, such triads include Odin, Vili, Vé, and Urd, Verdandi, Skuld, and Utgard, Midgard, Asgard, and Niflheim, Muspelheim, Ginnungagap. If pertaining to creation, these three Rays respectively symbolize an urge or intention, an energizing or activation, and a creation or forming.

Similarly, the Rays of Aspect relate to the three aspects of the mind: intention, awareness, and decision. In their turn, they relate to the three aspects of linear time. And in a mysterious way, they correlate to creation itself. Consciousness is movement caused by intention and creating memory.

In addition, the three Rays of Aspect correspond to the three colours of Bifrost. According to *Gylfaginning*, the Rainbow Bridge has three colours but mainly contains fire. According to *Esoteric Psychology*, the colours of the three first Rays are red, blue and yellow. The red of the First Ray corresponds to Thor. The blue of the Second Ray corresponds to Odin. And the yellow of the Third Ray might well correspond to Frey. These three gods were worshipped as a triad in the old Uppsala temple. Some say the colours are red, indigo and green, but it comes down to the same thing.

The Northern Mysteries Current

Dion Fortune's system of Rays is less lucid than that of Alice Bailey. Fortune assigns different names to the Rays referring to the exemplar schools of the Ray's qualities. Subsequently, she connects them with the planes of reality from which these schools draw their energy. In addition, she works with a colour scale to designate the Rays. Information on the Rays is found in her books *Esoteric Orders and Their Work* and *Aspects of Occultism*.

Her three Rays of Aspect stand out clear and are known respectively as the Ray of Power, the Ray of Devotion, and the Ray of Wisdom. Their colour associations are respectively orange, violet or purple, and indigo. Her first Ray is associated with the Abstract Spiritual Plane, her second with the Concrete Spiritual, and her third with the Abstract Mental.

Associated with the Ray of Power is the Green Ray. This Ray is on

Dion Fortune		Theosophy
Buddhic Ray (I)	Abstract Spiritual	Logoic Plane
Christian Ray (II)	Concrete Spiritual	Monadic Plane
Pythagorean Ray (III)	Abstract Mental	Atmic Plane
Hermetic Ray (V)	Concrete Mental	Buddhic Plane
Celtic Ray (IV)	Upper Astral	Mental Plane
Northern Ray (VI)	Psychic	Astral Plane
Etheric Ray (VII)	Physical	Physical Plane

the Upper Astral and its main expression is found in the Celtic tradition. She therefore calls it the Celtic Ray. This Ray and its tradition are associated with the faculty of imagination and the higher emotional self. It is also called the Ray of Beauty, the Ray of the Artist, and the Ray of Nature Worship. It seems to correspond to the Fourth Ray. Dion Fortune says of this Ray that it is a bridge between the so-called Rays of Aspect and Rays of Attribute.

Older than the Celtic Ray is the Norse Ray. It is called Nordic because the "purest contacts of this ... tradition which are available to us in the West are those of the Nordic mythology". She associates the Ray with the Lower Astral or Psychic Plane. It is the plane of instincts and passions, but which are transformed into heroic courage once sublimated. And as such do we know the gods and heroes from Norse mythology. This Ray is of particular interest to us, because it reveals the origins of the Northern mysteries.

According to Fortune, the archangel Michael guards "the gates of the Underworld, so that no uprush of chaos and old night may break through". The guardian is Thor, who defends man and god from the Jotun powers. The methods of this Ray, as Fortune explains it, correspond to what we know as Seidr.

A relationship between the Celtic Ray and the Norse Ray exists since they both operate on the Astral Plane. The one is older than the other and the other expresses different qualities than the one. Yet it is very clear from historical and contemporary traditions that the currents influenced each other if only because of their spatial proximity.

It is possible to trace the origins of the Northern mysteries to shortly after the last Ice Age 11,000 years ago. I have already discussed some of this in my book *Secrets of Asgard*. For example, the myth of Ask and Embla would refer to bow and arrow. The weapon appeared in Northern Europe in Mesolithic times, coinciding with the end of the last Ice Age. The same goes for the domestication of plants and animals, recorded in the Rune Alphabet. After the last Ice Age, the first deciduous tree to populate Europe was birch, which coincides with the position of the Berkana Rune in the Futhark.

In *Secrets of Asgard*, I pointed out that the invention of the runic alphabet as we know it might be a collaboration between Germanic initiates and initiates of the Continental Celtic tradition. This event blended the Nordic current with Celtic elements, softening it and making it compatible with the era. The methods from this era are known to us as Galdr. Later, about in the sixth or seventh century of our era, another event took place, again adding Celtic elements into the Nordic current. At this point in time, the Germanic peoples learned the art of poetry from their Celtic neighbours. The source of the skaldic tradition is found in the Celtic tradition, via the Primitive Irish or Old Irish people.

Lastly, when Christianity marched over Europe, it necessarily influenced all the indigenous Continental traditions. The Northern current, too, has been tinged by it and evolved into a tradition which was able to survive. The Christian clergy brought Western Occultism into Scandinavia and this further shaped the old currents. The latest expressions of this are found in the Icelandic grimoires of the seventeenth century. Some of these may yet survive as a living tradition.

Today, as a modern continuation of the old ways, the Northern tradition sails on the Ray of Intellectual Development, corresponding to the Third Ray. There is a very strong tendency in the modern expression of the Northern mysteries to study and research. The original mysteries were established on the Power Ray and were made gentle by the Devotional Ray in early Christian times, but the orientation today is especially mental. In the long run, this will round off the original current.

DOOR 2
ON THE SEAT
OF THE WILL

The mechanism of the human mind is represented by the life of the gods. Divine activity in the Nine Worlds symbolizes psychological activity. Some of that activity is apparent in our everyday dealings. Some of it presents itself in dreams. Some of it becomes clear when we listen a little deeper. But most of it is subconscious. That is why we study the myths. The life of the gods portrays the wide range of mental faculties.

The *Voluspa* poem relates the history of the Norse gods. The narration follows their collective activity from the very brink of creation to and beyond the end of the world. All the important moments in the life of the Aesir are told in that vision. From an esoteric point of view, these moments indicate progressive stages in the evolution of consciousness. I will give an outline of this supported by the events related in the *Voluspa* in the next chapter. First I shall briefly discuss the mythological context of the poem. In an additional section I will give a general interpretation of stanzas 3-26. In concluding, a few particular motifs found in *Voluspa* will be looked at in detail.

The translation and numbering of the stanzas will be based on the *Codex Regius* text.

The Context of the Voluspa

The words of the *Voluspa* are a direct reflection of a real channeling. We know this because the first person perspective is used throughout the poem. The seeress opens her session with a traditional request for silence among the gathered people. Only at the very end of the poem do we encounter indirect speech, as if a person guiding the seeress announces that she is no longer possessed by the spirits. This last half line of the poem runs like this: "Now must she sink back."

Since the channeling session is requested by Odin, we can imagine what this event must have looked like. The gods gather frequently to moot over difficult issues. Similarly, when Balder told his family that he had bad dreams foredooming his own death, a Thing or assembly was called and the issue mooted over. Subsequently, Odin left for the Underworld and conjured up a Volva from the grave. With the knowledge she imparted Odin returned; Mother Frigg acted upon the news.

In the case of *Voluspa*, too, the world is in great danger. At the moment of the channeling, the first signs of Ragnarok have already been consummated and war is upon the gods. Ragnarok is slowly becoming a reality. That is the reason why Odin has called a meeting and has invited the Volva to divine the future. The habit of entreating supernatural beings to learn the outcome of battle was an ancient Germanic practice and is recorded in many different forms in both the Migration Period and the Viking Age. Equally often, we find mothers and foster-mothers divining the wounds their sons will receive in battle. Sometimes the mothers wove magical shirts of nettle to give them added protection.

The moment of import has not escaped the writings of Snorri Sturluson. *Gylfaginning* 51 relates how Heimdal, the watchman of the gods, becomes aware of the military movements of the giants and then he "stands up and blows powerfully on Gjallarhorn and wakes up all the gods and they hold a Thing together. Then rides Odin to Mimir's Well and takes counsel from Mimir for himself and for his host." Snorri's prose rendering is based on stanza 45 of *Voluspa*.

Quite naturally, we can assume that Heimdal's tidings make the Aesir realize that they are on the brink of war. Consequently, an assembly is set up. I am supposing that the words of the *Voluspa* are spoken at that very meeting.

We imagine how the Aesir descend along the Bifrost Bridge and assemble in the shadow of Yggdrasil where they hold court. They assemble at the Well of Urd, which marks the most holy place in the Nine Worlds. From this singular location all destiny is controlled. But the signal of Gjallarhorn has not just awakened the Aesir. The Einherjar, too, wake up and are summoned. They will be present at Urd's Well. The occasion is hinted at in *Voluspa* 49. The stanza also reveals that the Elves will fight alongside the Aesir.

When everyone is present the Volva is summoned, and when she rises, she prophesies the outcome of battle. In the first stanza, the Volva explicitly states that she is summoned by Odin and will relate of the distant past, as he asked. Later she also speaks about the future. Odin obviously asked her about that as well.

The setting reminds us of the Ancient Germanic practice. A tribe riding for battle first supplicated the numinous forces at the lake side with promises of sacrifice in return for victory. Afterwards, weapon gear inscribed with the rival tribe's name was destroyed and dropped into the lake, bog or river. These Ancient Germanic people used the reflective water surface as an interface to communicate with their gods, either the gods of the Underworld residing under the water or the gods of Above reflected on the surface. A similar situation now befalls the Aesir as they assemble at the Sacred Well. It seems right to expect that the Well of Urd functions as an interface with the numinous Otherworld. Moreover, in many traditions, in dreams, and intuitively, water is associated with visions. The Volva personifies the divinatory attribute of the Well.

Possibly, the Volva is summoned from the waters of Urd's Well. After all, she is said to "sink back" at the end of the poem.

We can be fairly certain that the Well provided the medium through which the Volva of *Voluspa* materialized. But what spirit tranced the prophecy? Can we conjecture that Odin summoned Urd herself? Or maybe Frigg took the Volva's Seat and channeled the watery forces? Can it be Saga with whom we are dealing? Frigg and Saga both relate to water. Frigg's dwelling place Fensalir means Fen Halls. Saga's dwelling is Sokkvabekk. The second part of this word refers to a river bank, but the first part means 'sunken' and links in with the 'sinking' of the Volva. According to *Grimnismal*, Odin consults Saga every day, supposedly to drink from the river she represents. Some argue that she is a hypostasis of Frigg. Of the Queen of Asgard it is known that she knows the fate of all beings. This knowledge weighs so heavy upon her that she cannot speak about it. Might she, in her aspect of Saga, find an opportunity to speak about what she knows? After all, the name Saga is based on the verb 'to say'.

It is interesting to note in this context that stanzas 19-20 explain that the Norns themselves emerged from the Well of Urd. Among the three things they do, one is to "say Orlog". It means that the Norns indeed foretell the future.

How to Summon a Spirit

Stanzas 28-29 explain how the Volva might have been summoned. The seeress relates how Odin came to her and looked her in the eye. In this context, the eye is symbolic of water. In response of his approach, the Volva enquires into what he wants; why he "challenges" her. The word is *freista*, which means to put to the test, and what is put to the test is the Volva's ability to see the future. We read between the lines that Odin states the intention of his quest because we are told that he pays her in return for her visions.

Similar summonings are recorded in the lore. The text most akin to *Voluspa* is *Baldrs Draumar*. That time Odin rides to Niflhel to summon a Volva from the dead. He goes to a certain door and seeks out a burial place. Then he recites an incantation known as Valgaldr and the Volva rises from the grave. The passage is reminiscent of *Grogaldr* 1 and 15. Here Svipdag summons his dead mother from the grave, and she "stood in the door". Svipdag calls his mother with these words: "Wake up, Groa, wake up, mother; I wake you at the door of the dead." In *Hyndluljod*, Freyja summons Hyndla, who is identified as a Jotun bride. The goddess summons her with the words: "Wake up, maiden of maidens; wake up, my friend, sister Hyndla, who dwells in the caves." Dweller of Caves is a kenning for giant, and the word for cave is cognate with *hel*. Freyja tries to convince Hyndla by promising sacrifices to Thor. She says: "Thor must I worship (*blóta*), him must I pray to (*biðja*)." At the end of the poem, Hyndla ends the session by telling Freyja she wants to go back to sleep. In all cases an otherworldly being is summoned to acquire hidden knowledge.

The original heathen practice is easily deduced from these passages. Furthermore, it is possibly connected with such stanzas as *Havamal* 157. Each time, the practitioner wakes up an otherworldly being. The motif is also found in *Voluspa* 42, where a golden cock cries and wakes up the Einherjar, who are first and foremost dead warriors. Two more cocks cry, one at the gallows and another in Hel. Their call is strongly associated with waking the dead, and in popular belief a cock was able to bring the dead back to life.

The conjured spirit is coerced by payment of precious rings and trinkets (*Voluspa*) or through sacrifice (*Hyndluljod*) like in ancient heathen times. I take this coercing to be part of the *freista*. In *Voluspa*, this is accompanied by Odin's gazing. In *Hyndluljod*, too, Hyndla says that she can see in Freyja's eyes that she will lead her servant Ottar to his death. Moreover, in *Voluspa* 27-28, the Volva claims Odin's eye to be a well, either the one she is summoned from or Mimir's. She says that Mimir drinks from Odin's eye every day. It is this eye that Odin sacrificed in the first place to drink from the Well. Similarly, at the end of *Hyndluljod*, Freyja requests that the giantess offers Ottar a cup of memory, the

Minnisöl. This drink is associated with many other magical potions involving Mead, but in this context it is interpreted as a drink from the well. It corresponds to Odin's drink from Mimir's Well. Ursula Dronke interprets the sacrificial eye of Odin as the reflection of the Sun on the water.

There is one more parallel found in the poems. In the story of *Helreid Brynhildar* or Brynhild's Descent, Brynhild travels the road to Hel, because she died. On her way, a Gyg troll bars the way. They exchange words, but when Brynhild has had enough she commands the Gyg to go back to where she came from. She says: "Sink back, kin of Gygjar." The story reverses the normal process. Now the otherworldly being comes out uninvited and must be formally dismissed.

In all cases, we are dealing with the Underworld, more specifically the world of the dead. Yet, Hyndla and the Volva of *Baldrs Draumar* are of giant kind. Brynhild's Descent is interesting because the text clearly connects the giant race with the realm of the dead. In *Voluspa* 42, the realm where the cock cries is guarded by a giant named Eggther. He is defined as the king of the Gygjar. They are associated with Jotun giants. This raises the question whether the Volva of *Voluspa* is a giantess. Certainly, she claims to descend from Jotun giants (2). *Voluspa hin Skamma* 5 relates how the Volur connect with both the Jotun giants and users of Seidr.

Voluspa hin Skamma 5
All the Volur come from Vidolf
The Vitkar all come from Vilmeid
The users of Seidr all come from Svarthofdi
The Jotun giants all from Ymir come

Both in *Voluspa* and *Hyndluljod*, the verb *freista* is used to describe the summoning itself. Odin and Freyja seem to command the spirit to answer questions. In *Voluspa* and *Baldrs Draumar*, the verb *fregna* is used to describe the actual questioning. The verb means to ask, counsel, to inform, to be informed.

When the session ends, the being retires or "sinks back". In *Voluspa*, the sinking suggests that the Volva sinks back into the Well. The phrase recurs only one other time, in *Helreid Brynhildar*, and no water is overtly involved in this passage. Moreover, the summoned beings always express the desire to return to their original condition of sleep. We could therefore neutrally interpret the phrase as a formal way to close a channeling session. Sinking back can mean both to sink back in water or in the earth. Parallel to this are the words which Odin uses when he ends his trying time on the World Tree: "I fell after from it." This clearly signifies how Odin returns to his original condition after a self-induced trance session.

From stanzas 28-29 we deduce that Odin has already consulted the Volva at an earlier time. That the passage cannot refer to the current *Voluspa* session is inferred from what the Volva says about it. First of all, she speaks about Odin's request as if it is in the past. After that she reiterates what she said to him in that session. The stanzas following 28-29 recount Balder's death, which must necessarily be in the past. She specifically says that "she saw".

This earlier session is recapitulated in stanzas 30-38. Indeed, the information given in stanzas 31-33 neatly fits the text of *Baldrs Draumar*. From this we conclude that the Volva is referring to the time when Odin went to Hel in order to consult a Volva about the dreams of Balder. The Volva of *Voluspa* identifies herself with her but can hardly be the same person. Otherwise the entire divine family would have to move to the Underworld for the occasion. Hel is only accessible when you are either dead or riding Sleipnir.

So, how do you summon a Volva? Seek out a spring, a rivulet, a lake or a pond. Go there with a clear intention of what you want to ask. Have something of value with you. Prepare a short text and use it to invoke the spirit of the water. Promise to give something of value as payment. Ideally sit in the east so that you face west. Alternatively, sit in the south so that you face north.

Then summon the spirit by scrying the water. You can gaze at the reflection of the Sun or the Moon, or, if you dare, cast your precious object into the water and look at that. Take as much time scrying as you need, enough to get into a slight trance. Maybe close your eyes then. Ask your question, and continue to pray into the water. When you are done, offer your precious object to the water, if you haven't already. Retreat in silence once you have fully regained consciousness.

Changing Times

Because the *Voluspa* is recorded as one long direct speech, the present, the past and the future are discernible through the use of the tenses. What is more, the Volva introduces her visions of the past with "I remember" (2, 21) and "I saw" (30, 31, 34, 37, 38). The first section of remembering covers stanzas 2-26 and is an actual vision. The second section relates to what she saw the first time. This comprises stanzas 27-38. It implies that Balder is already dead and avenged by the time the Volva is invoked again.

After two or three more stanzas, we come to a point where the past tense changes into the present. This happens in the middle of stanza 42 and radically marks the point in time at which the actual session must be held.

Voluspa 42

Sang among the Aesir, Gullinkambi,
He wakes the heroes, at Herjafödr's
Another sings beneath the earth
A soot red rooster in the halls of Hel

The whole section comprises stanzas 41-49. Everything that happens in these stanzas is presented by the Volva as if taking shape in the present. The section opens with the three cocks crying (41-42). The section includes stanza 45 which says that Heimdal blows his horn to announce Ragnarok and stanza 49 which states that the Aesir meet in Thing. The acute moment of the present is underlined by a refrain that is inserted in the poem from here onwards and features the hellhound Garm (43, 46, 55). The refrain contains the Old Norse *nú* which means now. The whole section is written in the present tense.

From stanza 50 onward we are dealing with the future. The Volva introduces these visions with "I see" (56, 61). The events described in stanzas 50-62 cannot have happened yet because they entail the Ragnarok war itself. Obviously, the gods cannot be gathered in the assembly and be in the field fighting giants at the same time. The time aspect of these verses is stressed by the phrase *þá kemr* "then will come" at the beginning of several stanzas (51, 52, 53, 62). Stanzas 56-61 portray the distant future of a New World.

It is rather exciting to locate the exact moment of the present in the poem. The poem provides sufficient elements to say a little more. For example, cocks cry. That must mean that the Thing takes place in the morning. We also know that Balder's funeral ritually takes place at the Midsummer festival. At the same time, Ragnarok is associated with a long winter. That's why I suppose the Vision takes place at the end of summer.

The Mirror of the Soul

Traditionally, Volur were consulted for their power to divine the future. It is no different now. Yet, the Volva recounts things from the past first. The events of her discourse all relate to creation. This seems logical from a literary point of view, once we realize that the question is in fact about the destruction of that creation. In assuming that Odin asked the Volva to reveal the future we must interpret the past events as necessary in understanding the future.

Relating the ensuing war to the early phase of creation gives context to Ragnarok. The Past-section of *Voluspa* contains three significant events. Firstly, Midgard is created. This is a long process that entails the installation of time as well as the creation of mankind and the race of dwarves. What we see here is the creation of space, time, consciousness and life. Secondly, the war of the Aesir and Vanir is recounted. Thirdly, Balder's death is remembered, with all the events leading up to the present state of chaos. A few things can be said about these passages in relation to Ragnarok proper.

First and foremost, the creation process is implemented by a collective known as the Regin. They are decorated with the epithet Ginn-Holy. It links them to Ginnungagap; and possibly "the sons of Bur" must be interpreted as the Regin, too. From many texts, we know that Odin leads this host. The collective is named about four times (6, 9, 23, 25) and is implied in the refrain of Garm, mentioning Ragnarok as such. The word literally means destiny of the Regin. Hence the importance of giving context to these beings, covered in stanzas 3-26. The final destruction is only comprehended by realizing what the Regin originally created.

Secondly, the next most important event highlighted by the Volva is the war between the Aesir and the Vanir. The meaning of it becomes apparent when we read that this war is remembered as "the first war in the world". Accordingly, it creates a mythic precedent of any war human or superhuman that follows. Without this first war, there can be no last war. The image of the First War creates a mirror in the poem as it reflects the inevitability of Ragnarok. Ultimately, the First War is the prototype of war whereas Ragnarok illustrates its archetype. In scope, Ragnarok is more far-reaching, and that is the reason why the story of creation is included.

Thirdly, the final destruction makes it possible for Balder to rise again and create a new world. Thus Ragnarok is truly a mirror image of the Past. The Vanic War follows the events of creation, whereas Ragnarok precedes a second creation. The emergence of the New World precisely matches the creation of Midgard. The New World, too, rises up "from out of the sea".

Fourthly, Balder's dreams and his resulting death establish the axis around which the whole poem revolves. It is central to the framework of the *Voluspa* and links the Past to the Future. Moreover, Balder's death as a cause of war is mirrored by Gullveig's death as the cause of the Vanic War. In the same way, it is said of Gullveig that "she still lives". I assume, in an answer to Odin's question, that this is all he wanted to hear: Balder will live. The future is secured.

1.	Creation of Midgard	Past
2a.	Death of Gullveig	
2b.	First War	
2a.	Death of Balder	Present
2b.	Ragnarok	
1.	New World	Future

The Volva as Initiatrix

The revelations of the Volva represent the expansion of consciousness. That is why we can interpret the *spá* session as a form of initiation. The Volva acts as the Soror Mystica of Odin. She opens his consciousness. Her prophecies show a part of the Plan and cause Odin, the candidate, to take action. The presence of the seeress heralds the actual initiation represented by Ragnarok.

From her knowledge, Odin knows how to protect the integrity of the personality and the mind. This can only be done by slaying Balder. Here is the reason why Odin sent his son to the Underworld. He understands that it is the only way to safeguard the continuation of consciousness.

On Intuition

Contacting the Volva represents meditation. It is well known through meditational experience and teaching that the linear expression of time dissolves as one sinks deeper within the Self. That is why both the past and the future are included in the poem. The Volva represents a deeper aspect of ourselves. Listening to her words is like hearing our subconscious speak.

The words of the Volva can be interpreted as intuitive information. The individual is somehow informed of the future. Usually this manifests as premonition, insight, new ideas. Individuals who have travelled some length on the Path align themselves with their souls. In this way, information seeps in from the causal world into the mental world. Information travels from the Source to the Aesir.

In this interpretation, the Aesir represent the Spiritual Hierarchy, who mentally inform individuals across the globe. The individual is intuitively shown a part of the Plan, defining the course of evolution. Admittedly, as flawed as we are as human beings, we are usually unable to know the exact future, but some sense of purpose is roused, so that the individual understands his place in the scheme of things. As a result, the individual is able to manifest his soul's purpose and guide the evolution of mankind in a personal way.

Therefore, the intuition supports the reasoning faculty. Reasoning helps to predict the future. At the same time, when you try to capture the future it will help to understand the Law of Karma. Ultimately, you try to gauge the consequences of your actions. To understand the relation of cause and effect results in foreknowledge.

In the evolutionary scheme, the intuition only develops after the reasoning faculty. The Aesic race represents rational thinking. Potentially the Volva and what she symbolizes is present in the Vanic race. After the First War, both races become one and the latent faculty is given a chance to develop. Slowly but surely, the intuition awakens. In the *Voluspa* poem, the conscious registration of this faculty is voiced by Frigg.

Before the unfoldment of the reasoning faculty the human being is identified with the sensual side of life. This earlier stage of human evolution is also recorded in Vanic history. Freyja's abduction by the giants refers to the dominance of the animal life. Indeed, the war between the Aesir and the Vanir started because the rational Aesir tried to suppress the presence of Gullveig, who is a manifestation of Freyja.

We therefore see three subsequent phases in that short story. The First War marks the transition from emotional to mental consciousness. The former is symbolized by Freyja in stanza 25; the latter by Odin in the same section of the poem. The intuition is symbolized by Frigg (33, 51), but also by the Volva.

Body	**Instinct**	Freyja	Giants	Mass consciousness
Mind	**Intellect**	Odin	Aesir	Individual consciousness
Soul	**Intuition**	Frigg	Vanir	Group consciousness

DOOR 3
AN INTERPRETATION OF THE VISION

Creation reflects the self-development of an entity. When a unit of consciousness is able to generate intention, then it has the power to create change. This is equally true of a human being, a nation, a god, a solar system, or the universe. Again and again, every new intention evokes a response of everything around it. If purpose guides intention, then evolution proceeds. Purpose drives all creation.

When one intention finds its completion, the entity moves on to the next level. Thus, the evolution of any particular entity consists of many cycles. Likewise, the individual himself goes through a cycle and experiences lesser cycles within one incarnation. The process transforms an entity into its potential.

Everything in the Universe transpires in cycles. Herein lies the importance of studying the *Voluspa*. The text narrates one or more such cycle. It begins with the story of creation and ends with a phase of destruction, after which a new world emerges. It is the mystery of the Life/Death/Life cycle that Clarissa Pinkola Estés so profoundly talks about.

The *Voluspa* creation story comprises the first half of the poem. This panel is itself divided into different passages, corresponding to lesser cycles. Time periods or Ages are discerned in the story. The first Age consists of stanzas 3-6. It can be broken down further into a stage before and a stage after creation. Stanzas 6-16 encompass the second Age, of which stanzas 6-8 refer to an initial stage, but stanzas 8-16 express a succeeding stage. Stanzas 17-26 cover the next time period, of which 17-20 portray the start of the Age of Mankind. This Age continues throughout the poem and ends at Ragnarok. But stanzas 21-26 comprise a separate stage, depicting the events of the First War.

In the Days of Yore

Voluspa 3-6

Early was the age in which Ymir dwelled
There was neither sand nor sea nor cold waves
Earth was nowhere found nor upper heaven
The gap was like Ginn, but grass there was not

Soon the sons of Bur lifted the bottom
They shaped the famous Midgard
The Sun shone from the south on halls of stone
Then the ground was overgrown with green leek

From the south the Sun, in the company of the Moon,
Cast her dexterous hand about the edge of heaven.
The Sun did not know where she had her hall.
The stars did not know where they had their positions.
The Moon did not know what he had of might.

Then all the Regin went to the Stools of Reckoning
The Ginn-Holy Gods, and over this deliberated:
Night and the new Moon they gave names
They named the morning and the middle of the day
Tea and evening, to count the years

Symbolically, the Ages refer to stages on the evolutionary path. Everything begins with the stillness of Ginnungagap. In *Gylfaginning*, the void is described as a windless calm. This provides us with a strong image of timelessness, but it also signifies the impossibility of evolution. Conversely, time is the first thing implemented after the emergence of Midgard. The Sun, Moon and Stars and their paths across the sky cause a natural rhythm and eventuate evolution.

According to the text, the "gap was Ginnunga". The word *ginnunga* means nothing in itself, but it etymologically relates to our word 'beginning'. It accurately describes the state before creation. What is more, the Old Norse *gap* is often translated as 'void' but it can equally be translated as 'space'.

Ginnungagap is a world without "sand or sea or its cold waves, without earth or heaven, and without grass". A quick interpretation of these aspects shows that there was neither land nor water to form the matter aspect of creation. Neither were there waves, representing the flow of time. Or they might just as well symbolize light, sound or energy; Kvilhaug interprets the waves as sound. There was neither down nor up, nor was life present. Almost every aspect of manifested creation with which we are familiar is touched upon.

It is common to describe the state of affairs before creation in terms of negations. By definition, we cannot know anything about what causes creation to ensue. The First Cause lies outside creation, outside what we can know and describe. That is why the state is described by the absence of things.

The Babylonian *Enuma Elish* opens in the same way. Verses 1-8 describe how there was no up (heaven) or down (earth). There were no pastures, no gods, no names and no destinies. Only a dyad is present, namely Apsu and Tiamat. They represent the primal waters of chaos comparable to Ymir in Norse myth and Nun in Egyptian cosmogony. The Ancient Indian *Rig Veda*, book 10 hymn 129 stanzas 1-2, opens in the same way and mentions a primal being, identified with Purusha, who is interpreted as the First Cause. Furthermore, the topos of negation is comparable to the description of Dao in the *Dao De Jing*. The text states that the Dao cannot be named but is the source of heaven and earth. In a way, the concept of Dao is analogous to Ginn.

Many of these old texts explain that the onset of creation is immanent in a primal being. In *Voluspa*, the blueprint of creation is embodied by Ymir. Such primal beings represent the full potential of a future universe. They are the seed of the world.

The actual intention which kick-starts creation is the sacrificial death of that primal being. In Norse mythology, this is carried out by the Aesir. In the *Enuma Elish*, Marduk slays Tiamat. In the *Rig Veda*, the gods sacrifice Purusha.

The stanza about Ymir is immediately followed by the creation of Midgard. We therefore conclude that Midgard represents the manifestation of Ymir's potential. The primal giant links both sides of the mirror, the absolute and the manifest. He exists before creation, but lives on in creation. As a giant, he represents the seed of consciousness which the Aesir mean to nurture and harvest. Later, the Aesir will create mankind as a vessel for the evolution of consciousness.

But there is yet another link. The first object mentioned after the birth of Midgard is the Sun. The gods shape her from a spark of Muspelheim, which is a realm that existed before creation. She is therefore an aspect of the Absolute reflected in the created world. In the human being, the Sun represents the Monad, or divine spark, whereas Midgard represents the physical plane dimension. She is our link to the original source of all life. Esoterically, the goddess Sol represents the Logos of our solar system. Symbolically, her light and brightness herald the Golden Age ruled by the gods.

Voluspa 5 describes how the heavenly bodies are ignorant of their power and position. According to stanza 6, the gods change this apparent state of indefiniteness. They give purpose to the Sun and Moon and the heavenly stations are named so that time can be reckoned. It mainly produces the cosmic Law of Cycles.

Creation involves an intention towards the unfoldment of a seed potential, resulting in a space-time framework geared with the consequent set of cosmic laws. As aspects of this reality, we, as mere humans, are born and bound under the conditions of that continuum. However, it is this very framework of Space and Time that makes evolution possible.

The Golden Age

Voluspa 7
The Aesir met on the Idavoll
They wrought altar and temple high
Hearths they laid, forged riches
Shaped tongs and geared tools

When the gods move Midgard from the ocean, they create order. The earth symbolizes matter. By naming Midgard, they give it a destination. In the same vein, naming the times of day and night bestows Orlog or purpose upon the heavenly bodies. Up to that point everything is still in search of order and orientation.

The process of defining continues. In stanza 7, the gods are identified as the Aesir. Before, they were a nameless crowd of Regin, or, even more vague, the Sons of Bur. At the same time, the seat of the gods is named: Idavoll.

The world of the gods is separated from Midgard. Later, the diversification will become even more complex. Many lands will have names, such as the regions where the dwarves will have their homes; and a list of dwarf names is included.

In the Chinese tradition, this moment corresponds to the emergence of the ten thousand things. They have their root in the dualism of Yin and Yang, which in its turn is a diversification of an absolute, unified state

Wuji, *wu* meaning nothing. By the 'ten thousand things' everything that exists is meant. This stage of differentiation is reflected in the works of the gods. In the smithy, they forge many things.

We are faced with three labels to designate the gods. At first they are called the Sons of Bur. The term emphasizes the common source of these beings while their own identity remains unknown. They are defined by their common father. Esoterically, the sons of Bur represent the cloud of Monads who are as yet without a course, but who will incarnate through humanity in later times and attain individual consciousness. The expression 'the Sons of Bur' resembles the esoteric phrase 'the Sons of God'. Humanity is intended, hinting at their latent divinity.

In the next stage, the Sons of Bur are defined as Regin. They are an assembly of gods with the power of decision. They appear at different points in the poem and shape the course of the world. Esoterically, their work is to guide humanity. In the poem, their epithet is Ginn-Holy Gods. This somewhat delineates their personality. The morpheme *ginn* marks their origin, which goes back to Ginnungagap. It represents the life aspect. The term 'holy' describes their quality. The term 'god' explains their function in the service of humanity, but it also represents the form aspect. Thus, in three words, everything is described. Life. Quality. Appearance.

Lastly, the gods are known as the Aesir, and we finally enter familiar territory. As the Regin evolve, they will break apart into twelve Aesir with each his own function and specialty. At this point the process of individualization starts. Each of them takes on his own profession and the many functions of consciousness emerge.

As a stage in the evolution of consciousness, the Regin represent mass consciousness. From this, individual consciousness will arise, which is symbolized by the creation of mankind. Only then will the gods be able to differentiate themselves.

The development from Regin to Aesir is expressed by the unending zeal of the gods. They work in their smithies and build their temples and have time to play games and relax. In Idavoll, the gods build both their workshops and their homes. Their homes are places of worship and symbolize contemplation and meditation. Their workshops symbolize creativity, study and teaching. In tandem, their activities indicate the training and work of the initiate. From this, we infer that the Aesir represent mental activity.

In their role as Regin, the gods watch over the different needs of the world and its inhabitants. Once this is done, an Age of abundance and creativity follows. This marks an important step in the evolution of consciousness. When a human civilization has reached a certain point at which all the basic needs are fulfilled, time becomes available to devote life to inner development.

Voluspa 8-9
They played *tafl* in the garden and were happy
There was for them no want for gold
Until three came, Thurs girls,
Very much mighty, from Jotunheim

Then all the Regin went to the Stools of Reckoning
The Ginn-Holy Gods, and over this deliberated:
Who would shape the leader of the dwarves?
From Brimir's blood and Blain's legs

A long phase of construction precedes the Golden Age in which the Aesir find time and opportunity to enjoy their creation. It represents the height of a civilization ruled by order, peace and relative stability. Then comes a time when the balance tips and the homely world is challenged by a counterforce. In an Age of comfort, this is the only way to grow. Unsuspected difficulties are met with and overcome, and society finds a new age of peace on a higher plane.

The order of the gods is disrupted by three Thurs women from

Jotunheim. They represent an outside force that needs taking care of. The giants are an older race; they ruled the world before the gods. The Aesir push them to the very edge of creation. Consequently, the giants have no place in the world. As such, they represent all the elements big and small in our psyche that we suppress and ignore. These elements are oppressed by the sheer will of imposing order, routine and formality. After a while, this builds up so much pressure that the waking consciousness must at last yield and cope with it. Dealing with the giants symbolizes the refinement of consciousness. One by one, the unconscious forces in the mind are faced and integrated in the self. In an occult way, this process represents purification.

According to *Voluspa*, the Regin assemble to meet the need. Their response is to create a new race to maintain the balance. And so the race of dwarves is shaped from the blood and body of Ymir. It is not clear from the poem what the rise of the dwarves is intended to change. The closest connection with the giants is where they live. Their habitat is situated in the mountains. However, the dwarves are said to live in the earth, not on it. Symbolically, they represent the living energy of the planet. They represent the vitality of Mother Earth. Esoterically, they are the Deva or Elemental evolution, which is parallel to mankind's. These so-called Builders are intimately linked with physical and etheric substance.

The Age of Man

Voluspa 17-20

Until three came from that host,
Strong and affectionate Aesir, to a house
They found on the land with little main
Ask and Embla without Orlog

Breath they owned not; mind they had not
Vitality nor personality nor a good hue

> Breath gave Odin; mind gave Hoenir
> Vitality gave Lodur and a good hue
>
> I know where Ask stands; he is called Yggdrasil,
> A high tree sprinkled with white mud
> Thence comes the dew which runs in the valleys
> It stands ever over the green well of Urd
>
> Thence come the girls, conscious of many things,
> By three out of this sea which under the thole stands
> Urd is called one; the other Verdandi;
> They score the wood; Skuld is the third.
> They laid down the laws, they chose the lives
> Of the children of the Age, to say Orlog

Then something special happens. In stanza 17 we read how three Aesir disconnect from the host and wander through the world. On the beach they find two logs of wood and shape mankind from it. The passage conjures up the image of driftwood, which was a common sight in the sea-faring Viking society. The use of wood to shape man and woman also links in with Viking tradition in which representations of the gods were made from wood. Such pole gods were carved from wood and are known from the archaeological record. From textual material, we know such idols were painted and dressed. The analogy is light to make. What is special about the passage is that three Aesir decide to act without the cooperation of the group. The phase comes about by individual effort, or the application of will power.

In fact, in stanza 18, the three gods are identified by name. This symbolizes the transition from mass to individualized consciousness. Slowly but surely the animal herd mind is outgrown. This necessarily coincides with the creation of humanity, because symbolically man and woman are destined to become the vessels for the development of consciousness.

The passage is rich in symbolism. The Aesir find the logs at the beach. If we assume that these logs were brought to land by the sea, then we can rightly interpret this movement as another transition of consciousness. Water symbolizes the subconscious, land the tangible. Because land is more solid than water, the transition is a concretization of consciousness. Self-consciousness surfaces from the depths of the sea, so to speak. The locale thus represents the shift from subconscious to conscious life.

The whole transition is formalized by the ritual endowment of life and consciousness by the gods. The wood only serves as a physical vehicle to carry consciousness on the physical plane. Symbolically, wood represents material capable of life but not of consciousness. Certainly, wood lives, but it cannot act nor create. As it is described in *Voluspa*, the driftwood has no Orlog, no purpose. By enticing the human being toward self-consciousness, however, purpose is realized. In effect, the three Aesir may be interpreted as Ascended Masters who inspire mankind, impinging upon their consciousness as much of the Plan that the mind of the individual can bear. Through the faculties of the mind, the individual is able to register the subtler energies and contact the higher entities. The key faculty with which the gods bless humanity is termed Odr. It is usually translated as 'inspiration', but it also stands for that fervent drive to fight for one's ideals.

In the poem, the anthropogenesis is followed by an account of Yggdrasil and the Norns. Since it is not the origin of either that is recounted, it must relate to the creation of mankind. The connection is fairly straightforward. When the gods reach the sea, they find a log of ash and a log of elm. Then stanza 19 states that the ash is called Yggdrasil. We can only conclude that Yggdrasil is the name of the ash log. We see a correspondence with Jewish Mysticism, where the Tree of Life is equated with the representative of humanity, Adam, who is also the first man.

If the above is correct, then we must assume a female counterpart. No other stanza gives the name of the elm log, but the Tree has many other names, such as Mjotud, Mjotvid and Mimameid. Similarly, much debate persists as to whether the World Tree is an ash or a yew. The confusion stems from the fact that two different kinds of tree shared the same mythological importance. It supposedly means that the yew can be identified with the first woman. Indeed, there is a connection between yew and elm, since both were used for making bows. In remote times elm wood was used for hand bows, but because the tree's population had decimated, people changed to yew. Therefore, the elm log may originally have had a different name than Yggdrasil. Nowadays, we can use the name regardless of gender.

The change from Ask or Embla to Yggdrasil marks the same transition as mentioned before. Ask and Embla stand for the unrealized human being, ignorant of purpose, whereas Yggdrasil symbolizes the perfected individual, who is in control of his own life.

A person's destiny is symbolized by the presence of the Norns at the Well beneath the Tree. The Tree itself symbolizes the individual. The triad of Norns is an expression of a human's Free Will. The Well symbolizes what the individual feeds his soul with, because the Norns use the mud from the Well to nurture the Tree. As the only actors in the complex symbolism of the Tree, the Norns symbolize the decisions of the individual. From the Well he drinks the results of his past actions. And in runes he writes the future in his roots.

The individual is able to write his own Wyrd or Karma. At the same time, it bequeaths him with a great responsibility. Since Yggdrasil is a glyph to represent the connectedness of different worlds and dimensions, every Nornic judgement consequently manifests in every world and dimension. Whenever the individual makes a conscious decision and carries it through, it will influence his environment and initiate change in the matrix of reality.

The cycle of cause and effect is presented in the glyph as 1) the desire of the Norns, 2) the written formula which they carve in the tree, 3) the mud with which they feed their decision, 4) the roots that drink the decision from the well, 5) the life sap that communicates it to the Nine Worlds, 6) the branches, leaves and fruit which symbolize the product of the action, and 7) the dew that falls from the leaves and returns to the Well. According to the quality of the water the tree will grow. A clear well reflects clear intentions. The Tree will draw sustenance from this.

The identification of the human being with the World Tree has even wider implications. It means that a person is connected with each of the Nine Worlds. And not just that, the Nine Worlds permeate within him. The image demonstrates that the individual is not just a physical body. No, he is a being active on many planes. The Nine Worlds include the many states of mind that a person goes through or can access, from a normal waking consciousness, to trance, over meditation, dreaming and sleeping. It connects him firmly with his own subconscious realms as well as with his most enlightened states and Higher Self. What's more, through the image of the Tree and the Well the human being is not just connected with all the layers of reality but also with every other person on the planet.

The First War

> **Voluspa 21-26**
> This she remembers: The first war in the world
> When Gullveig with spears they studded
> And in the hall of Havi burnt her
> Three times burnt her; three times she was born
> Often, not seldom, though she still lives

Heidi she is called; wherever she comes to a house
Of the well done visions of the Volva, she charms the artifacts
Sorcery she can do; she charmed the possessed
Aye she was the perfume of evil brides

Then all the Regin went to the Stools of Reckoning
The Ginn-Holy Gods, and over this deliberated:
Whether should the Aesir pay the tribute?
Or should all of the gods own the payment of debt?

Flung Odin (his spear) and in battle shot about
That was the first war in the world
Broken was the plank-wall of the fortress of the Aesir
The Vanir knew how to trample the vision of the fight of the field

Then all the Regin went to the Stools of Reckoning
The Ginn-Holy Gods, and over this deliberated:
Who had all the air with treason blended?
Or to the tribe of Jotun giants Od's girl given?

Thor alone there fought, in a pressing mood
He seldom sits, when he of such is informed
To and fro went oaths, words and swearing
All speech did mainly middling fare

From stanza 21 onwards, a new episode begins. War is unleashed within the ranks of the gods themselves. The reason is a point of debate.

According to the poem, Gullveig is the cause of conflict; though it is not said what she is guilty of. Since the war is waged between Aesir and Vanir, it is assumed that she is one of the Vanir. Often, her name is interpreted as 'drunken of gold'. According to scholars, she brings discord among the gods over riches and wealth, much as in the Viking saying: "Wealth causes strife among kinsmen." In my own opinion, her name refers to Mead. The drink has a golden colour and *veig* is a kenning for Mead. Indeed, both money and alcohol are well known causes of trouble even among friends. Yet, stanza 22 clearly explains that Gullveig is accused of witchcraft. How she became a threat to the Aesir remains unknown.

Gullveig is accused of being a Volva. She talks to the spirits. She knows *seiðr* and is able to manipulate people's minds. Then she is said to have the support of evil women. While Seidr and *spá*, of which the *Voluspa* itself is an expression, are harmless, the second part of the stanza points out that Gullveig uses her powers for evil. Although the Vanir are sometimes associated with witchcraft, it is mainly Freyja who takes this role. She practices and teaches Seidr. The question then arises whether we are dealing with Freyja. Later in the poem, we are informed that Freyja is a prize of war.

The First War can be interpreted as a fight over the Goddess of Love. Then, the scene transforms into the grand theatre of a Sacred Marriage where the Aesir perform the masculine role and the Vanir the feminine. When Odin casts his spear, this becomes a sign of his virility. In this case, it makes sense to interpret Gullveig as a name for the Sacred Mead, because it was associated with the drinking horn. This, in its turn, is associated with the cup of Western occultism. The child that is to be expected from the union must be Kvasir, who is praised as a god of wisdom.

In relation to the earlier creation of mankind, the First War symbolizes the struggle of the male and female pole within the individual. Hypothetically, the Aesir fight for Ask and the Vanir fight for Embla. The inherent dualism with which mankind was originally created, either expressive of the left and right hemisphere, or of the personality and the soul, is overcome through a long struggle and consummated on a higher plane. The war is expressive of a long and enduring effort to integrate both poles in the Self. After much struggle, it results in the union of Ask and Embla. On a different level, it results in the alignment of the Nine Worlds. This is the meaning of the Sacred Marriage.

War is always the result of two conflicting forces. Something is out of balance, and there is a desire to restore it. Symbolically, war expresses the effort to integrate opposing types of energy. But the First War particularly represents inner conflict. Earlier, the gods were threatened by forces from Jotunheim and dealt with it. Now, they fight among themselves. The concept of the First War makes us aware that this event is symbolically very different from the earlier threat of *Voluspa* 8. However, there are many similarities. The Aesir are threatened by a female force, either the daughters of giants (8) or Gullveig (21). Both result in war, although the conflict with the giantesses is not specifically called war. If we read the poem correctly, the Aesir create the race of dwarves to deal with the forces of Jotunheim. The main difference between the two events is that the giants represent forces outside the sphere of influence of the Aesir, whereas in the First War, gods fight gods. The presence of the giantesses represents outer conflict, which is often easier to resolve than inner.

Inner conflict is one of the hardest things to overcome. Although you are internally divided, you can only rely on yourself. Like the all-out war between Aesir and Vanir, an inner conflict demands lots of time and energy to overcome. Frequently, it demands sacrifices, too. We can imagine how war is a metaphor of how an old opinion fights for its established position when an improved idea takes hold of the mind. For a time, both exist alongside each other, but eventually one or the other wins. If the new ideology has the upper hand, then the balances tip in favour of evolution. It is an opportunity to grow.

Expansion of consciousness
The whole section from stanza 3 to 26 deals with creation. The second

half of the poem deals with Ragnarok and annihilation. As discussed above, the first half of the poem sketches a certain chain of events that reflects the evolution of consciousness. Psychologically, each of the Ages symbolizes a method of personal growth. The four Ages are Ardagar or the Early Age, the Golden Age, Veröld or the Age of Man, and the First War.

(1) The Early Age represents natural growth. It stands for growth through creativity. Consciousness expands through study and meditation. (2) The Golden Age represents growth through external conflict. Pressure comes from friends and family, or from society as a whole. Unexpected events or disease put a person through a lot of trouble. The cause of the disruption is symbolized by the giants. The dwarves symbolize your inner resources, or, in the case of disease, your immune system. (3) The creation of man and woman is different, because it represents growth through ambition or aspiration. It symbolizes the application of Free Will. This includes devotion and dedication. The creation of mankind symbolizes the conscious effort to transform the Self. (4) The First War represents growth through inner conflict. This is the opportunity we are faced with most often. This state of mind turns up in the process of the three earlier methods. Yet, inner conflict presupposes self-consciousness. Any effort to personal growth will meet resistance in the old self. And so, inner conflict naturally arises. The First War shows that the conflict between the pairs of opposites eventually leads to synthesis on a higher level.

From the above, we deduce that personal development is mainly an internal issue. Only one out of four events represents expansion of consciousness through outer pressure.

DOOR 4
THE EVOLUTION OF CONSCIOUSNESS

The evolution of consciousness is tightly associated with the subject of initiation. As I interpret it, the *Voluspa* story represents the development towards initiation. The first section, of the past, contains the necessary preparatory work of which the individual becomes conscious only later. The middle section, the present, indicates the point in a person's life where he becomes aware of his own soul. He recognizes himself as a spiritual being and decides to turn his attention there. This marks the start of the Probationary Path. The future heralds those drastic transformational changes that typically accompany initiation. This is Ragnarok. Each of these stages contains tests or experiences that we must live through in order to attain a higher, more expanded form of consciousness.

The past, the present and the future are each subdivided in different phases. In total, we recognize nine Ages in the *Voluspa* that correspond to the steady unfolding. The nine phases are (1) Ginnungagap, (2) the Age of Giants, (3) the Age of Creation, (4) the Early Days, (5) the Age of Mankind, (6) the First War, (7) the Age of Portents, (8) Ragnarok, and (9) the New Age. Phases one to six cover the past. The seventh phase includes the death of Balder and therefore ranges from the immediate past to the immediate future. Ragnarok and the New Age deal with the future. Each phase has its own subdivisions and particularities. The assorted elements will be discussed per Age.

The outline of evolution is clear but very general. This means that the esoteric interpretation of *Voluspa* concerns both the individual and humanity as a whole. The emphasis lies on the individual development of consciousness, but a sporadic hint at the larger scale is everywhere included.

Some subjects will already have been discussed in the previous chapter. However, the overlapping cycles will be fine-tuned to the study of the evolution of consciousness. Moreover, the creation story will be integrated in the complete *Voluspa* story leading up to Ragnarok as an event of initiation.

Ginnungagap: The Age of Ginn

GINNUNGAGAP

Before creation, a stage of pure potential exists. Only the Ginnic forces are present. This comprises a purely abstract condition. The state corresponds to the state of being out of incarnation.

Ymir: The Age of Giants

YMIR

From the differentiation of Ginnungagap into its two most extreme states emerges the first seed of consciousness. The extremes are symbolized by Muspelheim and Niflheim. The electro-magnetic powers of Fire and Water create Ymir. He embodies the life principle, but also represents Monadic consciousness. This stage corresponds to deep sleep.

JOTNAR

As the embodiment of the life principle, Ymir spawns all kinds of primal beings. He is the ancestor of the giants. This class of beings represents a state of mind that is not fully awake yet. It coincides with the dreaming phase.

BUR

From the ice in Ginnungagap, Ymir also frees the ancestor of the gods. In a very basic way, the giants represent the unconscious and the gods the conscious part of the mind. The giants are associated with the instinct and the elemental, whereas the gods are creative beings with their own will. The giants are slaves to their circumstances, but the gods aim to act. The class of divine beings is represented by Odin.

Creation: The Age of the Regin

SPACE

The gods decide to create order. According to *Voluspa*, this is done by lifting the earth from the depths of the ocean. Other sources indicate that ocean and earth are created from Ymir's body. In any case, the act represents the creation of space.

TIME

The very next thing is the creation of time; an essential ingredient. Time makes evolution possible. Veered away from the abstract, creation is free to evolve in relation to its first impulse represented by the slaying of Ymir. The Sun and the Moon dictate the pace. Evolution follows the rhythm of cosmic tides.

MIDGARD

Afterwards the gods refine creation by differentiating and defining. This tendency symbolizes our reasoning faculty, our power to conceptualize. Definitions imbue things with a sense of purpose. This faculty is linked with the concrete mental plane. Object consciousness emerges.

Naming objects implies the creation of thought-forms. When things are named and defined, they can be contacted, used and wielded. The absoluteness of Ymir falls apart in an awareness of ten thousand things. A shift from unity to multiplicity is observed.

The creation of Midgard makes a separation between what is known and what is unknown, order and disorder, the wanted and the unwanted.

This sets up a sense of security, necessary to survive. Cultivating familiarity and building up a cosmological frame of reference supports the development of creativity. However, the immediate cost of harbouring a bubble of security, the so-called comfort zone, results naturally in the denial of the unknown, the so-called shadow. The problem is one of glamour.

The gods fight the giants and repress them to the corners of the earth. However, it must be noted that the giants know a process of evolution, too. They are metaphorically a part of the human consciousness. As the human being evolves, so does every part in him.

REGIN

The resulting civilization of gods is a reflection of consciousness in relation to itself. They become their own object of consciousness. Thus the individual arrives at a thought-form of himself: his *persona*. He identifies himself with what he thinks about himself and what he dreams of becoming. The astral and mental substance in his aura respond accordingly and create the ego.

But the gods are not individuals yet. When we study the *Voluspa* and its related sources, we discern that the creative work is completed by a collective. As a unity, the gods tend to build towards a common future. Everything is done as a community for the community. No-one is ahead and none is behind. There is no personal desire... yet. The Golden Age of the gods is characterized by mass consciousness.

Later, the Aesir will represent different functions in the human mind. But the incentive to differentiate will only be evoked when the comfort zone is challenged. A fine analogy would be the development of stem cells into specialized cells. In the individual, certain functions will be given more attention than others, according to personality.

The current stage of mass consciousness is a crude form of group consciousness similar to what a flock of birds or a shoal of fish or a colony of ants experiences. Although separate units exist on the physical plane, no sense of individuality has yet developed. We still speak of a flock of people when the herd instinct moves them.

Nonetheless, the institutionalization of a group of gods creates the possibility of individualization. When Midgard was first formed, the gods were vaguely called "the sons of Bur". After that event they adopted the name Regin. Among them, no chairman is named. All are equal.

The work of the Regin mostly consists of mooting over the next step of creation. They gather in their seats and discuss the problem at hand.

As a symbol, such an assembly suggests concentration. The individual contemplates a course of action. In other words, the mind gathers all the available energies in order to make a decision. As such, the Regin are an instrument of the Will. Incidentally, the seats they occupy are called *rökstóla* meaning seat of destiny. The morpheme *rök* means judgment or destiny. In this context, destiny is synonymous with evolution. Their decisions induce responsibility.

The Early Days: The Golden Age

TAFL

Voluspa stanzas 7 and 8 reflect the individual's inner development. The gods exhibit the process of learning, the appropriation of skill and the application of knowledge. The creative mind develops. The mind interacts with what it experiences. It recognizes its need, survival, desire, aspiration.

Three paths of experience emerge. These are symbolized by the temples, the smithies and the gaming pieces. The golden pieces represent attachment to pleasure and denote materially oriented people. It characterizes selfishness. Satisfaction of desire motivates them. The smithies represent catering for the basic needs of life in order to survive. The temple symbolizes the mystic path and reorientation to the spiritual vision. The three symbols represent a person's motivation to act. They are each expressions of the lower will powering the individual's consciousness.

On a higher arc, the temple and the smithy represent the split of paths. One person feels more attracted to the Path of the Priest whereas another chooses the Path of the Smith. The former represents the life of the mystic and the latter that of the occultist.

Smithy	Satisfaction of needs	Survival
Gaming pieces	Satisfaction of desire	Selfishness
Temple	Aspiration	Reorientation

THURSAR

The Golden Age is upset by the invasion of three lady giants. The security established by the Regin is breached. Within the individual we see the mental realm of the gods juxtaposed to the astral realm of the giants. *Voluspa* shows that the less refined person is centred in the emotional self and not in the mental self. Therefore the order of the Aesir cannot be sustained. The mind turns to selfish ends because it is governed by the lower will. Base desire overrides the sense of community and disrupts the balance.

The presence of the giantesses tests the established bubble of security. What has been ignored earlier will now surface again. It puts pressure on the emotional resolve of the individual. To find peace, the gods have to change and develop. Now the mind knows that it must reckon with forces outside the self. Higher faculties of mind need to be developed to cope with abstract situations and eventualities if another disruption is to be avoided. Indeed, Thor will specialize in dealing with such cases.

Herein lies the seed of individualization because the sense of self is consequently accentuated.

DVERGAR

The next stage offers a solution to cope with the upheaval. The dwarves are created. They represent the *persona*. The individual consciously or subconsciously creates masks to face the outer world. Depending on the circumstances, another mask is worn. This helps lessen the pressure that outer influences, such as other people, exert on the inner self. They are the logical result of the clash of the self-conscious unit with the unwieldy forces of society, symbolized by the giantesses.

This outside layer of the personality makes the inner world of the individual invisible. It makes him less vulnerable. Through the army of dwarves, the individual is able to retain a sense of self. Under pressure, such masks are automatically evoked. It is a mechanism of self-defence.

Mankind: The Age of Man

ODIN HOENIR LODUR

At some point, true individuality is developed. This is symbolized by the break-up of the Regin collective. Three gods remove themselves and go their own way. Notwithstanding, they walk together as a smaller unit. The process of individualization happens gradually. If we consider an original band of twelve Aesir, then a team of three makes a smaller group, but still a group. There is a stage between mass consciousness and individual consciousness comprising of smaller group units. The same group activity still reigns over all the members. The three gods still work together toward a common goal, but the fact that they separate from the source marks an important change.

It takes an effort of will to separate oneself from the group mind. It means to go counter to the opinions and moral codes of the congregation. In itself it represents an aspect of initiation. The decision itself is exemplary of wielding the power of individuality.

Somewhat later the three are called by name which finalizes the process of individualization. Odin, Hoenir and Lodur leave their comfort zone and explore what is outside their own consciousness. They necessarily expand consciousness. They venture into the unknown, Utgard, represented by the beach. The symbol of the beach is very interesting, since it denotes the vague and changing line between control and no control, between confidence and fear. The border changes continually as the tide moves in and out. Per definition, consciousness cannot venture beyond that point. The coastline represents the individual's Ring Pass Not, which on a grander scale is embodied by Jormungand.

The triad's adventure signifies a mission of bringing civilization.

ASK EMBLA

Odin, Hoenir and Lodur find two logs of wood at the beach, an ash and an elm, and shape the first man and woman from it. Man and woman are washed ashore from the subconscious unto the conscious. Their creation symbolizes the externalization of consciousness. The evolution of consciousness can only progress through the efforts of the physical person.

According to Woutersen-van Weerden, creation up to this point entails the preparation for the incarnation of the human soul. The gods have to create the right conditions first. Then, the human being will be able to become conscious. Before this point, humans were unconscious and were dependent on an encompassing group soul. The anthropogenesis marks the switch from the downward involutionary arc to the upward evolutionary one.

The inanimate wood symbolizes a lack of individual consciousness. Neither Ash nor Elm has Orlog. This means that they cannot make their own choices. Once the gods endow man and woman with life and mind they are able to make decisions. They become free and can choose their own life. They shape their Orlog. We might interpret Orlog as individual consciousness. Without it, the person is asleep. This stage in the story corresponds to our waking consciousness.

Now, the gods guide mankind and look on. Therefore, a further distinction must be made between the mental plane and how we experience consciousness in everyday life. The Aesir symbolize a person's higher self. In a sense, the gods become teachers. Evidently, it is the person's inner wish to reconnect with the realm of the gods. The individual has to realize his inner divinity, which is anchored in him by the gifts of life and consciousness. Then he will be able to manifest the Divine. Through devotional work, many people already feed back to the realm of the gods. This is evolution.

The downpour of life and consciousness results in the awakening of mankind, but it also means the death of awareness of a higher level. Very early, the Monadic consciousness of Ymir was slain. Subsequently the so-called buddhic consciousness represented by the Regin was affected. To the individual, their collective represents the causal body. Now, through the medium of the three gods, the person is awakened to self-consciousness and the mind centres on the three lower planes. It therefore loses contact with the higher planes. That is why the human being is not immediately conscious of his indwelling soul and its plane, represented by Asgard.

The metaphor can be taken further. The gods have access to all the worlds. This reflects how the human soul sees and knows all. It remains centralized in Asgard, which is the higher mental plane. On the other hand, the human has only access to Midgard, which represents his personality, his physical plane life. The gods reach out toward Midgard from time to time, but an upward movement is necessary to establish lasting contact with the Higher Self. Aspiration and a reorientation towards spiritual ideals lead an individual to the gates of Valhalla.

Here, the Aesir represent the overshadowing soul, reaching out daily, as the Aesir descend the Rainbow Bridge to moot over World affairs. At first, the individual is not conscious of this higher reality, but gradually, the Bifrost Bridge is built toward Asgard, and he is able to return.

YGGDRASIL

The subject of Orlog returns in the following stanzas. There is a tree named Yggdrasil and a well named Urd. At the well, three women shape the fate of mankind. They determine Orlog. There seems to be an immediate link with the creation of mankind.

The link is strengthened by the statement that the ash is named Yggdrasil. If the text is taken literally, it says that the gods find an ash and an elm, and that the ash is called Yggdrasil. It must be the name of the first man. Naming the logs of wood would have imbued them with Orlog. According to Woutersen-van Weerden, Yggdrasil represents the consciousness of I in any human. It is the medium of the ego and therefore represents individuality. The Yggdrasil myths are about mankind.

We can imagine two original trees at Urd's Well. Archetypically, the Well mirrors the beach of stanza 17. Analogously, the three Aesir are reflected by the three Norns. The picture is perfectly symmetrical. One body of water, two trees, three forces of fate. The Norns work in team with the Aesir. The individual is created by male and female forces. In addition, the scene reminds us of how magical thought-forms are created.

The Norns choose life and declare Orlog. These two aspects correspond to the life and consciousness aspect bestowed by the Aesir. But the Norns also impose laws. These include both the limitations of physical plane life and the cosmic laws or principles. The individual feels less free than the gods, because he is bound to the earth plane and its laws, but the gods and the Norns have no Free Will at all.

Orlog manifests as fate on the one hand, on the other hand it manifests as Free Will. The proximity of the Norns to the Tree of Life shows how intricately the life of the individual is intertwined with Orlog. Through the female forces of Karma, the divine Will and purpose are esoterically programmed in mankind. The evolution of consciousness becomes a conscious development.

The presence of the Norns teaches us that the individual must become conscious of the Law of Cause and Effect. These goddesses are the personification of this Law. They put it into practice through the power of decision and speech. Esoterically, these powers refer to a person's responsibility to right action and right speech.

Yggdrasil represents the implementation of Orlog in mankind.

The First War: The Age of Guilt

GULLVEIG

The main danger of individuality is the tendency to be separative. The ego increases in importance. The group connection recedes into the background. People cling to their own truths and opinions and no longer sympathize with the feelings of others. Conflicts between human beings or between aspects of the self consequently arise. In stories and myth, this is usually portrayed by war.

The First War shifts our focus back onto the world of the gods. However, everything that happens in the upper worlds inevitably works out on the physical plane. The war of the gods forms a mythical precedent of human behaviour.

There are three stages to the war and each has its importance. First there is a cause. Then the actual war is waged. Lastly, there is the aftermath. Similarly, any form of damage taken in the physical has a cause. Usually, the cause has long been present in the astral or the mental. The moment of damage can be relatively short, but the time it takes to heal typically takes much longer. In the story, the war is caused by Gullveig, is waged by the Aesir and Vanir, and results in the loss of the goddess Freyja.

Gullveig represents an alien element invading the comfort zone. Her presence causes the latent tendency to exclusion to appear. As a symbol, she first and foremost represents the Other, but she can also denote an aspect of the self.

Earlier, the creation of mankind heralded individuality. This resulted in a development of selfishness. This is only natural, because the individual needs to explore his own self. But a pressure such as Gullveig causes discord. If she represents other people, then the individual learns to deal with other people. But every person responds according to his own wits. Everyone acts for their own good. So do the gods.

The upset gods are called to order by one individual; in this case, Odin. He forces everyone to gather and think as one again. By seizing power, Odin incidentally creates a hierarchical system, but a form of government is necessary at this level. We observe how individuality produces inequality. Odin orders the mind to work as one again. He calls the meeting.

The task of removing the energy of Gullveig from the system appears to be a hard one. The gods kill the woman, but she revives every time. If she represents an influence from within the self of which the individual is not conscious, then we relate her to thoughts and emotions that surface now and then but are repressed every time. She shows herself when the mind relaxes and has nothing else to occupy itself with. She is an aspect of the self that cries out to be integrated in the personality, but the conscious mind does neither accept nor recognize her. Not yet. The motif shows how a person is faced with a part of his self, some element from his Jungian shadow, and how he ignores it every time.

VANIR

Gullveig shakes the foundations of the individual's personality. She tries his peace and disturbs his well-being. The war represents the personality reaction of the individual when faced with something unfamiliar. Because the Aesir repress Gullveig, the Vanir knock on Asgard's door and ask to settle things. The Vanir come and sue for peace, but the Aesir remain thick-headed. They need to learn the hard way. They rather fight than admit being wrong. They oppose the possibility of the Other. War results in the self. But in the end a pact of peace will be sealed anyway.

Psychologically, the Vanir and Aesir represent two aspects of the self. Or they can be two conflicting ideas in the mind, for example when a new paradigm is introduced, or when something traumatic happens.

The mind is centralized in Asgard, meaning that selfishness still has the upper hand. At some point the other side of the self needs to assert itself. Consciousness wants to express itself. The Vanir march on Asgard.

The Vanir will destroy the wall that protects the city of the Aesir. Their invading force intends to break down the walls that we imprison ourselves in. The wall represents longstanding habits, judgments and opinions. These need to be deconstructed before further growth is possible. As such, the old buildings represent thought-forms that have served their purpose.

In every respect, a wall represents separateness and isolation. Strong opinions inhibit an open mind. Tearing down the walls surrounding the mind creates a new openness towards the outside world. There can be no wall. Many mythologies from over the world speak about serial gates to enter either the upper worlds or the underworlds. Analogously, many a hero must travel seven mountains to get somewhere, and so on. Each time a gate or mountain is taken, the individual's view widens. Every time a wall is taken down, consciousness expands.

For a time, small thoughts and opinions are necessary and they temporarily give an illusory sentiment of self-confidence. They protect and shelter the ego. But they also close off the mind from new information and possibilities. They narrow. That is why Gullveig shakes the very centre. The presence of Gullveig puts pressure on existing patterns of behaviour which prove inadequate. Like Yeats says: "Things fall apart. The centre cannot hold." This is the Vanir's blessing. Mental rigidity is softened by a touch of loving understanding.

Here we see the basic process of self-development. Once a good degree of individuality is achieved it is necessary to return to a more inclusive vision. The path of individuality will have honed the individual skills which will only yield supreme results when the gods work as a team again. And after the war is over, a ritual of atonement will stretch the cooperation even further. Pacts of peace are vowed and a sort of universal brotherhood ensues so that the opposite camp will forever be included in the realm of the divine.

When war breaks out the Aesir still cling to their right. On those grounds, they initiate war. Odin of the Aesir casts his spear and declares war. He obviously wants to be in control. What is good about this act is that he takes on the challenge in a conscious way. I would almost say self-conscious. The spear represents his decision to cope with the situation. War is better than to keep trying to repress Gullveig. The war will eventually settle things. The mind takes up the challenge to stand and face something it would rather avoid. Within the context of self-development this is a big step forward. It means the superficial self starts to be honest with itself.

We see Odin emerge as the exponent of the Aesir. He is the leader. He is the aspect in the mind that makes decisions. He needs the others to contemplate the situation and carry out his orders, but the decision is entirely his. Remember the spear is a symbol of the Will. Now, the self is making conscious decisions about itself, about how it responds, how it can improve on itself.

FREYJA

At some point the mind realizes it cannot fight against itself. The war ceases and a new solution is looked for. What follows is the long process of integrating two apparently opposing aspects. This is symbolized by the truce settled by the warring camps. The Aesir and Vanir meet as Regin and decide to exchange hostages. We know this from other sources than *Voluspa*. The poem only says that the Regin gather in a meeting and oaths have been taken. From Snorri's material, we know that the gods enact a ritual of atonement.

The *Voluspa* poem, however, focuses on the aftermath of the war. In the meeting, the damage is measured. The gods are wounded in two ways. In general, the gods complain about poison. In particular, they become suddenly aware of Freyja missing. What does all this mean?

The main result of war is loss. We can say that the person is no longer whole or complete. A time of healing must follow. The fact that one of the Vanir is missing is significant, because they were the opposing force in the first place. Metaphorically, the goddess Freyja represents either sexual drive or creativity.

According to the poem, the giants took off with her. They represent the subconscious. Jotunheim is the realm of the physical needs and instincts. In quite a lot of myths we see how the giants want to kidnap one or other of the goddesses. This shows how what she symbolizes shifts from conscious to subconscious or unconscious. If she represents controlled desire in the realm of the gods, she becomes lust in the realm of the giants.

Later, Freyja moves to Asgard as part of the truce agreement. This symbolizes the integration of sexuality into civilization.

Only one god heals the loss. Thor immediately sets out after the goddess. He is the aspect in us that acts. His responsiveness also demonstrates the purpose of individuality. The mind would not have been capable of this had it remained unconscious of individuality and lacked mental differentiation.

The goddess is especially linked with Od. He is an obscure god known to be Freyja's husband. If his name is explained, he becomes the personification of one of the mental abilities that the gods gave man and woman. His name means inspiration. It couples Inspiration with Creativity. When Freyja is missing, Inspiration can no longer be channeled. The mind is no longer capable of expressing itself. She is in fact the manifestation of art, wrought by Creativity and caused by Od. Freyja is creative energy. That includes the drive to reproduction as well as the drive to artistic expression.

LAEVI

War leaves a bad taste in the mouth.

The mind is poisoned and no longer innocent. It feels unclean and wounded. Poison reflects a troubled mind, maybe even depression. According to esoteric tradition, the astral plane is formed as a byproduct of mind and matter. What the person contacts on this level is of his own creation and blots out the light of the soul. In a *Treatise on White Magic*, it says: "It is ... individuality which has brought humanity to its present condition (of world illusion). It is the consciousness of duality ... of 'I am God' and 'I am form' which has plunged mankind into the great illusion."

The wounds need cleansing before true recovery is possible. A sustained period of purification is therefore advisable. When the person no longer feels whole, he no longer feels holy. That is why so many esoteric traditions stress the habitual performance of a rite of purification.

Depression clouds the mind and makes clear thinking impossible. This condition might be even worse than war itself. Now there is doubt, regret, fear.

The Regin come together and evaluate events. When you go over all the happenings of the past, the causes, all that has brought you to this point, then understanding becomes possible. There may be decisions you regret, but there may be choices that you support as well. Perhaps this causes a form of self-doubt, but it also makes change possible. Here begins the long path of questioning yourself. The whole question of ethics bubbles up. Because you are self-conscious you are never one hundred percent sure whether what you do is right or wrong. Conscience starts to build.

A seed of self-confidence is always present. This is symbolized by Thor. He represents the integrity of the person, the aspect of yourself that never doubts. The giants impersonate fear, doubts, regrets and everything that takes us off balance. Thor deals with all this. He faces trouble believing in his own power. To assert yourself, you will have to allow the qualities of Thor to grow. Not just confidence but also the discipline to carry it out. Each for himself has to make the decision to go forward, improve and leave the dark clouds behind. Blow them away. That is what it means to work on yourself.

Freyja, too, represents self-confidence. Her abduction symbolizes faltering, when before you were so sure about everything. The first thing that happens with a person when he becomes more self-conscious is a loss of confidence. Opposing world views fight in his mind and make him victim to uncertainty and indecisiveness. When he takes a stand and becomes like Thor, then he regains the ground he lost when all was easy and comfortable in life. That is when Thor brings back the goddess.

Allegorically, the phase of growth before self-consciousness can be likened to childhood, when mom and dad take care of us and we have not much to worry about. Later, when we reach young adulthood, we fight away from that warm home and want to find out who we are. Then, all the troubles, cares and joys of life cross our path, but in the long run, the Lost Son will return home.

The Death of Balder: The Age of Portents

Voluspa 31-33
I saw Balder's, the bloody war god,
Odin's child, Orlog obscured.
It stood waxed higher on the field,
Slim and very fair, the mistletoe.

That beam, which slim seemed, became
A harm-flight, dangerous. Hoder took to shooting.
Balder's brother was quickly born.
He, Odin's son, one night old, took to fighting.

Though he never (washed) hands nor head combed
Ere he to the pyre bore Balder's adversary
But Frigg grieved in Fensalir
Over the woe of Valhalla.

BALDER

Up to this point, everything recounted in *Voluspa* has led mankind to develop individual consciousness. What happens next relates to the present and the future. The last phase of human consciousness is revealed at Ragnarok. That great event is itself divided into two great phases. The first one comprises the signs and portents of the Last War. The omens start with the death of Balder and the binding of Loki and end with the three cocks who call. The second phase comprises the war itself.

In my view, the Last War represents the consummation of consciousness. In other words, Ragnarok signifies initiation in an esoteric sense. Many different stages lead up to the actual war or initiatic event, but it is introduced by the death of Balder. A long time exists between the death of Balder and the onset of Ragnarok. In fact, the Eddic poems *Skirnismal*, *Hymiskvida* and *Lokasenna* and their related tales fit in between the two events.

It is particular of *Voluspa* to present the distant past and the imminent future, but nothing is said about what happens in between. There is also a long gap of history missing prior to Balder's death. However, we do not need myths to understanding what is in between, for that is where man and woman find themselves now.

The long time that passes between the death of Balder and the onset of War esoterically coincides with the Probationary Path. It says in *Initiation, Human and Solar*: "The Path of Probation precedes the Path of Initiation ... and marks that period in the life of a man when he definitely sets himself on the side of the forces of evolution ... He takes himself in hand, cultivates the qualities that are lacking in his disposition, and seeks with diligence to bring his personality under control." In other words, he consciously cooperates with the tide of evolution. In chapter 10, we will explore this section of the Path in relation to the exploits of Thor.

Balder's death marks the reorientation of the individual towards the spiritual Path. This early phase of preparation consists of two lesser stages. That is, Balder's death is followed by the binding of Loki. The events are directly related and both refer to something that is removed from consciousness.

When Balder is slain, the gods are shocked. As a son of Odin he was destined to become his successor. He was loved by all. Balder therefore is what one strives toward. The young god reflects the image of perfection that one constructs of oneself. He is the seed of perfection in us. His sudden loss tests the preparedness of the individual to take initiation. Balder symbolizes the promise of the individual's true Self developing.

To most people, Balder is what you hold dear. He is a person's reason to live. When a person is confronted with the loss of what he holds dear, his reaction varies in accordance with his level of development. Do you collapse under the loss? Or do you remain poised and can you guarantee a continuation of consciousness? The loss of Balder tests whether the individual is able to let go of his personal desires, especially the desire of achievement. Every act and thought of selfishness postpones the event of initiation. As long as the person holds on to his selfish desires he will be faced with loss.

Understanding the meaning of sacrifice is necessary to follow the path toward initiation. The god's death suddenly leaves the person free to act. He no longer feels attached to the innocence that Balder symbolizes. The god's purity is inferred by the *Grimnismal* stanza on his hall: "In that land, ominous staves are the fewest." Now, one is no longer bound by any moral standard or his own conscience. The dissolution of personal conscience helps develop the personality in a big way. The opinions and masks that you hide behind are sacrificed. "Naught else but selfishness is sacrificed," it says in *The Externalisation of the Hierarchy*.

In Bailey's book *Initiation, Human and Solar* we are told: "Each step up is ever through the sacrifice of all that the heart holds dear on one plane or another, and always must this sacrifice be voluntary. He who treads the Probationary Path and the Path of Holiness is he who has counted the cost, whose sense of values has been readjusted, and who therefore judges not as judges the man of the world."

The direct cause of Balder's death was the hand of his blind brother Hoder. They are thought to be twins and can be explained as such. Hoder's blindness symbolizes ignorance. His hand is guided by Loki. Hoder does not know that Loki gives him the one weapon able to kill Balder. He is blind to the truth. In a way, ignorance is a brother of innocence.

Both innocence and ignorance indicate a stage in a person's evolution where he has not awakened yet. Innocence implies a lack of experience which is necessary to grow in wisdom. Ignorance, willed or not, must be mended before the person can consciously tread the Path. The loss of innocence changes a person.

The death of Balder is avenged by Vali. This means the death of Hoder. Almost together the brothers leave Asgard and fare to Hel. They are eliminated from the waking consciousness but hide in the subconscious. Now, the individual opens his eyes and sees the world as it is. He is no longer blind to what happens around him, good or bad. And he acts, because he is no longer bound by the ideal of perfection either. In the meanwhile, the twin brothers stay in the Underworld and await their time. At some point the individual will have gone through all the necessary experiences to bring him before the fires of initiation and then real purity can manifest in the person. That is when Balder and Hoder will rise again.

That is the double meaning of the death of Balder. Firstly, it means sacrifice. Secondly, it ensures the continuation of consciousness.

Voluspa 34

A bound one she saw lying under Hveralund,
Treason-hungry, similar to the body of Loki.
There sits Sigyn, though not about her
Husband well gladdened.

LOKI

After Balder's death is avenged, Loki, too, is punished. The story is recounted in the *Lokasenna* poem, but reference is made in *Voluspa* in close connection with the murder. Loki is bound.

In the story, Loki represents the voice in our head inciting us to bad intentions. Of course, his words do not sound bad at all. In *Lokasenna* we are told how the gods finally become weary of Loki's doings. Consciousness can no longer bide with harmful thought and action. His distraction contradicts progress on the spiritual path. The mind no longer agrees to think in selfish terms. Instead the individual gains control over his thoughts. A sense of altruism grows. In the same vein, binding Loki stands for control over the astral.

Again, the gods strive toward a common good. They work together to bind Loki. As aspects of the mind, they each contribute their personal powers for the greater good. Information from the *Snorra Edda* shows that Loki is caught by the cooperation of many. Kvasir realizes that Loki has changed into a salmon. Thor is able to catch the fish. And Skadi exacts her vengeance. These are only a few roles. The joint effort makes it possible to shift consciousness to a higher level. The person no longer thinks in terms of theirself. On the contrary, he starts to appreciate group effort and group consciousness.

This event, too, is an example of the Law of Sacrifice. The lower, unnecessary thoughts are banned so that consciousness can rely upon itself. In that way, it can be trusted to receive the subtler information of the intuition. In a grander perspective, the person sacrifices himself in the service of his brothers and sisters. For one, there is Skadi, who is usually opposed to the gods. She is a giantess, but has been wronged by Loki. Now she puts her differences with the Aesir aside and works in team. The mind concentrates.

Both Balder and Loki are sacrificed. Both times the individual makes a decision to reorient his personality. In reality, one has to make this decision repeatedly. Balder frees you to act as you like, but Loki keeps you distracted. The giant god flees and hides and changes shape, but he will finally be caught. Then, one will know peace of mind and be able to channel the higher energies. The individual unselfishly strives forward for the good of all and lets nothing lead him astray or distract him. Everything that he gives up is summarized in Balder's death and Loki's binding. Why someone would do this is the Great Mystery. He sacrifices his life in the service of humanity.

Voluspa 41-42

There sat on a mound and beat a harp
A Gygjar shepherd, glad Eggther.
Sang over him on the gallow's wood
A fair red cock, which is called Fjalar.

Sang among the Aesir, Gullinkambi,
He wakes the heroes, at Herjafödr's
Another sings beneath the earth
A soot red cock in the halls of Hel

GULLINKAMBI

Three events signal Ragnarok. First of all, three cocks cry their morning song. Secondly, Heimdal blows his war horn. And in the meantime, Garm howls ominously. They happen not just in the world of the gods, but in the other worlds, too. All three awaken the sleeping hero. He must rise and make ready - for initiation is imminent.

First of all, we are told of three cocks. They are associated with early morning, the time of waking up, and therefore represent spiritual awakening. The first cock is Fjalar and lives in Jotunheim. He summons the adverse forces. The giants represent everything that is not refined yet on the Path of Probation, the attempts to purify one's body, thoughts and feelings. This process makes it possible for the Light and wisdom of the soul to pour through, find foothold and remain in the consciousness of the individual. But old habits die hard. A constant effort to cleanse the self from unwanted emotional and mental patterns puts pressure on the undesirable habits, and they are consequently activated. The giants prepare for battle.

The second cock is Gullinkambi. He lives with the Aesir and wakes the fallen heroes of Valhalla. The only reason for their existence is to battle the forces of darkness. The motif of awakening implies that the heroes have been slumbering all the while. The mind musters its energies to face the last battle with himself.

The mythologem is widespread in Western Europe. Many legends across Europe speak about dead kings and their armies sleeping in mounds and mountains who will awaken when their people are in need. According to Farwerck, many of these mountains are named after Odin. Examples are Onsberg in Samsø, Denmark, Odensberg in Schonen, Sweden, Godesberg in Bonn, Germany, Vaudemont in Lorraine, France, Woensberg in Huizen, the Netherlands, and Woodnesborough in Wiltshire, Great Britain. He names many more. Frequently, legends about ghost armies are associated with these places. Similar stories circulate about King Arthur, Charlemagne, Barbarossa and Holger the Dane in Kronborg Castle.

A third cock cries in Hel and wakes the dead. They, too, will oppose the mental realm of the gods. The aspirant has arrived at a point where he can no longer shy away of any impurity lingering in his personality. Every fault will be tested until the person is found perfect. The long dead traumas and the personality faults that have always been avoided now rise from the cellars of the mind.

In their entirety the three cocks are one's sensitivity. It borders on extrasensory perception. Their cry reverberates throughout the three layers of the world, the upper, the middle and the lower world. The threefold personality has therefore become an integrated whole. The awakening is the individual's response to intuition.

Voluspa 43
Now Garm barks mightily in front of Gnipahellir.
The leash shall be slit but Freki will run.
A lot of lore she knows – I see longer forward in time:
The bitter Ragnarok of the war gods of victory.

GARM

The last section of the poem is supported by a refrain which forewarns the doom of the gods. According to the stanza, Garm barks before the entrance of Gnipahellir. He is identified as the hellhound guarding the gates of Hella's domain. In *Baldrs Draumar*, Odin encounters him on the threshold of the Underworld.

The hound may originally have been a pet animal buried with its owner. Or it may have been one of those dogs buried under the threshold of the family farm when it died. Even in death, the dog guarded the house.

Its baying must be interpreted as a warning call. Dogs, like other animals, are sensitive to imminent danger. One example from history is the destruction of Pompeii. It is said that dogs had long fled the city before the lethal eruption of the Vesuvius covered the area. To the human mind, the baying dog symbolizes intuition. Birds have a similar sense for danger.

Gnipahellir means mountain cave. It is the typical place where the dead were believed to reside. The place name is connected with the stories of dead kings and heroes sleeping in the mountains. Clearly there is an overlap between them and the Einherjar roused by Gullinkambi.

Another overlap is found in the motif. The refrain says that Garm's fetters spring. This coincides with the unleashing of Fenrir. The wolf-son of Loki was bound by the gods in another act of mental discipline, but at Ragnarok, he runs free. On the field he fights Odin and then Vidar. Curiously, Garm, too, appears in the battle. He fights Tyr. But Tyr is the deity responsible for binding Fenrir. Therefore, Garm might be a kenning for Fenrir. Furthermore, the stanza confuses Garm with Freki. One wolf name was synonymous with any other wolf of Norse mythology in skaldic poetry. *Voluspa* mentions Garm only in the refrain. He is not mentioned as a participant in the battle. Snorri puts the dog on the battlefield opposing Tyr. In early times, Tyr might have been the one fighting Fenrir in the Last Battle.

The refrain is the only time Ragnarok is mentioned as such. The word is a composite of *regin* and the Old Norse word *rök*. Ragnarok is the last of the Regin gatherings. In response to Heimdal's war horn, the gods assemble one last time on their Seats of Judgment.

Voluspa 45

Mim's sons lick, but the Measurer is kindled

At the call of Gjallarhorn

High blows Heimdal, the horn aloft

Odin speaks with Mim's head.

The ash of Yggdrasil trembles standing,

The old tree howls, but the Jotun giant gets loose.

GJALLARHORN

Heimdal's sounding of the horn symbolizes the response of the individual to what Garm and Gullinkambi intuit. Heimdal is the guardian of the gods. His vigilance is famed.

The myths describe his keen senses. He is able to hear grass grow, or the wool on a sheep's back. This represents sensitiveness. The guardian god picks up information quicker than any other god. He therefore represents traits as sympathy, empathy, intuition and telepathy. He tunes in to the rippling disturbances in the fabric of Mother Earth's life pulse before it happens on the physical plane. The development of psychic abilities is a natural effect of the development of consciousness. In fact, the mind is sensitive per definition, but the individual must learn to become conscious of it, and recognises the Heimdal aspect in himself.

When Heimdal senses the movement of the giants, he blows his horn and the mind is suddenly awake. He registers every change within and without the mind. In a sense, he might be regarded as the aura which picks up any force that impinges on it. When a person tunes in to his own body awareness and from there expands his consciousness into the energy field around him, he creates a field of awareness in which it is easier to become conscious of any kind of impression. This includes the etheric disturbances, the emotional movements, and the mental currents. It is almost akin to second sight, touch and hearing. In the long run, the individual attempts to become sensitive to impressions from his own soul or Higher Self. If he is able to become aware of such impressions, chances are that he will be able to hear the gods themselves and consciously respond to their contact. Heimdal is the link between the human world and the realm of the gods.

MIMIR

In the same verse, stanza 46, Odin consults with Mimir. Allfather sets off to meet the giant when he has been informed of the looming war. It is an immediate response to the registered intuition of Heimdal. Odin understands what is happening and needs time to reflect. He does not act impulsively. The episode is all about the contemplation by the soul.

Mimir means memory. So Allfather makes an attempt to learn from the past. Odin represents a person's active intelligence seeking memory to make a decision. In fact, the awareness is an aspect of the mind associated with the past.

Voluspa 47-49

Hrym drives from the east, bears the linden (shield) in front
Jormungand coils in a Jotun mood
The worm knocks the waves, but the eagle screeches
Nidföl slits corpses. Naglfar gets loose

A keel fares from the east. Muspell's peoples shall
Come over the sea. But Loki steers.
Fare all the kin of monsters with Freki
The brother of Byleipt is with them on the journey

What's with the Aesir? What's with the Elves?
All Jotunheim resounds. The Aesir are at Thing
The dwarves groan before their stone doors,
Guides of the rock wall

THING

Visiting Mimir is Odin's personal way to deal with the events. On a larger scale he calls a meeting with the Elves and the Aesir. Supposedly, the Vanir are also present. Even the dwarves are mentioned. They know what is upon them and realize that death awaits. Total annihilation is prophesied. The near-immortal races are suddenly faced with the transiency of their existence. Together they created this world and now it is threatened with destruction. Will nothing remain of the old world? They seek the truth behind immortality, life and consciousness.

The meeting of the gods has been explained earlier as the concentration of the mind. It refers to mental work or meditation. The dwarves are mentioned separately, but they played a role in the creation story as a force to keep the giants at bay. They are also associated with stone and rock which are symbols of things that last. Now they grieve because even that will be wiped away. They represent our fondness of material things, objects, things that are owned. All of this will now disappear. The individual learns via a process of pain and suffering to let go of stuff.

In the complex of the self the dwarven race corresponds to the lunar lords from esoteric literature. They compose our lower self, with all its wants, urges and feelings. They are elementals residing in the threefold personality, meaning that they govern our physical plane body, our personal feelings and thoughts. Through them the soul attempts to express its qualities. In order to do that, the lunar lords have to be subdued. So long as the solar soul is not aligned with the personality, the lunar lords take over and move us in the material world. Consequently, the dwarves fear they will lose their place in the personality and no longer be able to rule.

Ragnarok: The End of the World

THE DWELLER ON THE THRESHOLD

Meanwhile the giants rise. They react to aspiration. When Loki is bound, all the giants fear this and rebel. The individual stands face to face with his dark side. The concept is sometimes personified as the Dweller on the Threshold.

In Bailey's *Esoteric Astrology* it is said: "This Dweller is the sumtotal of all the personality characteristics which have remained unconquered and unsubtle, and which must be finally overcome before initiation can be taken . . . The unconquered residue, and the ancient liabilities are numerous, and excessively potent, and ... there eventuates a life wherein the highly developed and powerful personality becomes, in itself, the

Dweller on the Threshold. Then the Angel of the Presence and the Dweller stand face to face ... and ... [the disciple] begins the battle between the pairs of opposites."

The Angel of the Presence is personified by Heimdal. The Dweller on the Threshold is Loki. He leads the army of giants to Asgard. But behind Heimdal a host of gods and heroes stands. Behind Loki, every family of giants follows. According to the *Snorra Edda*, Heimdal and Loki fight each other at Ragnarok.

It is significant that the giant force moves towards Asgard in ships. Water represents the astral world and the giants are masters of illusion. As a collective, they represent *maya* and glamour. One ship is sailed by Hrym, another by Loki, and a third is owned by Surt. They lead an open challenge over the waters of deception. Their invasion has a precedent in the beginning of the poem when three giant maidens uprooted the Golden Age of the gods.

The burning ground where both armies meet is known as Vigrid. The Aesir and Vanir make ready and both Odin and Frey lead. On one level this represents the harmonious cooperation of the left and right brain. On another level, it indicates the tendency to act as a group. The great conflict of Ragnarok causes parties to assemble and work together. This tendency from individual thinking to group awareness marks the next point in the evolution of consciousness. It no longer makes sense to fight amongst ourselves. Now is the time to stand together. The same motif is found in *Lokasenna*, which precedes the events of Ragnarok.

Those who can fight are on the battlefield. Most of the women, however, stay home. Allegorically, they take care of the body. Even under pressure, one has to take care of everyday life. That is what Frigg represents in the poem. She manages the home front while the men are out fighting.

Because Frigg is known as a goddess who knows the fate of every being, she is associated with foresight and intuition. She is a higher aspect of the self. From her union with Odin, Balder was born. He is the best of Aesir and Vanir and therefore symbolizes perfection. Odin realizes that his son's death will eventually conquer the transience with which the gods are faced.

Three forces endanger the lives of the gods: Fenrir, Jormungand and Surt.

Voluspa 50-54

Surt fares from the south with the treason of the bough
The Sun of the gods of victory shines from the sword
Grit clatters but fiends are reeling
Dead heroes tread the way of Hel but heaven is cloven

Then comes to Hlin another harm
When Odin fares with the wolf to fight
But the slayer of Beli (fights) against bright Surt
Then shall Frigg's sweetheart fall

Then comes the powerful kin of Sigfödr,
Vidar, to fight against the beast of death
Let he the kin of Hvedrung with his hands stand
The sword into his heart. Then he avenged his father.

Then comes the famous kin of Hlodyn:
Odin's son goes to fight with the worm
He hits in a mood, Midgard's templar,
All the dead heroes shall rid their homestead,
He goes nine feet, the son of Fjörgyn,
Chilled by the viper, by humility unconcerned

The Sun evinces to blacken. The field sinks into the sea.
Cast from heaven clear stars are

Smoke and life's sustenance chafe.

The heat licks high against heaven itself

FENRIR

Fenrir symbolizes fear. Odin faces him but he proves unable to vanquish the wolf. When he succumbs, his son Vidar takes his place and fights the wolf. Contextually, Vidar is responsibility. When his father dies, he does not think twice but takes his responsibility and stoically deals with the situation.

Vidar is known as the Silent God. He lives alone and no-one visits him. Yet he obeys his father without question. This is the individual's willingness to follow the Plan intuited without first caring about his own self. Another of his traits is indifference. This expresses his detachment from the material world and from his lower self. He acts with dispassion, but not without dedication or resolution. Because of his dispassion he is able to defeat the wolf.

A sense of sacrifice is evoked by Odin's death. Allfather sacrifices himself in the fight because he belongs to the old world. When he dies he makes room for the younger generation. Vidar is one of those promising gods.

The younger generation of gods is prominently present at Ragnarok. Apart from Vidar, there is also Frey, but the sons of Thor also fight in the battle according to the *Snorra Edda*. They are the seeds of new aspects of consciousness to be unfolded after initiation. In the battle, their influence is already present, but after the battle, they will have the time and space to develop. It is clear from the myths that the younger generation of gods is stronger than the elder.

JORMUNGAND

Jormungand is everything that limits us. Thor fights the dragon. While Jormungand tries to poison the world and to instill doubt in the mind,

Thor fights to break free from its influence. He fights for liberation. With Jormungand he removes from the personality all that hinders and limits. Slaying the monster means a shift of paradigm.

When the old god slays the dragon, Thor, too, dies. As Odin did, Thor sacrifices himself for the New Age. He is no longer needed. After Ragnarok the giants and their kind will no longer threaten the well-being of the individual. He has fulfilled his task.

SURT

Surt is introduced in stanza 52, but in the actual fight, he is no longer mentioned. From the *Snorra Edda*, we know he battled Frey. However, he makes his presence felt in *Voluspa* in a different shape. He represents the destruction of the world. The sea engulfs the land and fire burns the rest. The flood is originally an aspect of Jormungand, but the destruction by fire is brought about by Surt.

Jormungand and Surt are Water and Fire. In this respect, the dragon is the Ring Pass Not, the desire of form, of material possession, the desire to be in the form. Jormungand represents the workings of the magical formula TAU. On the contrary, the fire giant burns away everything that blots out the light of the soul. Surt embodies the magical formula AUM.

The destruction of earth by fire and water can mean physical death. From an esoteric point of view, it means purification by water and fire. Through Ragnarok, the focus shifts from the personality life to soul life. Initiation takes place and consciousness finds its completion. Up to that point the earth necessarily went through all the different experiences of personality life. The Aesir were able to develop. Midgard thus is all about the personality.

The destruction of the world is analogous to the death of the gods. Indeed, a divine being dies when the world ends. Sun and stars disappear.

A New World Rises: The New Age

> **Voluspa 56**
>
> She sees the Earth come up a second time
> Out of the Ocean, very green.
> The waterfalls flow. The eagle flies over it,
> The one who catches fish on the fell.

JORD

After the old world is flooded it sinks away in the ocean. Later, a new world arises much like the first. This new world represents a new form of consciousness. The fact that the same earth rises from the ocean means that we are indeed speaking about the same person, only on a higher level.

> **Voluspa 57-58**
>
> The Aesir find each other at Idavoll
> And the mighty earth-hoop they damn
> And they each remember there the mighty doom
> And the ancient runes of Fimbultyr.
>
> There shall afterwards the wondrous
> Gold *tafl* pieces be found in the grass
> Those of the clan they in the early days had

IDAVOLL

The resurrection of Mother Earth makes further progress possible. She picks up life where she left it. Everything is already there; plants, animals, landscapes. After the cleansing of fire and water, everything on the planet has attained a relative state of perfection.

The gods meet again on the planes of Idavoll, symbolic of the Inner Planes. In the story, this meeting is of significance, because it refers to the initial phase of creation. The Younger Generation repeats history, but on a different level.

The young Aesir reminisce about the past. They remember four specific things. First of all, they remember Ragnarok. This marks the initiation into the New Age. Their memory of it implies that they were fully conscious of the event. Secondly, they remember Jormungand. His death liberated consciousness.

Thirdly, the runes are remembered. In the old world, they were associated with secrecy. They were the domain of Odin the Magician. Now the gods rediscover the runes and they become available to all. The knowledge becomes public. Through Odin's experience, the Mysteries of how to enter the kingdom of the soul are open to all.

Lastly, the younger gods find the golden chess pieces from the Golden Age. They must have been forgotten since the first trouble unbalanced Asgard. The pieces symbolize the return of the joy and innocence of the Golden Age that was hampered for so long. That same peace is found and is finally truly theirs forever. The chess pieces are the tangible proof of a joy long lost which has been restored. The circle closes.

Voluspa 59

Unsown the fields shall wax
All wickedness shall get better. Balder shall come
They dwell, Hoder and Balder, in Hropt's Sigtoftir
The sacred space of the slain gods.

SIGTOFTIR

In this perfect world of mental poise and emotional peace Balder and Hoder make their return. Because they did not actively participate in the apocalypse, they are segments of the old world seeking home in this new world. As aspects of the old life they represent the continuation of consciousness.

But we can reverse the reasoning. Maybe Balder and Hoder are gods of the new world, who could not take root in the old. They hibernated. When the vibration of the individual was raised, this resonated with their true nature, and they were automatically drawn into the mind that is ready for them.

In this new world, Balder and Hoder are no longer separable from each other. They are now one entity. They are mentioned as a pair and they also occupy the same dwelling. Presumably, their return is invoked specifically by reclaiming the old peace of the chess pieces.

Their new home is Sigtoftir. In stark contrast to Valhalla, this new abode emphasizes the triumph over the lower self. *Sigr* means victory whereas *valr* denotes defeat. In esoteric astrology, we would equate *val-* with the fixed cross, the life of hardships before Ragnarok, but also of aspiration and orientation towards the soul. The morpheme *sig-* corresponds to the cardinal cross, referring to a life of compassion and understanding, but also of purpose. Interestingly, Sigtoftir is described as *vé val-tívar* or "the temple of the slain gods". By Val-Tivar, Balder and Hoder are meant.

Voluspa 60-61

Then Hoenir knows how to choose the lot-wood
And the sons of the two brothers settle
In wide Vindheim

A hall she sees standing, fairer than the Sun
Gold roofed at Gimlé.
There shall the doughty lords settle
And for all days make use of Joy.

HOENIR

Then we are told that neither Balder nor Hoder will rule the Younger

Aesir. Instead, Hoenir comes to the fore. He is a brother of Odin who assisted in the creation of man and woman. Hoenir is the first in line to inherit the throne.

Hoenir symbolizes some latent aspect of Odin. In the Old Age Odin ruled as a King of Asgard, but that era has ended. Now the second of three brothers comes in power. In the New Age, Hoenir is able to blossom. He succeeds his brother and equally guarantees the continuation of consciousness.

Moreover, because Hoenir belonged to the three gods who first developed individuality, he is regarded as one of the more advanced gods among the Aesir. He is described as a priest wielding the *hlautviðr*. The item emphasizes his spiritual capacity. He is moreover associated with *óðr*, which relates to consciousness.

In this way, Odin lives on. The brotherly succession means that a third era is hinted at. At the end of the New Age, Hoenir will die and Lodur will take his place. The latter represents the vision aimed at in the New Age. The three brothers and their Epochs correspond to humanity's personality life, soul life and Monadic life respectively.

VINDHEIM

The new kingdom of Hoenir will be called Vindheim. Essentially, Wind Home is a kenning for heaven. Symbolically, it emphasizes the mental realm. In the Old Age, the focus was on the astral and the physical. Now, heaven is on the earth plane.

Vindheim is the reincarnation of Odin's Gladsheim. In Vindheim, a hall is named Gimlé, corresponding to Valhalla. The new hall, too, is described as golden, which reveals a solar symbolism. In this hall, therefore, resides the soul. The individual associates himself with higher ideas and values. He has become one with the soul life centred in Asgard.

According to the stanza, the *dróttir* or lords will dwell here. These are the lords of every race of supernatural beings in Norse mythology. It means the unification of all the aspects of one's self. The Aesir are here, the elves, the dwarves, the Vanir and even the giants. When assembled under one roof, the integrated personality is fully aligned with the higher self. His thought life and his material life match flawlessly. He no longer feels conflict between his instincts, emotions, ideas and intuitions.

Voluspa 62

There comes the dim dragon a-flying,

The glistening viper, from beneath Nidafjöll.

He bears to himself in his feathers – he flies over the planes –

Corpses, Nidhogg does.

NIDHOGG

The *Voluspa* poem closes with the flight of Nidhogg. The dragon is a remnant of the old world which can no longer bide in the New Age. As a force of darkness, he represents the last trace of glamour that disappears. With this, the last possibility of going against the current of evolution is taken away. The last traces of *maya* dissipate in the standing light.

Nidhogg's presence means that the Underworld or subconscious still exists. But this realm no longer poses a threat.

The dragon can be viewed as the personification of a thought-form. As such, he is the aggravated form of all negativity ever created by humanity as a race. Through its age-long existence he has gained intelligence and has become a power keeping people from reaching out to the light. Fear and despair feed the dragon. He is a creature of the shadows, a creature of the Underworld, of Nidafjoll. In the myths, he is a threat to the well-being of Yggdrasil. Nidhogg coils around its roots and damages the tree.

Yet, in this last stanza, the dragon carries away the bodies of the old age. This is a good thing. All the dead thought-forms are disposed of. The soul and the personality are cleansed of the last remaining thoughts and harmful habits. Nidhogg takes it away with him. And with that, the human being is made anew and he can call himself an initiate.

Crises of Consciousness

In the complete story, the creation of man and woman marks the key point in the story of the evolution of consciousness. There is a clear progression from mass to individual consciousness. When the gods are first mentioned, they are a collective. Not one god is mentioned separately. Mass consciousness develops through the work of the Regin. Then a group of three detach themselves from the main party. They create man and woman and give them names. Afterwards, events culminate in the Ragnarok experience.

Lesser initiations take place in preparation of the Ragnarok initiation. They are always accompanied by a crisis. From an esoteric point of view, a crisis offers opportunity. In the words of Laurence Newey, "crises power the evolutionary process and are compulsory opportunities for growth."

A crisis evokes a response from the individual, which is either in line with or against evolution. In the first instance, the response is in accordance with the soul. The second is dominated by the lower self, resulting in the formation of conditioning habits. The tension or pressure that a crisis causes forces the person to look for a way to cope. In the Norse myths, the gathering of the gods is part of that problem-solving process. They inspire the individual to a creative expression. According to Newey, the person goes through the stages of crisis, tension and creative expression each time.

The *Voluspa* discusses five distinct moments of crisis. According to esoteric teaching, the five main crises in a person's life relate to initiation and pertain respectively to the physical, astral, mental, personality and soul. In the poem, the first crisis involves the lack of time. The second crisis involves the visit of the troll women. The third crisis ensues with the arrival of Gullveig. The fourth crisis deals with the disappearance of

Freyja. The fifth crisis is Ragnarok. Each is identified by the recurring words: "Then all the Regin gods went to their Seats of Judgment and mooted over this."

Esoterically, the meetings are the response of the personality to soul impact and the registration of the Divine Plan. The congregation is the ideal of group consciousness and group life; and the successive crises generate the process of transformation.

DOOR 5
A BEING OF
TWO WORLDS

The creation of mankind warrants some extra analysis. Men and women are shaped from logs of wood, but the gods endow them with all kinds of subtle features. The motif presents a duality and symbolizes the special position of humanity.

An ancient adage says that humans are beings of two worlds; the material and the spiritual. The two logs of wood represent concrete substance from the physical plane. This makes us mortal. The gifts of the gods are the intangible aspects of life and consciousness representative of the abstract mental and causal world. These make us divine.

Ash and Elm

According to esoteric teaching, two threads connect mortals with the spiritual dimension. They are the Sutratma and the Antahkarana. The former is the Thread of Life. It comes directly from the Monad and anchors in the heart centre. The latter is the Thread of Consciousness and anchors in the head centre. Most of the godly gifts relate to either Life or Consciousness.

Voluspa 18 explains that man and woman have no Orlog because they lack *önd*, *óðr*, *lá*, *læti* and *litu góða*. The same stanza lists what qualities mankind is endowed with and which god gives what. The same qualities are mentioned, but *læti* is omitted. The passage is paralleled by a prose rendering of the story in *Gylfaginning*. Snorri's list is more sophisticated and will be discussed.

The three gods involved are Odin, Hoenir and Lodur. Odin gives *önd*. Hoenir gives *óðr*. And Lodur gives *lá* and *litr*. A first impression tells us that the distribution of qualities is determined by the alliterative nature of the verse. However, the supreme god of Norse myth is mentioned first. Accordingly, Odin gives the most important gift: that of life. Without the breath of life, the evolution of consciousness would not be possible. Lodur is associated with the qualities that begin with the letter L. It seems fair to reason that these qualities are all synonymous with each other. That would explain the omission of *læti*. Esoterically speaking, the triad of divine blessings consists of life, consciousness or quality, and appearance.

Odin	*önd*	Life	Ray I
Hoenir	*óðr*	Consciousness	Ray II
Lodur	*lá/ læti*	Appearance	Ray III

All of these gifts are aspects of deity. Odin, Hoenir and Lodur endow mankind with divine aspects. It follows that nothing in the human being is not divine. Moreover, the aspects become the means of contact with the spiritual world.

A Comparison of Voluspa and Gylfaginning

The Northern anthropogenesis is based on a heathen ritual in which wooden idols were prepared to serve as a medium for the spirit of a god. These so-called pole gods were endowed with the breath of life. They were painted and clothed (*Havamal* 49). Similar practices are known from other cultures. The foremost example is the Opening of the Mouth Ritual from Ancient Egypt. I would therefore conjecture that the anthropogenesis is an old relic of an inauguration ritual.

More information on the cultic side of the anthropogenesis is found in the stanza about the Norns. Their actions refer to magical techniques and manifestations of energy. The work of the Norns applies to the creation of wooden idols in ancient times. As a metaphor, their function deals with the creation of magical thought-forms.

Presumably, the divine qualities mentioned in the poem refer to techniques of endowing pole gods with life and consciousness. It may explain why the list in the *Snorra Edda* differs so widely from the *Voluspa* stanzas. Snorri's listing sounds rather profane. He simply summed up the characteristics of the human being. He chose to replace the other terms with a terminology that he found clearer and more to the point. The concepts of the *Voluspa* are indeed poetic and difficult to interpret. The words are only used in poetry.

Snorri Sturluson still distributes the qualities equally among the three gods.

> Then they went to the seaward beach, the sons of Bur, they found two trees and took them up and shaped men from it. They gave firstly breath (*önd*) and life (*líf*), secondly mind (*vit*) and movement (*hræring*), thirdly countenance (*ásjóna*), speech (*mál*) and hearing (*heyrn*) and sight (*sjón*), gave them clothes and names.

Let us consider Snorri's vocabulary in relation to that of the *Voluspa*. *Önd* is the only quality that Snorri's listing has in common with the original verse. *Önd* literally means breath and refers to the breathing apparatus. Mankind shares this with the animal kingdom. In Christianized times, the term also referred to spirit, even to the Holy Spirit. The variant spelling is *andi*. The concept is similar to the Chinese *qi*, which also means breath but in its extended meaning includes 'life, energy' and even 'blood'. Life and Spirit are both associated with the First Ray in esoteric literature. Snorri adds *líf*, but it must be a synonym; it means life.

Óðr denotes understanding. The word has been translated as 'mind, wit, soul, sense' and has been equated with Latin *mens* and Greek *nous*. All of these point to consciousness, which is an expression of the Second

Ray. The Norse word is heavily associated with poetry and song and includes the faculty of speech.

Snorri lists *vit* and *hræring* as the second god's gifts. He may have found these concepts more straightforward than the poetic *óðr*. *Vit* is cognate with English 'wit'. Its first meaning is consciousness, in particular the waking form or superficial mind. In a stricter sense, it refers to reasoning and in particular understanding. Therefore, *vit* is associated with the concrete mental plane, whereas *óðr* relates to the abstract mental plane. In its wider sense, *óðr* stands for inspiration. It feels like the berserk rage that comes over a person who is overflowing with ideas. This aspect is peculiar for the human kingdom. *Vit* is primarily associated with Ray III and secondly with Ray V.

The other word is *hræring*. The word means motion, which is a faculty usually associated with the gifts of Lodur. However, the concept also relates to the astral and mental realm. Movements in the astral realm are experienced as emotions, but those in the mental realm manifest as inspiration and enthusiasm. The word stems from *hræra*, *hræra* meaning to stir. The concepts *óðr* and *hræring* are connected in the well known name Odrerir, the Stirrer of the Mind. *Hræring*, either emotional or mental, is linked with Ray Four and secondly with Ray Six.

Lodur bestows *lá*, *litu góða*, and supposedly *læti*. In the *Snorra Edda*, these are explained as *ásjóna*, *mál*, *heyrn* and *sjón*. It seems that everything that was not mentioned under the first two headings appears under the third.

The meaning of *lá* is unclear. It is treated as a *hapax legomenon* in *Voluspa*. Cleasby and Vigfusson transliterate it as *læ* and translate it as 'craft'. According to the word lists in the *Snorra Edda*, *lá* is synonymous with hair. Literally, the word refers to the borderline of land and sea where the surf rolls over the sand. As a *pars pro toto* it denotes the sea and as a kenning it becomes a word for blood. Symbolically, the concept indicates a person's vitality or life energy.

Læti means manner and denotes a person's character. The Thulur or word lists in the Edda explain it as the voice (*rödd*) on the one hand and as manners (*æði*) on the other hand. *Rödd* corresponds to Snorri's interpretation of the concept as *mál* 'speech'. It includes the faculty of hearing or listening, which is *heyrn*. *Æði* is cognate with *óðr*, rage. *Læti* and *lát* are related to Dutch *gelaat* meaning countenance. In Snorri's list, the countenance is called *ásjóna*, related to Dutch *aangezicht*. The Old Norse word includes a person's total appearance. The term *sjón* means sight. It is obviously related to the face, but particularly indicates the faculty of seeing.

There is an Old Norse expression *skipta litum ok látum* which means to change one's opinion. The alliteration connects *læti* with *litr*; *lát* being the singular form of *læti*. Old Norse *litr* refers to the colour of the face. In my opinion, a healthy colour is what is meant by the expression *litir góðir* or good colours. Conversely, *skipta litum* implies the shift of hue owing to strong emotions such as embarrassment or anger. All of this is due to the blood in the face but also to the person's vitality.

All the concepts pertaining to Lodur deal with a person's physical or etheric body. The quality of the vital body dictates a person's health. It is a lower expression of the more abstract concept of life, but it comes down to the same thing. Freya Aswynn equates *læti* with Reiki. *Lá*, *læti* and *litir* symbolize the flow of life that persistently pumps through the body. Moreover, the life stream makes him a part of the etheric grid of Mother Earth and connects him with every living being on the planet. Vitality is a Seventh Ray reflection of a First Ray power and is shared with both the animal and vegetable kingdom.

Læti is an interesting concept because it denotes personality. It is more prone to change than either consciousness or life. It is also more tangible and we are faced with it every day. Through our outer appearance we interact with other people. Furthermore, understanding why people are so different makes it easier to deal with them. Not incidentally, *læti*, as well as *litir*, is a plural noun. From an esoteric point of view, the personality is the congregation of the colours of thoughts, feelings and outer appearance. Moreover, a person's character is determined by his Rays. His personality may be on a certain Ray, but his mental, emotional and physical Ray may all three be very different, too. This explains the difference in character among people.

As a whole, these three gifts bestow Orlog upon mankind. Man and woman are given life, consciousness and a personality. This does not only make them individuals, it also grants humanity self-awareness and consciousness. That is what it means to have Orlog.

7.		
6.	Monad	Gneisti / Sia
5.	Atma	Önd / Andi
4.	Buddhi	Odr
3.	Mental body	Minni / Ged
2.	Astral body	Hamr
1.	Etheric body	La / Laeti

An Age of Opportunity

It is interesting to interpret the later *Voluspa* stanzas of the Present from the perspective of how mankind evolved. What does humanity do with the gifts of the gods? It says in the poem that people lie. There is conflict, whoredom. Poison is in the air.

Voluspa 36-38

Toward the north on Nidavöll stood

A hall of gold of the family of Sindri

But another stood at Okolnir:

The beer hall of a Jotun giant, but he is called Brimir

A hall she sees standing far from the Sun
At Nastrand. North faces the door.
Drops of poison flow in from the vent
That hall is wound with worm-ridges

There she sees wade through heavy streams
Oath breaking men and murdering Varg wolves
And those who others confuse with ear-secrets
There sucks Nidhogg corpses of those who passed away
The Varg wolf slits husbands

Stanzas 35-38 and 44 give a pessimistic picture of what mankind has done with the gifts of the gods. A world of conflict and deceit is portrayed. Glamour and *maya* chain the minds of many who struggle to free themselves. But humanity's present faults simultaneously contain its opportunity for growth.

Voluspa 44

Brothers shall beat each other and become each other's slayer
Sisters shall spoil their siblings.
Hard it is in the world, much whoredom.
An Age of Axes, an Age of Short Swords, shields are cloven.
An Age of Wind, an Age of Varg Wolves, ere the world stoops.
No one man shall respect the other.

Stanza 44 seems to herald the self-destruction of humanity. At the same time, it provides an image of how spiritual reorientation is reflected in the world of mankind. The first line announces that the described events will be expected in the immediate future. This present or future is designated as an Age of Axes, an Age of Swords, a Wind Age and an Age of Wolves. These Ages are to be understood as synonyms. The general idea is one of strife; internal as well as external. There is imbalance. The individual is tested and *karma* has to be tackled.

The strife entails the working out of *karma* that has been accumulated up to that point. Taking full responsibility of your actions is the only way to be free. That is what Ragnarok is about. Again, it is a process of purification. The lower self is reined in so that the Light and wisdom of the Higher Self can shine through and bring truth and compassion.

In particular, the various names of this Age underline the different aspects of conflict. The axe and the sword are both weapons. They represent physical war, real pain and suffering. Metaphorically, they stand for deliberately hurting people. The sword is so-called double-edged. On the one hand it is the sword of reason. Decisions are made in the clarity of the rational mind and so the redundant is sacrificed. On the other hand it is the sword of the tongue. Wrong speech hurts people. In a society that claims civilization, war is looked down upon, but the tongue still carries criticism and sows discord. This, too, must disappear before one can stand free before the door of initiation. When one learns to cultivate right speech (*mál*), he will still be faced with thoughts of criticism and jealousy and hypocrisy and gossip. Learning to control the mental realm corresponds to the Wind Age.

Wind refers to storm. In simple terms, this is a kenning for war. Symbolically, it refers to a period of rapid growth associated with initiation (*óðr*). Events follow each other without cease. Things move quickly, and the mind is constantly stimulated and inspired. Information, forces and energies rage through the person's life like a storm. A lot is happening and it is difficult to keep pace. Things move fast and change rapidly. Such storms in life carry an initiatory aspect and initiations are usually accompanied by such periods.

Lastly, there is the Wolf Age. This Age refers to the social aspect of unrest. As a person grows in self-understanding and takes the occult path, he suddenly realizes that he has moved away from his brothers and sisters.

Not many can follow him. Less understand him. He becomes an outcast, a *vargr*. But he is content with his fate and understands his position on the path of evolution.

The Present Decides

The time period reaching from before Balder's death to the present moment coincides with the Path of Probation. Not incidentally, this section is interspersed with information about how humanity is faring. It portrays a most difficult time of life. But the same can be said of humanity striving for a collective expansion of consciousness. The situation matches our present world conditions. In other sources, this period is called Fimbulvetr, the Great Winter, signifying an Age of distress and crisis.

In the poem, the present stretches from stanza 42 to 50, but there is a vague time interval between the death of Balder (31) and the moment of the *spá* session. Therefore, I would include the immediate past and the near future into the present moment.

After stanza 42 it is not very clear which events take place in the present or in the future. This is because the Germanic languages do not have a clear future tense. An auxiliary verb is employed to conjugate the main verb. Stanzas 42-50 are all in the present, but the verb *munu* in stanza 44 indicates a future event. Yet, the content of this stanza has already been mentioned in stanza 38, which takes place in the immediate past.

In *Voluspa*, the exact moment of the present falls on the morning of Ragnarok. This determines the structure of the entire poem. It also underlines the importance of spiritual opportunity. The story portrays the process of decision making. When you understand the relation between the past and the future, then you can fully live in the present. The reasoning leading up to making a decision is symbolized by the words of the Volva. Regardless of Odin's question, the Volva not only speaks about the future but also of the past. Only through the past can the future be reasonably understood. That's why Odin consults Mimir, and the Volva.

As the head of the gods, Odin represents the power of decision. This mental faculty is specifically associated with the present. The will to do something projects the mind into the future (Vili), but the safety of a sacred space is created by an expansion of awareness in the past (Vé). Using both aspects, Odin calculates his best solution. In this way he reaches a rational decision. His actions are neither based on an emotional whim nor on a mental bias.

Fear of Destruction

As a person takes opportunity, he becomes more sensitive and less self-centred. He gradually starts to realize that he will have to let go of the lure of his lower self. An instinctive reaction seizes him. He has become so attached to the comforts and discomforts of his personality that he completely identifies with it. The thought of leaving himself behind fills him with fear. Ragnarok embodies this fear.

War foretells the destruction of Midgard. This symbolizes the decomposition of his ego. He will no longer be swayed by emotions or the appetites of the body. But he fears the loss of his identity. He cannot give up what he lives for or lives through. Yet would he yield to the soul's power, more happiness would ensue. It is this basic fear that makes a person want to know the future. Again, this is why Odin consults the Volva, and Mimir.

Literally, Ragnarok means the destiny of the gods. It means a shift in consciousness. From the soul's perspective, the personality has almost no importance. It serves solely as a vehicle of expression on the denser planes of reality. To the indwelling self, this feels wrong, because the person goes through all kinds of emotions in his life which add to the wisdom of his soul. Still, the personality is a transient thing and the soul is more permanent.

The current state of unrest in the world inspires uncertainty. This makes him project his mind into the future to gain knowledge. At the same time, his intuition feeds back the realization that Fimbulvetr is only a passing stage towards something better. He sees himself as a participant in a great theatre. Turmoil and crisis always lever a person to a next level of development.

How to Create a World

From a magical point of view, the creation of mankind is analogous to the creation of Midgard. Esoterically, both pertain to the technique of creating thought-forms. From this respect, and with the concepts of the anthropogenesis in mind, *Voluspa* stanzas 3-6 require a little more thought.

The term thought-form is used in esoteric slang to denote ideas, opinions, and archetypes. A thought-form is an idea clothed with mental and/or astral substance. Much of our preconceptions are essentially thought-forms. Ideas gather substance because we think about them, regardless whether the idea is correct or not. Ultimately, the thought-form with which each of us is most familiar is what we think of ourselves.

Magically, a thought-form is created to substantiate an envisioned goal. In doing so, the magician makes the ideal accessible to others. People around him unconsciously contact the thought-form.

The conception of his idea gains momentum when it gathers substance. The magical work of creating a thought-form consists of three stages. The first stage is to build the form. In the second stage, the form performs. Lastly, it disintegrates.

Two energies, wielded by a magician, help create the form. As *A Treatise on White Magic* puts it, the individual needs the "dynamic energy of purpose" as well as the "magnetic energy of desire". Seeing a need, the individual wishes to help and inspire others. The magnetic force that assembles the necessary substance relates to the energy of Niflheim but the energy of purpose comes flying from the fire world of Muspelheim.

The emergence of Midgard from the ocean symbolizes the manifestation of a thought-form. The process is likened to an actual birth and to the universal ritual of baptism. The comparison makes it clear that the creation of a thought-form happens before the actual birthing. The thought begins to form in the same way as Ymir materializes from ice and fire. The aggregation of matter and energy reflects the process of building a thought-form. As a matter of fact, the process is always the same, whether we are talking about building a thought, a human being, or a solar system.

If we read the Norse myth of creation, then Ymir represents the thought-form that is built and the Aesir represent the creators of the form. More specifically, as the head of the pantheon, Odin symbolizes the creative individual.

In building a thought-form, the substance needed is mental matter. In the myths, it is Ginn, the quality of potential with which the space around Ymir is filled. Ginn feeds the form. Ginnungagap is the 'ether' or the waters of space within which a form is conceived. In the incarnated life of the human being, the waters of space refer to the amalgam of all those energies that constantly impinge upon his subtle bodies. The complex of twelve rivers known as the Elivagar represents this on every level.

The implementation of the thought-form is the sacrifice of Ymir. The giant is disassembled into its various parts, each with its specific function in the manifested world. From this point onwards, the thought-form enters the phase of its functional performance. Yet the link with its creators continues. The Aesir who sacrifice Ymir find a place and settle in Midgard. Ymir as an entity existing before creation embodies only the visualization of the thought-form or, in this case, the world-to-be.

The sacrificial act causes a flood in Ginnungagap. Ymir's blood fills the space and becomes the vast ocean. From this ocean, the Aesir lift the earth. According to legend, the giants that Ymir had begotten by then are drowned. This latter motif signifies the purification of the form before it can safely be brought into the world. It symbolizes the reorientation of the thought-form. The form must be pure, true, clear and balanced. All this is implied by the element of ice that makes up Ymir.

In addition, the ocean would be the waters of desire which "become so potent as to cause ... the consequent appearance of the desired form of expression". The role of the Aesir as creators of a thought-form emphasizes the importance of creative work on the mental plane.

Once airborne, the thought-form must be vitalized. This might be represented by the continuous care of the Norns toward the World Tree. Bifrost Bridge represents the steady link of the creators with the form and its life. It is both the necessary distance to be kept and the enduring connection. The Aesir watch, but do not intervene.

Once the purpose of a thought-form is achieved, it naturally disintegrates. Realizing this makes it easier to accept Ragnarok as an integral part of Midgard's creation. In the words of *A Treatise on Cosmic Fire*: "In all creative work in mental matter, man is ... to be seen as a Trinity at work; he is the creator, preserver, and destroyer."

In conclusion, one must realize that every human thought gathers Ginn and resolutely clothes it in the waters of Niflheim seeking expression. Always.

The story of creation proves to be a good image of how a thought-form is constructed. In the same way, Ragnarok explains how a thought-form is deconstructed. *A Treatise on White Magic* teaches that the destruction of such a form comes about through inhibition, disintegration and absorption. These correspond respectively to the works of Jormungand, Surt and Fenrir. Inhibition is a technique whereby a thought-form is not allowed to gather substance on the astral plane. This is symbolized by the watery dragon encircling the world. Disintegration is a technique whereby a harmful form is countered by a gentler thought of love. This is Surt's consuming fire. Absorption is a technique whereby the person absorbs the harmful form into his energy body and deconstructs it with the power of love; the Sun-eating wolf.

So, how do you create a magical thought-form? Determine what you want. Write down the purpose of the thought-form on a sheet of paper. For example, healing, warding, world peace. Write your own name on the paper to remind you of your responsibility. Think about how you would like to name your thought-form. Note it down on the paper. Think about a symbol to represent the purpose of your thought-form. Note it down.

All the above will plausibly go together with a meditation. Therefore, before you begin, create a sacred space and time. For example, you can cast a magical circle. Light a candle and invoke your patron deity, your personal guides or Norns, and any gods that affiliate with the purpose of your work. If you like, ritually enter Asgard, Vanaheim or Alfheim to connect with the higher worlds. For example, you can circumambulate your sacred space while you imagine climbing a mountain; at the top you enter a door of light with the name of the world on it. Then you contemplate the what and the why. Have your pen and paper ready. When you finish your contemplation, use your pen to draw a circle around the name and the symbol of the thought-form.

Choose a medium to house the energies of the thought-form. For example, a crystal, a slip of wood, clothing. Mark it with the symbol on a new Moon day and start feeding the medium with attention. Rub your hands and send power into it, or either use Reiki. On the day of the full Moon, go out to a pond, river or well and submerge the amulet in the water. When you take it out, name it and state its purpose and lifespan. Carry it with you or place it somewhere where it can operate properly. When the purpose has been achieved, or the lifespan attained, or when you start disregarding it, decide to ritually destroy the thought-form.

DOOR 6
THE GERMANIC TRINITY

The Germanic Trinity is one of the most underestimated mysteries of the Northern tradition. In it we hear of Odin and his two brothers. Together they constitute a mystical triad.

In *Voluspa*, the three brothers are named Odin, Hoenir and Lodur. They create mankind. In *Gylfaginning*, they are Odin, Vili and Vé and they create the universe. The same triad is mentioned in *Lokasenna*. Similarly, when Gylfi enters Valhalla in the *Gylfaginning* story, he is introduced to three kings: Har, Jafnhar and Thridi. Their names mean High One, Equally High, and Third One.

Snorri claims that Odin, Vili and Vé are the children of Bor, son of Buri. In *Voluspa*, the creator deities are called "the sons of Bur". They are not specified, but we assume they are the same three brothers.

Not many myths about the Odinic triad are extant. The lack of stories must be due to their ancient roots. In Ancient Germanic times, the names were linked by alliteration and sounded like Wodanaz, Wiljon and Wihaz. The names are clearly connected. The sound change from *woðan-* to *óðin-* occurred somewhere in the sixth century. The trinity must therefore have been a living part of the mystery schools before that. At the time when the Eddic poems were composed, myths surrounding the Odinic triad were already fading from memory.

Hypothetically, an original triad might have been Od, Vili and Vé, thus emphasizing the abstract nature of the names and keeping the name Odin as an enveloping concept. The elder form of Od sounds like Wodiz and a god with this name exists and is usually interpreted as a hypostasis of Odin.

Odin, Vili and Vé are personifications of abstract concepts. The Old Norse concept *óðr* covers what we understand as consciousness. Vili means will. The spear is its symbol. In the mind, this aspect is linked with the intention. Vé refers to sacred space. Such a space separates the sacred from the profane. Metaphorically, it indicates a meditative state of mind.

1.		Har	Od	Odin	Consciousness	Ray II
2.	Odin	Jafnhar	Vili	Hoenir	Life	Ray I
3.		Thridi	Vé	Lodur	Body	Ray III

The more reliable *Voluspa* features Odin, Hoenir and Lodur in the story of creation. However, their names do not alliterate. Their names and appearances in other myths seem to indicate that they were less interdependent than Odin, Vili and Vé. Maybe they can be viewed as a more individualized stage of the Odinic triad. They are the externalization of the earlier, more abstract triad.

	Odin	Vili	Will	Ray I
Odin	Hoenir	Od	Consciousness	Ray II
	Lodur	Vé	Appearance	Ray III

Yet another triad appears in the myths. In *Skaldskaparmal* and *Reginsmal*, Odin, Hoenir and Loki travel together. Contextual information indicates that this happens shortly after the creation story. The threesome is therefore taken as an alternative version of Odin, Hoenir and Lodur. In *Skaldskaparmal*, Snorri mentions the three gods again at the start of the tale of Idun's kidnapping. In Snorri's mind, these three gods and their travels formed a classic start of many a myth. In *Loka Tattur* the same three gods travel together. According to *Lokasenna*, Loki and Odin swore blood brotherhood in some ancient time. This might well explain the triad.

What stories have survived about the Germanic Trinity? In *Lokasenna*, Frigg is accused of sleeping with Vili and Vé. This seems to indicate that Vili and Vé were supposed to rule Asgard whenever Odin was away. This motif is paralleled in a section of Saxo Grammaticus' *Gesta Danorum*. At one time, when Odin is gone, Mithothyn rules Asgard, and at another time Ull takes his place. Mithothyn or Mit-Odin means 'with Odin' and is equated with Ull. Scholars usually see a reflection of the complex Od/Odin in the analogous Ull/Ullin. But the specific relationship between Odin and Ull remains unclear. Snorri's *Heimskringla* supports the notion that Vili and Vé look after Asgard when Odin is abroad.

Another hint is found, surprisingly, in the folktales of the Karkonosze mountain range on the border of the Czech Republic with Poland, which is known as the Giant Mountains. One of the local stories relates how three brothers, Slez, Vil and Van, found the state of Silesia. Slez is the main character and the eldest of the three. He is both a farmer and a magician. He can read the stars and heal the sick. Vil and Van are clearly variant forms of Vili and Vé.

As the story goes, Slez is wise, but his brothers only care about money. They fall out with each other, as in *Lokasenna* and the *Gesta Danorum*, and Slez starts to travel. Eventually, he becomes the first settler of Silesia, from which he takes his name in the first place. According to the story, Slez fathers thirteen sons. They correspond to Odin and the twelve Aesir. The name Slez stems from the same root as *schles* in Schleswig-Holstein. The original Danish Slesvig means Bay of Sles.

The Fifty Names of Odin

Odin is known by many names. For instance, the names of his brothers are used frequently to refer to him in skaldic poetry. According to Snorri, he adopts a different name in every country. *Grimnismal* contains the most complete list of Odin's various names. Among them, we find Har, Jafnhar and Thridi, but neither Vili nor Vé, nor Hoenir and Lodur are mentioned. However, Vili and Vé were certainly used as Odinsheiti in skaldic poetry.

Grimnismal gives scant information on the meaning of these heiti, but it is clear from the stanzas that each alias refers to a particular myth, feat or job.

More names are found in the *Snorra Edda*. When Snorri introduces Odin he offers a list of twelve names. The number is significant, because it refers to the number of Aesir, or sons of Odin, all of who represent aspects of the One God. Many more names, heiti and kennings are found in skaldic poetry.

From this collection of names we are able to deduce a little about the god's nature.

Gylfaginning 3

He is called All-Father in our speech, but in the old Asgard he had twelve names. First he is All-Father, second he is Herran or Herjan, third is Nikar or Hnikar, fourth is Nikud or Hnikud, fifth Fjölnir, sixth Oski, seventh Omi, eighth Biflidi or Biflindi, ninth Svidur, tenth Svidrir, eleventh Vidrir, twelfth Jalg or Jalk.

Grimnismal 46-50, 54

Hétumk Grímnir, hétumk Gangleri,	I am called Grimnir, I am called Gangleri
Herjann ok Hjálmberi,	Herjan and Hjalmberi
Þekkr ok Þriði, Þuðr ok Uðr,	Thekk and Thridi, Thud and Ud
Herblindi ok Hár.	Herblindi and Har
Saðr ok Svipall ok Sanngetall,	Sad and Svipall and Sanngetall
Herteitr ok Hnikarr,	Herteit and Hnikar
Bileygr, Báleygr, Bölverkr, Fjölnir,	Bileyg, Baleyg, Bolverk, Fjölnir
Grímr ok Grímnir, Glapsviðr	Grim and Grimnir, Glapsvid and Fjolsvid

ok Fjölsviðr;	
Síðhöttr, Síðskeggr, Sigföðr, Hnikuðr,	Sidhott, Sidskegg, Sigfodr, Hnikud
Alföðr, Valföðr, Atríðr ok Farmatýr.	Alfodr, Valfodr, Atrid and Farmatyr
Einu nafni hétumk aldregi,	By one name I have never been called
síz ek með fólkum fór.	Since I fared among the folk

Grímni mik hétu at Geirröðar,	Grimnir they called me at Geirrod's
en Jálk at Ásmundar,	But Jalk at Asmund's
en þá Kjalar, er ek kjálka dró;	But Kjalar when I drew the cheek-sledge
Þrór þingum at,	Thror at the Thing
Viðurr at vígum,	Vidur in fights
Óski ok Ómi, Jafnhár ok Biflindi,	Oski and Omi, Jafnhar and Biflindi
Göndlir ok Hárbarðr með goðum.	Gondlir and Harbard among the gods

Sviðurr ok Sviðrir er ek hét at Sökkmímis,	Svidur and Svirdrir was I called at Sokkmimir's
ok dulðak ek þann inn aldna jötun,	And I concealed that one, the old Jotun
þá er ek Miðvitnis vark ins mæra burar	When I of Midvitnir's famous son had
orðinn einbani.	Become the one slayer

Óðinn ek nú heiti, Yggr ek áðan hét,	Odin I am called now, Ygg I was called then
Hétumk Þundr fyr þat,	I was called Thund before that
Vakr ok Skilfingr,	Vakr and Skilfing,
Váfuðr ok Hroftatýr,	Vafud and Hroptatyr
Gautr ok Jálkur með goðum,	Gaut and Jalk among the gods
Ófnir og Sváfnir, er ek hygg at orðnir sé	Ofnir and Svafnir which I think are words that be
allir af einum mér.	All one in me

Let us discuss the many names and string them together according to function.

First of all, many of the heiti call Odin 'father'. He is the father and ancestor of gods and men. Secondly, many names describe him as a war god. Lastly, Odin is depicted as a god of magic. Evidently, the different categories overlap or need subdivisions. For example, some of his names describe his outer appearance but refer to his different capacities at the same time.

FATHER

Odin is called Alföðr, Valföðr, Sigföðr, Sigfaðir, Herföðr, Herjaföðr, and Aldaföðr. He is the father of the gods. He is the supreme god of the Norse pantheon. All the gods spring from him and in him they unite. In *Baldrs Draumar*, Odin is called *galdrs föðr*. In a way, Odin is the god of fatherhood.

Alföðr	Father of All
Valföðr	Father of the Slain
Sigföðr/Sigfaðir	Victory Father
Herföðr	Host Father
Herjaföðr	Warrior Father
Aldaföðr	World Father / Father of Men
Galdrsföðr	Father of Magic

TYR

Heiti for Odin often contain the *týr* element. Examples are Hapta-Týr, Her-Týr, Hanga-Týr, Farma-Týr, Hropta-Týr, Rúna-Týr, Vera-Týr, Gauta-Týr and Fimbul-Týr. Odin is called Sig-Tyr and Val-Tyr. They are personifications of the *sig-tívar* and *val-tívar* which are designations of the collective of gods who fight at Ragnarok. *Sigr* means victory whereas *valr* means defeat.

Sometimes the compounds are made with *guð* or *gautr*. *Gaut-* refers to mortal men, sometimes to gods. By 'Goth' a warrior is meant. Odin bears names such as Val-Gautr, Her-Gautr; and Farmaguð, Hangaguð,

Haptaguð, and Hrafnaguð. *Hapt* or *haft* means 'bond' but denotes the gods when plural. Hropta-Týr is based on the name Hroptr. Odin is also simply called Gautr or Áss.

Sig-Týr	Victory Tyr
Val-Týr / Val-Gautr	Tyr of the Slain or Goth of the Slain
Hapta-Týr / Haptaguð	Tyr of the Bonds or Bond God
Her-Týr / Her-Gautr	Host Tyr or Host Goth
Hanga-Týr/Hangaguð	Tyr of the Hanged or Hanged God
Farma-Týr/Farmaguð	Tyr of the Freight or Freight God
Hropta-Týr	Shouting Tyr
Rúna-Týr	Tyr of Runes
Vera-Týr	Tyr of Men
Gauta-Týr	Tyr of the Goths
Fimbul-Týr	Great Tyr
Hrafnaguð	Raven God
Alda Gautr	World Goth or Leader of Men

Patterns become apparent. Odin is called a god of war and a god of death and a leader of gods and men. The freight or cargo refers to the Mead he steals from Suttung. Runa-Tyr and Hroptr refer to Odin's magic.

WARRIOR

Many of Odin's heiti call him a god of war or a god of death. He is Herjan, Herteitr, Sigarr and Viðurr. The names mean Warrior, War Joy, Lord of Victory and Feller. The latter is based on an Old Norse verb that means to cut wood. Possibly, Atridi originally meant rider or charger.

More names portray Odin as a battle god. He is Biflindi or Biflini and Hjálmberi. Simek translates Biflindi as 'painted shield' and the alternative Bifliði as 'trembling host', but both names refer to the shield, as the N is sometimes dropped before a consonant. *Lind* means lime tree; its wood was used for making shields, which were usually painted.

Metaphorically, *lind* can mean both 'shield' and 'spear'. The trembling or shaking is associated with wielding weapons. Hjalmberi means Helmet Bearer.

As a battle god, Odin is associated with wind and storm. He is Virdrir; Weather. He is Svölnir; Cooler. The wind cools the summer air. The name is related to Svalinn, which is the shield that cools the Sun's heat. Odin is also Hlé-Freyr; Lee-Lord.

As a god of death, Odin is called Hrafnaguð and Hrafn-Freistuðr; Raven God and Challenger of Ravens. Maybe Ýggr the Terrible also refers to Odin as a war god.

YGGDRASIL

Odin is Hangi and Farmr-Galga; Hanged One and Freight of the Gallows. These names refer to his hanging. The myth of his hanging relates to Odin as a god of death and a god of magic.

ONE EYED ONE

Quite a few names give information about Odin's appearance. Obviously, names frequently discuss his eye, but other facial traits are also revealed. He is often called the Old One. Just as often, his hat or helmet is mentioned.

Odin is Blindi or Blindr, Helblindi, Bileygr, and Báleygr. These names mean Blind One, Blind One from Hel, Flashing Eye and Flaming Eye. He is also Gestumblindi; Blind Guest. Gunnblindi means Blind One of the Battle. Odin's blindness relates to the myth of Mimir's Well. Therefore, the heiti refer to his wisdom.

Odin's one eye is explained by the fact that he is a solar god. In cultures across Europe, solar beings were typically depicted with one eye only. This eye represented the Sun. Celtic solar deities have one eye, and the Greek Cyclops has one eye for the same reason. The Cyclopes are associated with lightning. In the Indonesian language the Sun is called Matahari, the Eye of the Day. In Medieval Scandinavian manuscript drawings, Odin is always depicted with the Sun connected to his neck by a leash.

Odin's facial features focus mostly on his beard. He is Hárbarðr, Síðskeggr, Síðgrani and Hengikjöptr or Hengikeptr. The names mean Hairy Beard, Long Beard, Long Beard and Hanging Jaw. The Old Norse *gran-síðr* means long bearded. *Kjaptr* means mouth or jaw; the name is a kenning for beard. Sidskegg is also a name of Bragi. The long beard is a wisdom symbol. He is also Langbarðr.

One of Odin's names is Síðhöttr, literally 'side hat' but most often translated as 'slanting hat'. Nowadays, Odin is often pictured with a drooping hat for that reason. The manuscript tradition of Medieval Scandinavia, too, shows Odin wearing a hat, but I doubt that we are dealing with an original aspect. As a battle god, the hat may well refer to a helmet. But a better explanation can be offered. The description of the god's outer appearance has bearing on his profession as a magician. His long beard is a sign of wisdom. His one eye refers to wisdom and trance magic. Lastly, the 'hat' points to a magical technique.

MAGICIAN

Odin is Grímnir and Grímr.

In the *Grimnismal* stanzas, the name Grimnir occurs three times. The name opens the list (46). This is probably so because Odin introduced himself by this name when he entered Geirrod's court. The name appears again in a traditional alliterative line (47). Lastly, the name is explained in the context of the Geirrod myth (49). The first reference is possibly a later addition to an original list when it was included in the final editing of *Grimnismal*.

It is interesting to notice that Odin lists the names Grimnir and Gangleri first. There is a thematic connection, since Gangleri is the name that king Gylfi uses when he enters Valhalla in the beginning of the *Gylfaginning* story. Odin calls himself Grimnir in *Grimnismal* because he visits Geirrod's court in disguise. In Hnitbjorg, Odin introduces himself as Bolverk. Each time, Odin adopts a new name, one that is appropriate to the circumstances. Each time, Odin desires to remain incognito. Gylfi may not directly be a name of Odin, but it refers to wolves in poetry; a power animal of Odin.

The Grimnir name is often translated as Hooded One or Masked One, but it does not refer to a normal hat. The translation 'mask' is apt because the *gríma* is meant. It was used to disguise the person.

The Old Norse word means cowl, hood. The Old English cognate *gríma* means both mask and spectre. By poetic substitution the word also meant helmet. In skaldic poetry, it is furthermore a kenning for night. The Indo-European root **ghrey-* means to dye.

The 'mask' refers to the practice of dressing up for cultic purposes. It applies especially to the Wild Hunt. Every autumn tide, members of a secret society dressed up as the dead and rowdily visited the villages of their community. Someone represented the mythical leader of the host. The folk tradition staged Odin leading his band of chosen warriors. Faces were dyed black to represent the dead. Thence derives the folk tradition in the Lowlands of Saint Nicholas and his host of Moorish people. Members also dressed as animals. Farwerck assures us that the animals, too, represented beings from the Otherworld. That is why Odin was called Grímr. He is a god of the dead and the leader of the Wild Host.

Farwerck says that members of the Host had a measure of legal authority and sometimes officiated in their cultic dress-up. This explains the Viking Age law term *grímu-eiðr*. The concept refers to an oath of innocence witnessed by six hooded people. The use of *gríma* in the concept infers that it relates to the custom of the Wild Hunt and their members.

In a broader sense, the cowl refers to trance magic. It is associated with both Galdr and Seidr. In *Grimnismal*, we find Odin in a very peculiar setting. His dark cloak, his seated position and his alias give away the ritual implications. The setting is completed by the two fires surrounding the god. Analogous to his ordeal on Yggdrasil, Odin is deprived of food and drink. In both rituals he must endure nine nights. A vision ensues during the ordeal. The similarity between both myths is striking. The ritual induces the trance vision. A descent into the Underworld is necessary to obtain the vision.

In the Yggdrasil myth, it is clear that Odin enters the World of the Dead, but the same metaphor is found in *Grimnismal*. Being a giant, Geirrod's home equals an Otherworldly location. The antagonist of Geirrod is Agnar, and in the prose prologue of *Grimnismal* Odin says that Agnar *elr born við gýgi í hellinum* "begets children with a troll wife in the Underworld". Geirrod's brother Agnar is therefore equally associated with the Otherworld. Odin reaches Geirrod's place by covering his face with his cloak and going into a trance.

The method is found a number of times in myth and saga. Bits and pieces of trance lore can be retrieved from the sources. For instance, *Havamal* 134 offers information on the practice of trance-wrapping. Moreover, it speaks about the Thul office. Indeed, Odin is called Þulr and Fimbulþulr. A *þulr* is a ceremonial priest responsible for reciting formal verses in rituals. Fimbulthul also happens to be the name of a river. I suppose that the river's murmuring sound resembles the Thul's recitation.

Havamal 134b

At hárum þul hlæ þú aldregi	At the bearded Thul you will never laugh
oft er gótt þat er gamlir kveða	Often is good what the old one sings
oft ór skörpum belg skilin orð koma	Often from a goatskin a skilled word comes
þeim er hangir með hám	That hangs with the skins
ok skollir með skrám	And sways with the hides
ok váfir með vílmögum	And waves with the slaves

Let us take a brief look at the stanza.

According to the verse, "skilled words come from the skin". The expression *skarpr belgr* refers to a skin that is worn on the body. The Old

Norse word *skarpr* particularly means parched goatskin. Presumably this was used to cover the head.

The skin "sways and waves". The verb *váfa* 'to wave' refers to the act of wrapping a cowl. The verb *skolla* 'to sway' reminds us of Odin's hanging, as does the explicit word *hanga* 'to hang'. *Skolla* is used to describe the image of a body dangling from a tree. Therefore, 'skin' is a metaphor for a person who goes into trance. The word is synonymous with *gríma*.

More importantly, the second word used for 'skin' is *hamr* which is the designated term for the astral body. The expression *skipta hömum* means to shift shape. *Hamr* primarily means shape. The word is cognate with Dutch *hemd* 'shirt'.

From this stanza and other sources, mentioned in chapter 5 and chapter 7, it is gathered that synonyms for *hamr* include *belgr*, *héðinn*, *líkr*, and *litr*. All these words mean skin, if not in their primary meaning than at least secondary. The words refer to the complete range of shapeshifting practices, including the berserker cult. Animal skins were put on the body to effect the shift. Additionally, *Ynglingasaga* 7 associates *litr* with the concept *lá* in the context of shapeshifting.

Clearly, the cowl-wrapping technique formed part of the original Wild Hunt ceremony. Participants used this technique to incarnate the dead as well as to shapeshift into animals. In costumes, sometimes only attributes were appropriated, like goat horns, tails, etcetera, if one dressed like a goat.

Late medieval sources also tell of people who dress up like wolves. The animals often feature in the Host. Indeed, the wolf skins are still remembered in the sagas and in werewolf legends from across Europe. Presumably, wherever we encounter werewolves, we should think of shapeshifters. They dressed in the animal's skin.

More scraps of the custom are found in character names from Icelandic sagas. The best example is Skalla-Grim, Egil's father. He was nicknamed *kveld-úlfr* 'evening-wolf' because he changed shape at night.

But his real name already gives away his occupation. *Grímr* refers to the cult mask. In *Njalssaga*, the names of Njal's sons have a bearing on the topic. The eldest son is called Skarphéðinn which means Goatskin, and the second son is Grímr. Now, Grímr and Grímnir are names of Odin, but they are also names of goats in Snorri's Thulur. The goat skins have cultic significance. Moreover, Skarphéðinn is a direct synonym of *skarpr belgr*. These character names imply shapeshifting.

The last verb in the *Havamal* stanza, *váfa*, is cognate with *veifa* and *vefja* 'to wrap'. These words are frequently used to denote the trance-wrapping. From it derives the heiti Váfuðr; Waver. The same element is found in the giant name Vafthrudnir. According to the story, the giant travelled to the Otherworld. A pattern arises whereby a person wraps his face in a goatskin in order to go into a trance.

A passage in *Njalssaga* elucidates the practice. In chapter 10 of the saga, the "mighty sorcerer" Svanur is introduced. In chapter 12, he shelters a man. At some point, Svanur starts yawning and tells the man he sees the Fylgjur of his enemy looking for him. Yawning is a sign of light trance. Then Svanur "takes a goatskin and waves (*veifa*) it over his head". Next, he sings a Galdr and mist envelops the enemy. In the passage, the cowl wrapping is overtly associated with magic.

Similarly, in *Eyrbyggjasaga*, Katla protects Odd. Arnkell and his friends are looking for him. When they come to Katla's place, they cannot find Odd because of some sorcery. Arnkell muses "whether Katla had a skin and waved (*veifa*) it over our heads?" Arnkell and his comrades leave. On the way back they meet Geirrid and she offers her help. She covers herself in a blue cloak; *hafa blá skikkju yfir sér*. When they arrive at Katla's place, she knows Katla's sorcery will no longer work. *Skikkja* means cloak.

The most famous instance is found in the *Islendingabok*. When Olaf Tryggvason imposes the Christian faith on the Icelanders, the island is divided on how to respond. Thorgeir Lawspeaker is asked to settle the matter and he consequently isolates himself and wraps his cloak about his head; *breiða feld sinn á sik*. He remains quiet the remainder of the day and the following night. In the morning he announces his decision. Here, Thorgeir is explicitly called a heathen. Moreover, the Thul description from *Havamal* suits him rather well. *Feldr* is interpreted as a sheep's skin. The same story is repeated in *Njalssaga* 105 with the words *breiða feld á höfuð sér*.

It is sure that the practice of 'going under the cloak' aided one to enter the Underworld. It is equally sure that this technique is implied in *Grimnismal* and is the reason why Odin calls himself Grimnir.

Furthermore, the expression *falda sítt* means to cover the head so that the face and the eyes cannot be seen; *sítt* is a variant spelling of *síðr*, often used in kennings for Odin. I presume Odin uses his cloak to hide his face. The Old Norse word for cloak is *feldr*. According to the *Grimnismal* poem, Grimnir wears a dark blue or black cloak (*feldr blár*). *Feldr* and *falda* derive from the same root.

Therefore, 'hat' is a kenning for trance-cowl. Suddenly, a name such as Slanting Hat becomes meaningful. The hat 'droops' because it covers the face.

According to *Havamal*, the Thul is old and bearded, two attributes of Odin. The Thul was also known to be seated on a special chair known as the *þularstóll*. The seat was raised on a dais. There is the reason why Odin is called Hávi; High One. The seat particularly refers to his throne Hlidskjalf, which he uses for scrying. According to legend, Odin is able to peer in each of the Nine Worlds from this throne. This is the seat he uses to reach the Otherworlds. From the same seat, Odin would utter his words of wisdom. From the cited examples, wording the vision formed an integral part of the experience. *Grimnismal* is such a speech.

Odin is also Hroptr and Rögna-Hroptr, the Crying One or the Shouting One. The names refer to his chanting. He is also Ómi, which means sound, voice, but also resonance. Possibly related are Unnr and Uðr meaning wave, and Þunn, þundr and Þuðr, because they are names of rivers. Again, I see a link between the murmuring river and the Thul's intoning.

The Odinsheiti refer to the Old Man's magical practice. In particular, Seidr is associated with trance techniques. Odin is associated with this womanly practice in *Lokasenna* and in *Harbardsljod*. Additionally, the name Jálkr may have bearing on the topic. The word means gelding. Kvilhaug reasons that initiates were said to be gelded, because Seidr was thought to be unmanly. In that case, Gelding is a suitable name for a horse god practicing Seidr. The name appears twice in the *Grimnismal* list, but the spelling is a little different (Jálgr).

Odin is Sváfnir and Ófnir. They are also names of snakes in *Grimnismal*. The Svafnir name is based on a word for sleep, possibly a reference to the apparent sleeping condition of a person performing Seidr. In *Ynglingasaga* 6, Odin is said to look asleep or dead (*sofinn eða dauðr*) when he performs shapeshifting (*skipti hömum*). It is uncertain what Ofnir means. Otten suggests 'loop', either referring to the noose of the gallows or the snake's shape. Titchenell translates the name as 'opener'. If the name derives from *opinn* or *opna*, then it would mean opening. Grim, too, is a snake name.

Odin is also Vakr; Wake One. According to Cleasby and Vigfusson, the word denotes a certain type of horse in modern Icelandic. The word is found as a morpheme in the horse name Árvakr.

Additionally, Odin is Göndlir; Sorcerer. The root *gandr* means artifact. His name Óski means Wish. He is also Göllnir and Göllungr. The names are cognate with *galdr*.

So, how do you trance-wrap? If you do this inside, use a special chair to sit on. Make a diagram on the floor representing the Nine Worlds. Light a candle at each side of the chair. Have a cloak or shawl ready. Maybe smudge with mugwort. Sit down, cover yourself with the cowl, and get into a sleepy state. When you start yawning or daydreaming that is the time to recite a verse carrying your intention to contact the Spirit World. Either sing the names of the Nine Worlds or the names of their Guardians. Then give yourself a moment and then start saying out loud what you see and experience. We highly recommend having another person in the room to watch over you.

If you prefer to do this outside, look for a height in the landscape. Sit on the top. Maybe light torches to your right and left. Address the spirits of the quarters and/or call upon your ancestors. Then cover yourself with the cloak so that all becomes darkness and start the meditation in the same way as described above.

WISE ONE

In old times, knowledge was profoundly associated with magic. Odin is therefore called Fjölnir, Fjölsvinn and Fjölsviðr. The names mean He Who Knows a Lot. The morpheme *fjöl-* means much; *svinnr* or *sviðr* means swift and indicates someone quick of mind; Wise One. The names Sviðarr, Sviðuðr or Sviður, and Sviðrir may all be related. Alternatively, the names derive from *svíða* meaning to singe, to burn. The latter interpretation might refer to *Grimnismal*.

There is also the name Svipall. It derives from *svipr*, which denotes the ghost of a deceased person. In saga and folklore, the word is used when a spirit is sighted. Its relation with the dead makes it an appropriate name for Odin.

Other interpretations are possible. The adjective *svipall* means changeable, unstable. It would refer to Odin's shapeshifting abilities or his association with water. In any case, *svipa* and related words mean something that happens suddenly. The word is cognate with English 'swift'. A swooping movement is intended. In that case, the name again means Quick Minded One. The name can also be translated as Flashing One, referring to Odin's solar aspect.

The morpheme *svip-* appears again in the mythological hero name

Svipdagr. *Svipdagr blindi* is a heiti of Odin in *Ynglingasaga* and means Blind One of the Sweeping Day. The word *dagr* points to a solar deity as does the epithet 'blind' as earlier explained.

Odin also bears the names Hnikarr or Nikar and Hnikuðr or Nikuz. The translation is problematic. Simek translates as 'instigator'. But the names may be derived from the same root as *nykr*, a water sprite; German *Nix, Nixie* and Dutch *nikker, nekker*. Old English had *nicor*. Possibly, the British expression Old Nick for Devil derives from this heiti.

Odin is Þekkr, Sannr, Saðr, Sanngetall. The first name is an adjective meaning pleasant, agreeable, and likeable. However, the word derives from *þekkja* 'to perceive' and is related to English 'to think'. It therefore means Knower. Sannr and Saðr mean true. The word is cognate with 'sooth'. The morpheme *–all* is an intensive marker. The verb *geta* means to get. In its secondary sense it means to guess. Therefore the last name translates into The One Who Verily Gets True or The One Who Guesses Very True. Either explanation refers to Odin's skill to acquire wisdom and knowledge.

His name Ginnarr may mean Lord of Ginn. The energy of Ginnungagap is alluded to. This may be a reference to Odin as the Lord of the Ginn-Regin. However, the verb *ginna* means to deceive. In certain expressions the verb means to intoxicate. Either explanation rings true for Odin. He is known to deceive Suttung and he carries away the Mead of Poetry in eagle shape. Indeed, Ginnar is the name of an eagle. Odin is also Fengr; Catcher, because he fetches the Mead.

In the story of Gunnlod, Odin calls himself Bölverkr; Bale Worker. It means that he likes to cause trouble, which he does in Suttung's court. At another time he is Gagnráðr, Gain-Rede, which means that he always contradicts another's point of view. He simply cannot be trusted. The heiti Viðrímnir suggests the same; Counter Rhymer. Odin is called Glapsvinnr and Glapsviðr. The element *glap-* seems to mean accident or confusion. The name indicates deceit.

From *Havamal* we learn that wisdom is gained by travelling a lot, which is exactly what Odin does. That is why he is called Gangleri or Ganglari, and Vegtamr. The former means Weary of Journey, the latter Ready for the Road One. Bolverk and Grimnir have already been mentioned.

Odin is also Kjalarr, which means keel. Most probably, it refers to the ceremonial ship that was drawn about in Midwinter processions. However, it may just as well be a reference to the Mead of Poetry, since Odin is called God of Cargo.

NAMES

More names are given. Odin is Skilfingr, meaning Rock Dweller, which is a common designation for giants. The name might refer to Hlidskjalf if it derives from *skjalfr*.

Odin is also Þrór and Sigþrór. I do not know the meaning. Thror appears as a dwarf name. Þekkr is also a dwarf name, so are Hár and Ginnarr.

In Jón Árnason's collection of folktales, the names Fjölnir, Fengur, Þundur and Þekkur are remembered. Fjölnir appears in the Galdrabok. A runic Viking Age amulet employs the name Thund. The names Hengikjöptr and Fjölnir both appear in *Grottasongr* as Odinsheiti.

A Triad of Mothers

The Odinic triune constellation returns among the goddesses. We first encounter them as the Matronae or Matrones of Ancient Germanic times. Many finds from the archaeological record show votive altars dedicated to these matrons or Mother Goddesses. Typically, the Matronae are depicted in threes. Sometimes they have additional attributes, such as a basket of fruit, a dog or a baby.

The inscriptions are in Latin but the Matron names usually give away their native Celtic or Germanic origin. The Latin *matronae* refers to married women. Two of the three women always wear a bonnet, which is traditionally a mark of motherhood, or at least of wedlock. Unmarried girls wear their hair loose. Curiously, the altars show how a young lady is flanked by two married women. In medieval literature, such girls were so-called virgins.

The constellation of women corresponds to the triad of Norns known from *Voluspa* and *Gylfaginning*. Three Norns appear, one of which is a young lady.

The Norn Urd is associated with the past. She is therefore the eldest. Verdandi embodies the present. Skuld represents the future. Their relative age is inferred by the associations of time. The names Verdandi and Urd both derive from *verða* meaning to become. Therefore, Urd and Verdandi are closely related but Skuld stands out. Snorri remarks that Skuld is a Norn and at the same time a Valkyrie. In passing he also reveals that she is the youngest of the Norns. He means that Skuld is the youngest of the Nornic triad. The mothers are identified as Verdandi and Urd.

The three Norns, Urd, Verdandi and Skuld, are all aspects of the archetypal Norn Urd in the same way as Odin, Vili, and Vé are aspects of Odin. The Matrons are three different entities, but can be viewed as aspects of one principle.

The Norns are associated with fate and destiny. *Urðr* means fate cognate with English 'weird'. Skuld means debt, but the primal meaning of Old Norse *skuld* is bondage. Somehow she embodies Law, Karma, what is bound to happen. In the *Voluspa* stanzas, the Norns assign Orlog to the first man and woman.

In *Nornagests Thattr*, another group of women is associated with Orlog. According to the text, those who know *örlög* are called *völur*. Evidently, the Volvas are related to the Norns. In the story, three *spá*-women appear. They are termed *nornir*. The match is perfect. In *Helgakvida Hundingsbana hin fyrri* 37-38, *völur* are furthermore linked with *valkyrjur*. The Matronae were in fact *völur* and *nornir*, while *valkyrjur* were associated with the same group.

From the above, it follows that the female Mysteries consisted of separate groups; one made up of married women and one made up of unmarried women. The Valkyries embody the latter group. It is clear from myth and saga that Valkyries forsake their vocation as a warrior when they marry. This is the meaning behind the marriage of Sigurd and Sigrdrifa. The Matronae are therefore interpreted as retired Valkyries. They are initiated in the magical Valkyrie society but are no longer active as such. However, they gain a new role. Becoming a wife and a mother opens them to new avenues of life. Thus they become guardians of the women's Mysteries. In support of this we recall the Dutch word for midwife, *vroedvrouw*. It literally means wise woman. The morpheme *vroed* is cognate with *fróðr*.

In her analysis on the story of *The Ugly Duckling*, Clarissa Pinkola Estés points out the importance of support to a young mother. In the old times, a first-time mother was received into a social network of experienced mothers. The elders incarnated an age old source of instinctive knowledge and wisdom. Today, all of this is given too little time and thought. But this circle of what Estés calls *todas las madres*, the many mothers, is essential to human society. What is more, their pool of wisdom never exhausts. Her reasoning explains the existence of Norns and Volvas.

The close tie between Valkyries and Norns is corroborated by Snorri's quotation of the Thulur. When he sums up the names of the Asynjur in his *Skaldskaparmal*, he ends by saying: "But there are others, the maidens (*meyjar*) of Odin: Hild and Gondul, Hlokk, Mist, Skogul. Then Hrund and Mist, Hrist, Skuld are tallied. Norns are they called, who shape Need (*nauð*)." Need is synonymous with fate. Old Norse *mey*, *meyja* and *mær* are often translated as 'maiden' or 'virgin' but are better rendered as 'unmarried woman'.

In this respect, it must be remembered that many if not all of Frigg's servants are termed virgin. Consequently, they classify as Valkyries. The appellation takes on symbolic meaning. In her work on the Greek goddesses, Jean Shinoda Bolen uses the term 'virgin' to designate independent women.

Among the Norse goddesses, Fulla is said to wear her hair loose. Moreover, she keeps Frigg's basket, which is one of the Matron's attributes. The young goddess Idun keeps a basket in which she stores the apples of life. She can therefore be identified with one of the Matrons. Dogs and children are attributes of Frau Holle or Hella, who in her turn is identified with Freyja. Hella impersonates one of the Mothers, but Freyja would be a Valkyrie most of the time.

Another hint is found in medieval Continental sources. In Meransen, South Tyrol, there is a legend about three women. In times of peace they dedicate themselves to housekeeping, but in times of war they fight in the front lines. One of them is portrayed with a spear, but the other two have farmer's tools. The description reminds us of the Norns and the Matrons.

The names of these three women have come down to us in many legends. In the above story, they are called Ampet, Gaupet and Gewerpet. They are better known as Anbet, Wilbet and Barbet. Alternatively, they are Aubet, Kubet and Guerre. In modern Germany, they are known as *die Beten* or *die Bethen*.

Their names are found all over Germany, Switzerland and Italy, though most records stem from the Meransen region. Usually, the names are given in their native tongue, but sometimes the Latin transcription appears.

The sources disagree on the second name of the trio. Sometimes she is Gaupet or Kubet; sometimes she is Vilpetta or Willibeth. Kubet and Cubet are certainly Latinizations of Gaupet. It may derive from German *Haube* meaning bonnet. The meaning is uncertain. However, the alternative has the morpheme *vil-* in it, referring to 'will', and incidentally to Vili, Odin's brother.

The meaning of the first name is derived from the German sources.

There we have Ainpett, Ainbeth and Einbede. *Ain-* or *ein-* must mean one and is cognate with *ein-*, as in *einheri*.

Meransen		Aubet	Kubet	Guerre
Latin manuscript	ca.1500	Aubet	Cubet	Guerre
Meransen	ca.1382	Ampet	Gaupet	Gewerpet
Meransen	ca.1603	Anbetta	Vilpetta	Gwerpetta
Latin manuscript	ca.1650	Ambett	Cubet	Guerrae
Plawenn		Aubete	Carona	Bavina
North Bayern		Ainpett	Fürpett	Gwerpett
South Bayern		Ainbeth	Willibeth	Barbeth
Worms		Einbede	Willebede	Warbede

The last name seems to be derived from an old Frankish word for war, indeed, cognate with English 'war'. Under the influence of French and Italian tongues, the morpheme *war-* changed into *guerre* and *gwer*. This *bete* corresponds to skuld.

The second part of the name – *bet* or *–pet* refers to battle, according to Lucillo Merci. It corresponds to the morpheme *–heri*. The name might well have been a feminine equivalent for Einherjar. Alternatively, the suffix *–bet* is a diminutive marker. In that case the names mean Little One, Little Hood and Little War.

The names are clearly associated with the Valkyrie tradition. Moreover, these legendary girls are said to be members of Saint Ursula's host.

A Latin recording of the legend connects them respectively with the Christian Saints Fides, Spes and Caritas. Freya Aswynn links the goddesses with the Earth, the Moon and the Sun respectively. According to tradition, they were honoured every Monday.

DOOR 7
THE MEAD
OF POETRY

Central to the Northern Mysteries is the story of the Mead of Poetry. The story contains an initiation motif that consists of two components. Firstly, the candidate for initiation unites with his bride. Secondly, he drinks from the Cup of Wisdom. The former symbolizes alignment with the Higher Self. The latter symbolizes the transference of knowledge.

The story has come down in two versions. A poetic version is given in *Havamal* 104-110, although stanzas 13-14 are also part of the story. Snorri Sturluson records a different version in his prose *Edda*. His account is divided into two parts. The first part relates the creation of the Mead. The second part relates the stealing of the Mead and coincides with the *Havamal* account. Snorri's account naturally contains more detail.

I am of the opinion that the *Havamal* version is closer to the original story or ritual. Snorri Sturluson retained all the necessary elements but misinterpreted or deliberately changed information. Then again, Snorri's account must be based on traditional lore since he utilizes the myth to explain traditional kennings.

The poetic version of the Mead of Poetry will be quoted in full.

Havamal 13-14
The Heron of No Memory is called he who lingers over the ale
He steals man's consciousness
By that bird's feathers I was fettered

In the garden of Gunnlod

Drunken I was. I was overly drunk
At wise Fjalar's
Best is ale when back home
Takes every man his consciousness

Havamal 104-110
That old Jotun I sought. Now I have returned
Little did I get there by keeping silent
Many words did I speak to my advancement
In Suttung's halls

Gunnlod gave me from her golden chair
A drink of that dear Mead
Ill recompense did I let her have afterwards
For her sincere thoughts
For her strong affections

I let Rati make me room
And gnaw grit
Over and under me stood the Jotun ways
So did I risk my head

Well bought I have used my complexion well
Little is wanting for the wise
Because Odrerir has now come up
To the edge of the people's temple

A doubt it is to me whether I would have come back
From the Jotun's garden

If I had not used Gunnlod, that good woman
Who laid her arm around me

The next day, the Rime-Thurses went
To the High One, asking for advice
In the High One's halls
They were looking for Bolverk;
If he had come amidst the Bond Gods
Or if Suttung had sacrificed him

An oath on the ring, I think, he has granted
How shall his trustworthiness be trusted?
He broke his promise to Suttung to leave the symbel behind
And made Gunnlod weep

If we reconstruct the story line we obtain the following. Odin travels to Suttung's hall, where he introduces himself as Bolverk. He is well received by Suttung and they discuss business. At some point, Suttung and Odin come to an agreement. Odin consequently swears a ring-oath. Gunnlod is present in the hall. She serves the Mead to Odin. Odin gets drunk and sleeps with Gunnlod. Because of his oath, he is unable to leave the place. Eventually, he escapes by boring a hole in the mountain. He shapeshifts and leaves for Valhalla. Suttung goes after him. The day after, the giants find Bolverk and Suttung gone and they knock on Valhalla's doors for an explanation.

Now, a brief summary of the prose story is due.

The first part starts after the Vanic War (*Voluspa* 25) when a truce is arranged in two ways. First and foremost, hostages are exchanged. Secondly, every one of the Aesir and Vanir spits in a pot (*ker*). This symbolizes their union. From this liquid, the gods create a man called Kvasir. Much later, two dwarves, Fjalar and Galar, invite Kvasir and kill him (*drápa*). They catch his blood in two pots (*ker*) and a cauldron (*ketil*), the names of which are Son, Bodn, and Odrerir. They mix the blood with honey and brew Mead from it. This becomes the Mead of Poetry. Later, the dwarves invite the Jotun giant Gilling and his wife. The three men go out fishing but the boat capsizes. Gilling drowns. When Fjalar and Galar tell his wife, she becomes hysterical. Fjalar becomes annoyed with her wailing and kills her with a millstone. Afterwards their son Suttung demands recompense. In exchange for the murder, the dwarves hand over the Dear Mead. He hoards it in Hnitbjorg and puts his daughter Gunnlod in charge.

The second part goes as follows. Odin travels to Jotunheim to retrieve the Mead. He meets nine mowers. Odin offers his help but causes discord among the workers. They fight and kill each other. At night, Odin arrives at Baugi's house and calls himself Bolverk. The giant tells him business is going bad since he lost his mowers, but Odin offers his help. In exchange, he wants a draught of Suttung's Mead. Suttung and Baugi are brothers, but the giant cannot promise anything. Yet Baugi says he would *freista ef þeir fengi mjöðinn* "test if they could fetch the Mead". When Odin has finished his harvest job, Baugi goes to Suttung and asks him for a drop of the Mead on Odin's behalf. Suttung refuses. Still Odin demands Baugi to help him. This time they turn to illicit means. Odin takes out an auger (*nafarr*) called Rati and they set out for Hnitbjorg. Baugi makes a hole in the mountain, and then cheats Odin, but to no avail. The second time Baugi bores a hole through the mountain. Odin changes himself into a snake (*bregða í ormslíki*) and enters the mountain. Again, Baugi tries to cheat Odin, but to no avail. Inside, Odin finds Gunnlod. He lies with her for three nights, at the end of which Gunnlod allows him to drink three draughts. In the first he drinks Odrerir, in the second Bodn and in the third Son. Then he changes himself into an eagle (*bregða í arnarham*) and flies to Asgard. Suttung finds out and changes himself into an eagle and chases after him. When Odin arrives in Asgard, the Aesir are ready to catch the Mead in containers. That is the end of Snorri's account.

On Words

In the *Havamal* stanzas, the word *öl* is used. It literally means ale but allegorically refers to any kind of intoxicating drink. In a broad sense the word indicates a drinking bout or party. As such the word is used here. The word *sumbl* is used once as a synonym. According to *Alvissmal*, *öl* is called *sumbl* by the sons of Suttung. Typically, a 'symbel' represents a formal drinking ritual, but in *Alvissmal*, it refers to Odrerir as a drink. The words *öl* and *sumbl* therefore have a double meaning. They simultaneously refer to Odrerir and to a drinking ceremony.

The section about the sacrifice of Kvasir contains some mystical elements. The dwarves prepare three pots to capture the blood of Kvasir. Snorri chooses Old Norse *ker* which is a generic word for pot. However, it also occurs in the names of mythical rivers, such as the twin Kerlaug Rivers over which Bifrost Bridge is built. The second element in Kerlaug refers to water and is considered a kenning for Mead.

In *Havamal* 107, Odin transports the Mead to Asgard. The stanza specifies the place as *alda vé jaðar*. The Old Norse *jaðarr* literally means edge, but as a figure of speech it denotes the best. Therefore, *ása jaðarr* and *goðs jaðarr* are kennings for Odin. Similarly, *fólks jaðarr* is translated as "the best of men". Therefore, the kenning *alda-jaðarr* means "the best of people" which I interpret as a kenning for Odin. Then the Old Norse line translates as "sanctuary of the best of all people" or "the best among the shrines of men" and becomes a kenning for Asgard.

According to stanza 109, Odin comes *með böndum* "among the gods of binding". *Bönd* is the plural of *band*, meaning bond or fetter. As a plural it denotes the gods. Similarly, the gods are called *haft* or *hapt*. This word is derived from *hafa* 'to have'. The singular means handcuff or bond; Hafta-Guð is a name for Odin. Again, as a plural, the gods are meant.

The concept of binding either refers to contracts or to war magic. Binding the hands was used for formalizing contracts. In contrast, in magic, we hear of spells that can shake off bonds and fetters. The First Merseburger Incantation is an example of this and involves the Disir.

In relation to our story, there is an Old Norse expression of interest to us. The expression *haft-sæni* means atonement of the gods. It is a kenning for poetry and specifically refers to Odrerir. The concept of binding consequently refers to the contract between the Aesir and the Vanir. *Haft* implies that the gods atoned themselves.

The Old Norse *með* 'with, among' also translates as 'with the help of'. More precisely, we read that Odin escapes with the help of the residential Aesir. This translation is in keeping with the other sources.

Stanza 109 features the name Bölverkr. It means instigator of evil. Snorri explains the name by relating the story of how the nine mowers meet their end. He 'works bale' amongst them. The story is not found in the poetic version, implying that in all probability the name originally pointed to Odin's oath-breaking.

Gunnlod must have been conscious of Odin's plan to escape. In stanza 108, he admits that he would not have returned if it wasn't for Gunnlod. She helped him. Svava Jakobsdottir interprets the last line of the stanza in this way. From other fragments we also know that Gunnlod is with child. She will give birth to Bragi, the god of poetry.

A Difference in Perspective

The two accounts differ in many respects. In both stories, Odin visits Suttung's court. But in Snorri's, he never enters Suttung's hall directly, whereas in *Havamal* he does. According to the *Havamal* stanzas, Odin not only discusses business with Suttung, he also swears an oath.

Conversely, Snorri's account explains or tries to explain many aspects of the poetic version.

Havamal 105 relates how Gunnlod gave Odin a drink of the Mead and how Odin did not give her what she deserved in return. Snorri explains that Odin and Gunnlod slept together for three nights and that Gunnlod offered him the Mead after that. From the poem we surmise that Gunnlod trusts Odin well enough to share the Mead after those three nights. Snorri also explains that Odin takes off with the Mead. Nothing further is related, but we deduce from the poem that Gunnlod expected Odin to stay. However, it contradicts her helping him. In any case, Gunnlod regrets Odin's leaving. Stanza 108 agrees with the fact that Gunnlod slept with Odin.

Havamal 106 mentions Rati. Snorri explains that Rati is the name of an auger. The instrument bores through the mountain wall and Odin enters the hole to either leave or enter the mountain. Snorri explains that Odin has this instrument with him but asks Baugi to handle it. The giant bores from the outside and Odin changes into a snake to enter. In the poem, Odin clearly uses the hole to leave the hall. Turville-Petre considers this difference the most significant discrepancy between the story of *Havamal* and Snorri's account. In the poem, Odin first visits Gunnlod and then uses Rati to crawl out. In Snorri's account, the auger is used to enter Gunnlod's room.

Stanza 107 relates how Odin changes shape. And that is the reason why he can escape. He brings the Mead to the "holy place of the people". Whether these people are men or gods or initiates is never unveiled. Snorri tells us that Odin brings his booty to Asgard, where everyone is waiting for his return. He explains that Odin changes into an eagle to escape. The poem, however, does not say into what Odin shapeshifts. *Havamal* is silent on that point except for the fact that Odin must go 'up'. A handful of Odin's nicknames are also names of snakes and eagles.

The Promise

The key focus of the *Havamal* stanzas is the ring oath. The oath is not mentioned in Snorri's account at all. He only alludes to it by introducing

Baugi. Snorri's character is a reference to Odin's oath because his name derives from the ring on which the oath is sworn, for which the Old Norse word is *baugr*. Baugi is its personification. The *baugr* was made of gold or silver and kept in a sacred space. At sacrificial ceremonies the ring was blessed with the blood of the sacrificial animal. The priest had to wear the ring when he performed his duties. Oaths were sworn on this ring by touching it. The ring was associated with law, meaning that the administered oaths were binding. The ring-oath is called *baug-eiðr*.

Havamal 13-14 may indicate that the oath was sworn when Odin was drunk. We know from the sagas and the Heroic Poems that sometimes oaths were sworn on the spur of the moment but regretted when the person sobered up. The oath was binding. In the case of our current story, Odin broke his promise. The theme must have been familiar.

What did this oath involve? Since Odin's leaving is regarded as ill recompense for Gunnlod's care, we suppose that an agreement was made to marry the girl. Marriage is a standard motif in initiation stories, and the Mead of Poetry Mystery is such a story.

In stanza 106, Odin confesses that he risks his head by escaping. The words imply that he breaks his oath by leaving but is ready to suffer the consequences. In the prose story, Odin takes a risk when he tries to infiltrate the mountain hall. In the poetry version this is impossible, because Odin pleads his case with Suttung. But he takes a risk when he cheats Gunnlod by leaving.

Snorri furthermore relates a story in which Odin has dealings with Baugi, the personification of the oath. Their agreement backfires. Therefore, the gist of the original myth is preserved. Odin asks Baugi to help him. He keeps his promise, then Baugi asks Suttung for a drop of the Mead, but he refuses. Baugi is still compelled to help Odin, but when Odin enters the auger hole, Baugi attempts to stab him with the instrument. That is what it means to risk his head. The episode allegorically explains the agreement between Suttung and Odin.

Atonement

Suttung and Gunnlod are giants. Hnitbjorg is therefore situated in Jotunheim. When Odin arrives, he finds Suttung, Gunnlod and Odrerir assembled in Hnitbjorg. The scene changes after he steals the Mead.

At the end of the story, Odin and Suttung disappear from Jotunheim. The giants follow suit. They arrive at Valhalla's doors and inquire after Bolverk and Suttung. The question remains whether they knew that Bolverk was Odin.

The giants believe that Suttung slew Bolverk. They regard Bolverk's death as his atonement for breaking his promise. From *Havamal*, we deduce that Suttung is slain. We infer this from the words spoken by Odin himself: Suttung died and Bolverk survived.

Havamal employs the verb *sóa*. This Old Norse verb refers to a ritual killing, usually of an animal, to atone towards the divine. The Old Norse is cognate with Dutch *zoen* 'kiss' and *verzoening* 'atonement' and German *Sühne* 'atonement'.

The concept of ritual atonement is known in many traditions, especially in Judeo-Christian traditions. Nevertheless, an original working may be found in the shaman culture. In his ceremonies, the shaman atoned for all the food his tribe gathered from game and field. We would now call it thanksgiving. The principle goes back far in time. In heathen times, the *són* ritual was associated with official court sittings, doom and judgment. The context seems to drag the powers of the Norns into play.

The atonement restores a certain balance. Peace ensues. The story of the Mead of Poetry begins and ends with such a ritual. It begins with the sacrifice of Kvasir. It ends with the sacrifice of Suttung. Kvasir's ritual death is relevant to the story because it symbolizes the truce between the Aesir and Vanir. Consequently, one of the Mead pots is called *són*. It means atonement.

In the Gunnlod story, the reason for atonement is obvious. The giants believe that Suttung would kill Bolverk because he broke his promise.

It was, however, Suttung who was sacrificed. The question then arises what the gods had to atone for. Does it somehow compensate for Odin's crime against Gunnlod? Or is it the giants who atone for something? What does Suttung's death compensate for? Must we conclude that he killed Kvasir in the original story?

If we carefully read Snorri's version, we realize that the Mead is a symbol of atonement to Suttung. When he arrives at Fjalar's, he demands the Mead as compensation for his father's death. The text has the word *sætt* 'peace' to denote atonement.

Therefore, the Mead symbolizes 1) atonement between Aesir and Vanir, 2) atonement between the dwarves and Suttung, and 3) atonement between the gods and the giants, specifically between Odin and Suttung. The meaning of the latter is unclear, since we do not know who atones for whom or for what reason. On top of this, the possibility exists that all three events originally covered one and the same motif.

The Origin of the Mead

No mention is made in the poetic Edda of how the Mead of Poetry came to be. In fact, Kvasir's name does not occur at all in the poetic Edda. Conversely, his name appears frequently in Skaldic poetry. *Voluspa* mentions the truce but not the existence of the Mead. However, Snorri conjures up Kvasir in his *Heimskringla*, in which he appears in the context of the war between the Vanir and Aesir. This time, Kvasir is one of the Vanic hostages (*Ynglingasaga* 4).

Kvasir is the personification of drink. His name originally derives from the name of the drink. Etymologically *kvas* refers to any intoxicating drink. He is the same as the Mead. Therefore, the creation of Kvasir is related to the creation of the Mead. But we have one story about how the drink is created from the spittle of the gods, and we have another story about how the Mead is brewed from Kvasir's blood.

The motif of spitting in a brewing pot reminds us of the ancient technique of using saliva to ferment honey or other substances to obtain an alcoholic drink. Some native people of Central and South America still chew maize to start the fermentation process. And in Japan, rice grains were originally chewed and spat into a vat to produce *sake*. Evidently, the life force and energy signature of the participants mixes with the brew. Saliva contains a person's DNA. The same symbolism is therefore found in Kvasir, whose make-up consists of the energy of each of the gods.

Kvasir's blood is obtained by killing him. Fjalar and Galar gather the blood in three cauldrons; Odrerir, Son, and Bodn. The appearance of *són* suggests that we are dealing with a sacrificial death.

In *Havamal* 14, Fjalar appears in connection with the Gunnlod story. This is our only poetic reference to the story of the two dwarves. However, from *Havamal* we cannot deduce whether Fjalar is a dwarf or something else. From the context, we would rather suppose we are dealing with Suttung and that Fjalar is another name for the giant. Does this mean that Suttung killed Kvasir?

There is good reason to equate Fjalar with Suttung. In *Harbardsljod*, Fjalar appears as a giant name. Odin mentions the name when he speaks about Thor's encounter with Utgarda-Loki, who is a giant king also known as Skrymir. All the names are plausibly synonyms. This makes Suttung a leader of giants.

In his own home, Suttung clearly hosts an army of *hrím-þursar* or Frost Thurses (*Havamal* 109). The notion is in keeping with his appearance in *Alvissmal* 34, where the giant race is termed "the sons of Suttung". *Skirnismal*, too, summons the "sons of Suttung". In *Voluspa* 42, Fjalar is the cock of Jotunheim who wakes up the giants.

Whether Fjalar is a dwarf or a giant, the name certainly refers to magic. Fjalar is probably cognate with Fjölnir, based on the morpheme *fjöl-* meaning 'he who knows much'. The other dwarf is named Galar. The name is cognate with *galdr* 'magic'. It is also the name of a giant in

Snorri's Thulur. Would they be Suttung and Baugi? Interestingly, Suttung and Baugi are consistently termed Jotun in the Eddas.

The three names of the Mead of Poetry each have meaning. Son has already been explained. Bodn comes from Old Norse *boðn* 'vessel', possibly ceramic. Anglo-Saxon *byden* means cask or barrel; *beór-byden* is a beer-barrel.

The mystical name of the Mead is *óðrœrir*. The word means Mind-Stirrer. The first part of the name, *óðr*, primarily means rage, and refers to Odin. Secondarily it indicates the mind complex. The kind of rage implied is that of inspiration and enthusiasm, passion. Note that the English words are actually based on words for 'spirit' and 'god'. Someone inspired by Od is therefore rapt in ecstasy. The second part of the name contains the verb *hrœra* or *hrœra*. It primarily means to move, but secondarily means to stir. Something is caused to move. The compound implies that the mind of the individual is caused to move. In other words, the Mead causes the inspiration. The mental movement translates as an influx of ideas, insight, and a tendency to create. Hence the Mead's association with poetry.

In a magical context, the drink must be regarded as a sacrament. Many rituals from many countries incorporate the sacrament of spirited drinks to connect with the subtle dimensions. Even in the Christian Mass wine is served. Odrerir is a sacrament to cause divine inspiration.

In the Eddic poems, Odrerir is only mentioned twice; once in *Havamal* 107 and once in *Havamal* 139.

The Maiden and the Mead

Within the corpus of Norse mythology, quite a few texts contain motifs similar to the Gunnlod story. Elements of it are found in the myth of Idun's abduction, in *Hymiskvida*, and in *Volundarkvida*. Maria Kvilhaug correlates even more myths and sagas with the same motif, such as *Skirnismal*, and the Helgi poems.

An example of a myth with a lot of correspondences is *Volundarkvida*. At some point in the story, Volund comes home and sits on a bear skin (*ber-fjall*). When he wakes up he finds himself bound hand and foot. King Nidud isolates him on an island named Saevarstod; Sea Stead. Further on in the story, Bodvild, the king's daughter, visits Volund. They drink and sleep together. Afterwards, Volund is able to leave the island. According to the text he soars up (*hófsk at lofti*), meaning that he changed into a bird.

Volund has also been maimed. According to Farwerck, in Germanic rituals candidates for initiation were symbolically maimed; as a ritual death. Moreover, the setting of the Volund story represents an Otherworld. That is what the island represents. The fact that Volund is bound is a further sign that he is a candidate for initiation. Similarly, Odin was bound by the feathers of the Heron.

Comparable to Odin (*grætti gunnlöði*), Volund leaves the girl behind to grieve (*grátandi böðvildr*). Just like Gunnlod, Bodvild carries the hero's child. Volund can only leave after he has slept with the maiden. Nidud, corresponding to Suttung, appears in a kenning for giant.

The main difference with the Gunnlod story is the motivation. Volund is held prisoner against his will. Yet he resolves all the tests and passes initiation. The fact that he betrays both father and daughter is similar to the *Havamal*.

The story of Thjazi and Skadi also reads like the Gunnlod story. The latter part of the myth goes as follows. Loki rescues Idun from Thrymheim, Thjazi's abode in Jotunheim, but Thjazi follows in pursuit. When Loki arrives in Asgard, the gods lie in wait. When Thjazi enters Asgard, they kill him. Odin and Suttung suffer a similar fate. The only real difference is that Loki retrieves a goddess and Odin a drink. If the correspondence is meaningful for the Gunnlod story, then we have to assume that Suttung was killed by the gods. Thjazi chases Loki in eagle shape. Loki escapes in falcon shape.

Afterwards Skadi, the daughter of Thjazi, comes knocking on

Valhalla's doors and demands compensation. She is granted one of the gods in marriage and chooses Njord. This is a Sacred Marriage. Thus, Skadi is like Gunnlod. The is also reminiscent of the Rime Thurses who come knocking on the same doors.

Hymiskvida only contains the motif of stealing the Mead. In the poem, Thor travels to the realm of the giants to fetch a cauldron used for brewing Mead.

Kvilhaug sees *Skirnismal* as a different interpretation of the same motif. In *Skirnismal*, Skirnir travels to the Underworld on horseback. Once arrived, he is invited to drink the Mead (16). So far, it coincides with the story of Odin, who would otherwise ride Sleipnir to reach the World of the Dead. Skirnir meets a guardian giant. Maybe he is like Baugi or Suttung. Frey's nine nights of yearning compare with Odin's nine nights of privation.

In *Grogaldr*, one of the charms that the mother teaches her son is one that enables him to converse with a Jotun giant (14). Apparently this is needed to be allowed entry into the Underworld. It applies to Skirnir's conversation with the guardian, but also to Odin's business with Suttung. Many other *Grogaldr* charms give instructions of how to enter the Underworld.

Kvilhaug sees a further similarity in the *Hyndluljod* story. The entire poem follows the format of an initiation ritual. The hero Ottar is introduced to Hyndla by his promotrice Freyja. He enters the Underworld and is presented a cup of memory and mythical information is imparted. Moreover, the *Hyndluljod* reminds us somewhat of *Rigsthula*, where the initiation ritual is associated with sacral kingship.

Svipdagsmal, which contains *Grogaldr* and *Fjolsvinnsmal*, follows the same format. The hero Svipdag enters the Underworld, converses with a guardian giant and unites with his eternal love Menglod. This happens at a certain tree called Mimameid, identified as Yggdrasil. Svipdag is also known as Fjolsvinn which is a name for Odin. Menglod is interpreted as Freyja.

Menglod's home is located on a mountain top. The story of a princess living in a glass castle on top of a mountain is well attested in fairy tales. In *Svipdagsmal*, the mountain is named Lyfjaberg, which means Healing Mountain.

I would dare associate this mythical mountain with the concept of KUR in the Mesopotamian mysteries. In Late Assyrian iconography, the Tree of Life was frequently rooted in the cuneiform sign for 'mountain', which consisted of three triangles. In Mesopotamian symbology, the mountain signifies the foundation on which the Tree is built. In later times the Judean tradition borrowed the glyph and from that stems the Sefirotic Tree of Life. The Sumerian KUR corresponds to the current Sefirah Yesod, which word means foundation or fundament and refers to the horizon. The symbolism coincides well with the Lyfjaberg. The aspects of life and healing refer to the immortality found in this mythical place.

The Celtic Link

In her research, Svava Jakobsdottir explains the *Havamal* story in the light of Old Irish traditions. She is able to draw parallels by isolating the central themes; the Mead and the Marriage. She further defines the story of the Mead as a rite of sacred kingship. Similarly, in his work *The Lady with a Mead Cup*, Michael Enright claims that the Mead-offering is Germanic and forms part of a royal consecration ceremony. He says that offering Mead gave authority to the king.

In the Celtic tradition, the king was considered to be a descendant of the gods. Divinity was installed upon the king-to-be by a formal ceremony, analogous to Ancient Egyptian and Mesopotamian rituals. In the ritual, the king married the goddess of the land over which he was to rule. The goddess was generally called Flaith or Sovereignty. In the ritual,

Sovereignty offered Mead and slept with the king. This consummated the consecration.

According to the *Bailé in Scáil*, Sovereignty married each successive king. We can hypothesize that the land lived everlasting but not the king. Yet the king's office lasted. A new king therefore incarnated the immortal archetype through the ceremony.

In the Celtic vernacular, the Sacred Marriage was termed *banais rígi* or *banais ríghe*. The Irish is translated as 'wedding-feast of kingship' and consists mainly of two elements according to the *Oxford Dictionary of Celtic Mythology*, namely "the libation offered by the bride to her husband and the coition". The conditions coincide with the central themes of the Mead story.

The Old Irish word for kingship is cognate with Heimdal's alias Ríg in *Rigsthula*. Moreover, in the Irish story *Bailé in Scáil*, the king to be consecrated bears the name Conn. Although this is a common name in the Celtic tradition, it seems to correspond to the initiate candidate Kon who appears in *Rigsthula*. In the Eddic poem, Rig travels to the world of mankind in order to teach wisdom. He sleeps with three couples successively. The first couple represents the class of slaves, the second that of workmen and the third that of the nobility. The classes must be interpreted symbolically. From sleeping with the highest class, he fathers a son Jarl. The name means prince or earl and derives from Ancient Germanic *erilaz*. Rig teaches Jarl about the runes and tells him to claim the land of his ancestors. Later, Jarl's son Kon is initiated in the Mysteries by Rig. According to *Rigsthula*, Kon was consequently bestowed the *ríg* title. The names and motifs correspond to the Irish story. Can we assume that the name Conn denoted an initiate in the Celtic Mysteries? The name was common but only used in families of power.

If the *Havamal* myth is interpreted as a ceremony of royal consecration, then Gunnlod represents Sovereignty. Like Sovereignty in the *Bailé in Scáil*, Gunnlod is seated on the high seat. According to

Jakobsdottir, the high seat was the "inviolable place of the goddess" in the royal consecration ceremonies. In a pagan Scandinavian setting, the hall had a dais on one side of which the seats of the lord and lady were placed. On these, Suttung and Gunnlod would be seated. In the Irish story, Sovereignty is accompanied by a phantom that appears to be a shadow of Lugh. He represents the royal archetype.

From her seat, Gunnlod bestows the sanctifying drink. And when Odin sleeps with Gunnlod he ritually marries the earth. If this is true, it explains the union of Odin and Jord known from other sources. Jord, or Mother Earth, is Odin's first wife. Their son is Thor, defender of Midgard and Asgard. Indeed, bedding Jord would install Odin as king of the world and Lord of Men and Gods. Earth may be referred to in *Havamal* 107. *Alda vé jaðar* then means "the temple of the land of the people".

In the Northern tradition, the notion of a lord sleeping with the land coincides with the concept of Folk Hamingja. The king was responsible for the prosperity of his people. That is why it was important for a king to marry a woman with good Hamingja. Not just her ancestry but also her energy was considered.

Many more instances are known from the Celtic tradition. First of all, there is a legend about Queen Medb that states that a king cannot be king of Connacht unless he sleeps with Medb first. In later Celtic traditions, stories are told in which the hero must first sleep with an old hag but will then be granted the Grail. When the hero has the courage to sleep with the ugly woman, she becomes a beautiful lady. This is symbolic of one of the tests of initiation. Comparable is the story of *Lugaid Laígde*, in which the hero is met by an ugly sorceress. She offers him ale and invites him to sleep with her. He refuses, and she tells him he has forgone Sovereignty. A similar thing is found in the story of *Niall of the Nine Hostages*.

Svava Jakobsdottir concludes that the *Havamal* story refers to a ritual of a royal consecration, which is either akin to or inspired by the Celtic tradition. The parallel with the *Rigsthula* story seems to corroborate this.

A widespread Tradition

The *Snorra Edda* story contains many more mythologems than the poetic rendering. Jakobsdottir hypothesizes that the long myth compares to other Indo-European myths about the theft of a sacred drink. These stories centre on the aspect of immortality. I agree that the theme is better found in many Indo-European traditions, for instance in stories about the Vedic Soma, the Greek Ambrosia, and the Mesopotamian plant of life.

In the Vedic sources, the Soma is sometimes called *madhu*, which means honey and is cognate with 'Mead' and Old Norse *mjöðr*. In Persian mythology, the drink is called Haoma, cognate with *soma*. The Vedic drink is also known as Amrita, meaning immortality. This is analogous with the *nektar* and Ambrosia of the Ancient Greek gods. Both drinks grant immortality, and Ambrosia literally means immortality. The word is actually related to Sanskrit *amrta*. Furthermore, the Nectar is a honey-based drink and thus related to the Sacred Mead of Northern Europe.

The cultic drink also reminds us of the *kukeon* of Ancient Greece. This drink plays a role in the Eleusinian Mysteries. The name of the drink is based on a verb meaning to stir, to mix, analogous to *hrœra*. Curiously, when Circe serves the *kukeon*, she adds honey to the drink.

Jakobsdottir reasons that the Soma myth is closest to the myth about the Mead of Poetry. But the Hindu Soma is not just a drink. It is also the plant from which the drink is made. On top of that, it is the numen of the drink. In the Persian Avesta, Haoma is the name of the drink, the plant from which it is made, and the indwelling deity. In Snorri's account, the numen is Kvasir. The Soma deity is a god of wisdom; so is Kvasir.

Persian and Indian traditions agree that the plant is found in the mountains; as with the quest of Gilgamesh for the plant of life. In Sumerian mythology, Gilgamesh is in search of Immortality. His quest leads him to the mountains (KUR). In Ancient Sumer, an actual mountain range was seen on the eastern horizon. This location acquired mythical qualities. This place is analogous to the European Underworld concept. The mountains correspond to Hnitbjorg and *jötna vegir* of *Havamal* 106.

Gilgamesh has to pass certain tests and then goes in search for Utnapishtum, who lives on an island. This man has gained Immortality in an earlier Age. The man's name refers to the Hebrew Nefesh. In the Qabbalah, this is one of the three aspects of the soul. At long last Gilgamesh arrives at a woman named Siduri. She is a key figure in the myth. She is a so-called ale-wife, *sābitu*. Siduri is a goddess of beer, in particular of the fermentation process. This reminds us of the Norse stories. She gives Gilgamesh all kinds of advice, but when he asks where he can find the plant of immortality, she says it grows on the bottom of the ocean. Can we interpret the ocean as the Mead of Immortality?

In comparing the *Havamal* story to the Soma myth, Jakobsdottir mentions a hymn from the Rig Veda. In the hymn, Apala, the daughter of the Sun, wants to marry Indra. She starts chewing *soma* and offers it to the god. In the process, Apala changes herself into a snake. The shape is at once a solar and a chthonic symbol. The marriage and the offering of the drink link the myth with the Germanic and Celtic traditions.

In another myth, the gods obtain the Soma via Garuda. He is an eagle god and nicknamed Soma-Thief. Garuda is an enemy of snakes and associated with the Sun. He is like the solar eagle of Norse mythology who carries the Mead. In the myth, the Soma or Amrita is guarded by a flaming wheel. Somehow Garuda gets past. Behind the door a guardian keeps watch. In the world of Norse mythology, we would expect a giant. Sometimes Naga serpents guard the drink. In addition, the Soma is located in a mountain.

The flaming ring corresponds to the wall of fire found in many heroic tales from the Germanic tradition. In *Skirnismal*, Skirnir has to pass both a wall of flames and a guardian to reach Gerd. Moreover, the lady is a daughter of the sea. This reminds us a little of the Sumerian story of Siduri. The wall of fire also features in the *Nibelungenlied*, where it shields a maiden, and in *Fjolsvinnsmal*, guarding Menglod. In *Fjolsvinnsmal*, the hero also encounters a giant guardian.

In Old Norse, the fire is called *vafrlogi*; 'waving fire'. The verb *váfa* might relate to the practice of Seidr, as explained in the section on Odin's heiti. The *Grimnismal* story links the concepts of Seidr and fire.

Piercing this wall marks a proof of courage. In other tales, the obstacle is a wall of shields or thorns. In *Sigrdrifumal*, Sigrdrifa is surrounded by a wall of shields. In *Sleeping Beauty*, the lady is walled in by thorns. The meaning is always the same.

Esoterically, fire cleanses and purifies. It burns away the dross. The giant guarding the entry to the *anima* of the individual symbolizes the confrontation with the Dweller on the Threshold. The message is clear. Can you stand the blazing fires? Do you possess the courage to continue? Only those pure of heart will pass.

The Sumerian story of Gilgamesh is equally clear in its outline and symbolism. Gilgamesh travels to the mountains, the Otherworld. There, he meets Huwawa, representing his shadow. Then he travels to the sea and meets Siduri, his *anima*. Eventually he finds immortality, which means that the individual aligns his mortal personality with his immortal soul. Gilgamesh never drinks anything, but he does dive into the Abzu, which is the watery abode of Enki. AB.ZU literally means Liquid of Wisdom. Furthermore, this ocean realm has also been deified.

The Path is always the same. To reach the soul, you have to face your deepest fears.

The Soma-Thief of Hindu myth is also found in Sumerian stories. In Sumerian, the bird is called Anzu or Anzud. There is a story about the Anzud bird in which he steals the ME from Enki. The ME are the essences or principles of the universe. In a different version, they are visualized as the Tablets of Destiny. The word for destiny, NAM.TAR, is etymologically derived from ME 'to be'. The bird is defeated by the hero Ninurta, who returns the ME to Enki, the god of wisdom. Later, Ninurta steals the ME himself.

Another Sumerian myth relates how the goddess Inana gets Enki drunk and then deprives him of the tablets. Two things are interesting about this myth; the appearance of the goddess and the involvement of the alcoholic drink. Here, Inana is Freyja, Gunnlod, or Sovereignty. Enki literally means Lord of the Land. What is more, Enki's abode Abzu is situated beneath the earth's surface and equals the Northern notion of the Underworld. It mirrors Odin's account. Analogous to Anzud stealing the ME, Odin steals the Mead from the Underworld in the shape of a bird.

Garuda furthermore is like the eagle of the Etana myth. In this myth, a snake and an eagle dwell in a tree. They quarrel a lot but eventually make peace. Later, the snake becomes angry because the eagle deceives him, and he throws the eagle into a pit. The bird is finally saved by Etana who desires a kind of plant of life in exchange. So the bird takes Etana on his back and they fly to the mountains.

There are lots of parallels. First of all, the snake and the eagle are both shapes of Odin in the *Skaldskaparmal* story. The peace-making atonement is a recurring theme in the Gunnlod story but specifically refers to the ring-oath. The eagle breaks his promise. Pits were moreover used in rituals to represent the Underworld, according to Farwerck. If the eagle is Odin, then his movement mirrors his descent and ascent. Etana never shifts shape, but at least he rides the eagle. In addition, Etana looks like a homonym of Odin. Lastly, the tree is Yggdrasil.

The Inana myth about the Hulub tree also shows elements of the mystery of the Mead. Inana wants a tree cut because she wants her bed and throne made from the wood. She waits and waits, until someone helps her out. In the myth, Gilgamesh comes by and builds her throne and bed. Only when both are ready can the Sacred Marriage be consummated. The Sumerian Sacred Marriage Rite is recorded in the Joy of Sumer hymn (Iddin-Dagan A).

Here, too, the king is asked to build a throne for Inana. The motif resembles the Celtic consecration ritual.

That these myths are so manifold and universal has one reason only. In origin, the rites were intended to increase fertility.

Effects of the Mead

One can ask oneself: What does the drinking of the Mead amount to? According to *Havamal* 107, Odin is able to shapeshift because of it. Snorri's account associates it with poetry. In both readings, Odin changes shape immediately after drinking the Mead. *Havamal* stanzas 140-141 further imply that drinking it makes one wise.

In *Havamal* 141, the Old Norse *fróðr* means wise. The adjective is found in *Havamal* 14, associating Fjalar with the Mead and calling him 'wise'. Odrerir was therefore associated with Wisdom.

Havamal 140-141

Nine mighty songs did I take from the son
Of Bolthorn, the father of Bestla
And I got a drink from the dear Mead
Sprinkled from Odrerir

Then did I take the fruits and wise became
And waxed and had it well
Word me from word to word led
Work me from work to work led

But we have access to a lot more information. Piecing together input from the different Indo-European traditions on the sacred drink helps us to understand the symbolic nature of Odrerir.

Wisdom and poetry are traits frequently found in connection with the cultic drink. Moreover, poetry itself was heavily associated with wisdom, lore and magic in both Celtic and Germanic traditions. In the Celtic tradition, the initiates of the Mysteries were first and foremost bards or poets.

In her paper on the Precious Mead, Svava Jakobsdottir associates the Mead with kings, poets and wise men. She links it with the Irish Flaith, which means both authority and ale. The Soma was equally associated with kings, poets and Brahmins, the latter being the Hindu priests. The Vedic drink is heavily associated with the art of poetry.

The Mead of Wisdom seems also connected with the Celtic cauldrons of magic. The Welsh goddess Ceridwen owns a cauldron of wisdom. Briefly, the story goes as follows. Ceridwen prepares a potion and sets the young Gwion Bach to guard it. In the end, three drops of the liquid touch Gwion's skin and he licks it, thus gaining the wisdom contained in the drink. Since the drink was not meant for him, Ceridwen gets rather mad and chases after the boy. In the chase, both Gwion and Ceridwen change shape often. His ability to shapeshift was gained from the drink. Later, Gwion becomes Taliesin the Poet. The effects of the potion coincide with those of Odrerir.

In Celtic lore, the cauldron is called Awen or Amen and is associated with poetic inspiration. Awen is therefore Odr. The root of *awen* means to blow, like wind. The same idea is found in the root of *óðr*. In medieval times, this old symbolism was bestowed on the Grail.

The story of Ceridwen and Gwion is reminiscent of that of Sigurd and the dragon's heart. Sigurd is asked to cook the heart for Regin, but Sigurd burns his hand and licks the fat. Thus he gains the wisdom and learns that Regin wants him dead, but Sigurd kills Regin first. The motif is different from the offering of the Mead because the wisdom is gained by accident. Yet, the core motif is the same.

In the Hindu tradition, the Soma grants immortality. In the Persian tradition, according to the Avesta, the Haomo bestows physical strength, acute awareness, sexual prowess, healing, and it strengthens the soul. Apart from all that, it is intoxicating.

In the Germanic tradition, the potion had the power to either make one forget or remember. For instance in the *Volsungasaga*, Grimhild serves Sigurd a drink which makes him forget his promise to Brynhild. In the *Nibelungenlied*, Grimhild offers her daughter Brynhild a drink of forgetfulness.

The forgetfulness is paralleled in Greek myth. When Circe prepares the *kukeon*, she also adds herbs and magic to cause forgetfulness. The mind numbing quality of alcohol was already hinted at in *Havamal* 13.

Conversely, drinking the Mead restores lost lore. In *Sigrdrifumal* we read that Sigrdrifa fills a horn and gives Sigurd the *minnisveig* or cup of memory. In *Hyndluljod*, the goddess Freyja means to give the hero the *minnisöl* or ale of memory. After drinking from that cup, the hero is given all kinds of relevant information. The line of ancestors that Ottar is made to remember in *Hyndluljod* reminds us of the king list of *Bailé in Scáil*.

The concept also reminds us of the Helgi poems in the Edda. According to Kvilhaug, Helgi incarnates life after life but marries the same Valkyrie every time. Kvilhaug interprets the Valkyrie as the immortal soul going through a series of mortal lives. From an esoteric school point of view it refers to apostolic succession. Initiation into an order marries the candidate into the group mind of the tradition.

The individual gains access to his inner wisdom after drinking. Everyone possesses this innate wisdom, but only few are able to tap it. The awakening to the inner memory of truth is likened to the self-remembering suggested by Gurdjieff. It lifts the veil of glamour and illusion. The intuition of the Buddhic level now passes unhindered into the mind of the individual. As Jakobsdottir puts it: "From the giant's point of view, the removal of treasures in the land of the immortal is theft, but from the gods' viewpoint, it is redemption, or freedom from enchantment."

In conclusion, we can safely posit that the Sacred Mead proffered wisdom. This included poetic inspiration, maybe immortality, and certainly the ability to shapeshift.

Initiation

The main element of the story of the Mead of Poetry is the Mead itself. The drink is in possession of the giants but becomes the aim of the efforts of the gods. The second most important theme is the union of the maiden and the hero. Jakobsdottir associates the rite with sacral kingship analogous to the Celtic tradition. Kvilhaug widens the view and interprets the story as a rite of initiation. When she explains her view, she cites Gro Steinsland saying that initiation consisted mainly of three themes: death and rebirth, esoteric knowledge, and sacred marriage. In my own opinion, the marriage signifies the union of the individual with his Higher Self. The union results in a widening of consciousness. The intuition awakens and esoteric knowledge arises. It therefore implies initiation.

Initiation is essentially an expansion of consciousness. It is usually paired with the acquisition of secret knowledge. The first is symbolized by the sacrament of alcohol, the second by the art of poetry.

To the candidate, the giantess represents the unconscious which is seemingly of the opposite gender. She embodies the person's *anima*, or Higher Self. From a woman's perspective, the soul would be represented by a man. Archetypically there can be no gender discrimination. At this point, I have to add that Estés says that women, too, consider their soul as feminine.

The hero is the candidate for initiation, either a man or a woman. The relation between man and woman in the myth acts out the pairs of opposites that need to unite with the higher self. He feels a certain degree of magnetism and attraction towards his deeper self, yet it is still completely different from him. After the union, the inner pairs of opposites will be overcome. As Kvilhaug puts it in the introduction to her *The Seed of Yggdrasil*: "In the myths, sex is a metaphor for union with the divine."

This explains the Sacred Marriage. Soul and personality become aligned. The Mead symbolizes inner wisdom. The associated art of poetry represents inspiration and intuition, which presupposes soul contact. It also explains the cup of memory. The inherent wisdom of the soul is finally unlocked and the initiate is able to change himself into an eagle. In other words, he knows how to reach the higher planes. He understands the principle of meditation. In particular, he now has free access to the abstract mental and Buddhic plane.

Kvilhaug's profound analysis of the Dear Mead examines the different recurring themes in the variations of the initiation story. She discerns six themes: a vision quest theme, a vision theme, a descending theme, a trial theme, a maiden theme, and a result. Using those elements she traces the key motifs of the Sacred Marriage in many Norse myths and sagas.

In my opinion the vision quest and the vision do not belong to the ritual itself, but reveal how an altered state of consciousness necessary to perform an initiation ceremony would be obtained. The descent coincides with the opening section of the ceremony. The locale is ritually defined and the candidate is led into it. Kvilhaug mentions a trial, but whether this would form part of the same ritual is uncertain. The maiden theme is vital to the ceremony, since this symbolizes how the candidate is brought face to face with his soul, represented by the gender opposite to his own. She corresponds to the High Priestess of the Tarot.

Lastly, Kvilhaug mentions a result theme. This corresponds to the results of initiation. In the ancient Mystery Schools, this concretely meant secret knowledge. In *Havamal* and *Sigrdrifumal*, this is exoterically expressed by the long section of advice giving.

In my opinion, the basic motif consists of three parts. Firstly, the candidate enters the Underworld. Secondly, he becomes initiated. And thirdly, he returns. The first part is of paramount importance. A ritual of initiation would first recreate the mythical setting. Then the initiand is guided into the Underworld. Images abound in the stories. In the Northern tradition, the world of the giants is most often regarded as the Otherworld. The Sumerian and the Indo-Iranian traditions feature the same boundary-crossing.

To enter the World of the Dead means to die. Farwerck states that you had to be dead before you were allowed participation in the ceremonies of the cultic bonds of old. Kvilhaug suggests that the realm of Suttung and Gunnlod can be identified with the world of the dead. In her interpretation, the giant world is synonymous with the Underworld. The attributes of the giants are, among others, the snake and the wolf, symbols of the Underworld.

I would like to expound on this notion. *Vafthrudnismal* 43 reveals that Vafthrudnir descended into the World of the Dead in order to gain secret knowledge, in particular runes. Since his name refers to a trance practice, I would suggest that the method generally involved a sort of 'dying' to reach the Spirit World. Consequently, mock dying was a means to enter the right ritual atmosphere and the right state of mind. This might be the reason why *Havamal* 140 repeats the Mead of poetry story right after Odin's ritual hanging. Self-sacrifice pays Odin's entry into the world of the dead. Kvilhaug certainly interprets the acquisition of Odrerir in *Havamal* 140 as a result of Odin's death rite on Yggdrasil.

Farwerck gives numerous examples indicating that only the dead were allowed to participate in the Mysteries. Binding, maiming, hopping, and being slain by club, sword or hammer lead a candidate into the world of the dead. Accordingly, initiation involved a descent into the Underworld.

Sporadically, the myths reveal the archetypal location of the rite. In *Volundarkvida*, the ritual takes place on an island. The setting incidentally corresponds to Circe's abode. She lives on an island in the east, which location emphasizes her solar aspect as a daughter of Helios. In *Fjolsvinnsmal*, the ritual takes place on a mountain in the vicinity of Yggdrasil, which makes sense if we follow Kvilhaug's interpretation about Odin's ordeal. In Indian, Persian and Sumerian mythology, the myths are set on a mountain. According to esoteric tradition, climbing the mountain symbolizes the effort to tread the Path of initiation. In *Esoteric Astrology*, the Mountain of Initiation is associated with Capricorn. The star sign coincides with Yule Tide, when most, if not all, the initiatic ceremonies were held.

As for the ritual setting, Farwerck mentions pits, caves and hills as places for initiation ceremonies. In particular, he discusses labyrinths and so-called Troy Towns or Troy Castles in relation to initiation. These labyrinths and Troys were often situated on hills. You had to walk to the centre of such a maze to enter the holiest of holies.

In Scandinavia, these constructions are called Trojaborg. In Finland they are known as *jattulintarha* "giant garden" or *jättiläisen tie* "giant road", thus associating these constructions with the Jotun giants. Shall we visualize Jotunheim as a labyrinth?

Hnitbjorg might well have been such a place. When Odin says that "the Jotun Ways are all about him" he may well mean such a labyrinth. He escapes by backtracking the maze. Symbolically, a movement from the Underworld to the surface is imagined. He entered as a snake, but leaves as an eagle.

Jakobsdottir explains the Jotun Ways from the perspective of Greek mythology. She translates Hnitbjorg as Collision Cliffs and interprets stanza 106 as the danger of getting crushed. She likens Hnitbjorg to the Symplegades of Greek tradition. Myth relates how Jason and the Argonauts have to sail through the Symplegades in order to get to the Golden Fleece. The Symplegades form a narrow strait, the opposite rocks of which clash together. Jakobsdottir interprets this as an entry into the Otherworld. Passing this is a proof of courage.

Let us examine the Greek myth for a minute. We note that the Golden Fleece is a symbol of authority, which coincides with the Celtic Sovereignty, and that Jason gets help from Medea, the maiden in the story. She is an enchantress and the granddaughter of Helios. Moreover, she helps him on the premise that they will marry. The myth seems to belong to the category of sacral kingship.

In the same vein, the monsters Skylla and Charybdis that Odysseus needs to pass are analogous to the Symplegades. Earlier in the Homeric *Odysseia*, Odysseus dug a pit to connect with the world of the dead (*nekuia*). Jung uses the term *nekyia* to describe the process of deepening the mind to access "the deeper layers of the unconscious psyche".

There is therefore reason to consider the place name Troy as the mythical presentation of a magical location. Such a site was built in the real world and used as a representation of the Germanic Otherworld.

The Greek story about Helen complements the Norse myth under discussion. The legendary war over the hand of Helen fits all the elements of the Germanic myth. The king travels to a far-off world to rescue the princess that was to be his. Helen is herself a half goddess and she represents the hero's *anima*. The war symbolizes the test to take initiation and is itself reminiscent of the Vanic War.

Helen's future husband Menelaos sends his brother Agamemnon to woo the girl. This parallels the *Skirnismal* story in which Frey sends his servant Skirnir to woo Gerd. As Kvilhaug remarks, the same custom is found in other Germanic stories, such as the *Nibelungenlied*.

From the gathered material we may doubt that Troy was indigenously Greek. Rather, it may have been an original Germanic place name which was remembered throughout different time periods. The name got into Greek myth via the Homeric epics. There may be evidence that these stories came to Greece via the migrations of Northern European tribes. This explains the blond hair and blue eyes of Greek deities, heroes and heroines, apart from many other close links between Greek myth and mystery with Ancient Scandinavian ones. Felice Vinci has written extensively on this topic. In his *The Baltic Origins of Homer's Epic Tales*, he analyzes the *Iliad* and *Odyssey* as if they were of Northern European origin. Some of his conclusions are very elucidating.

Last but not least, Troy is alternatively known as Ilion. The name derives from the name of the city's founder. Linguistic evidence shows that it originally sounded like **wilion*. The word is possibly cognate with Vili, which derives from the Ancient Germanic **wiljo-*. If this is correct, then Troy is the City of Odin.

In her turn, Maria Kvilhaug suggests that the introduction to the *Snorra Edda* contains more truth than hitherto acknowledged. She puts forward the thesis that the reference to Troy and Turkey reflects migrations in early times. In my opinion, the Troy of Greek myth was originally an Otherworldly place in Northern myth. However, it may be worth examining the passage.

The Faulkes translation of the prologue to *Gylfaginning* runs as follows:

> Near the middle of the world was constructed that building and dwelling which has been the most splendid ever, which was called Troy. ... This place was built much larger than others and with greater skill in many respects, using wealth and resources available there. Twelve kingdoms were there and one high king... The twelve rulers of the kingdoms were superior to other people who have lived in the world in all human qualities.

The description reminds us of Valhalla, which is larger and more beautiful than any other building. Troy is visualized in the centre of the world. This situates Troy simultaneously in Midgard and in Asgard. Moreover, twelve Aesir rule in Asgard and they are superior to any other people. We imagine a well and a tree in the environs of which the twelve rulers assemble. In his work, Farwerck remarks that sometimes a tree was in the centre of these Troy labyrinths. The mythology about Troy and

Valhalla reflects the existence of actual Troy towns used for ceremony and initiation.

From an occult point of view, the twelve rulers are initiates presided over by a hierophant. Troy is a place of initiation. It is the Otherworld.

So, how do you perform a Sacred Marriage? If we are to reconstruct the rite, then I would isolate the separate elements from the stories. Three roles are played; that of hero or candidate, that of bride or initiatrix, and that of Underworld king or initiator. Mainly two actions complete the rite; the offering of the Mead, and sleeping with the bride. The locale of the ceremony must be defined as the Underworld. This will either be the world of the giants or of the dead. Kvilhaug reasons both worlds are one and the same thing. These are the elements, and from these it is fairly easy to reconstruct a modern ritual of initiation to a satisfying degree.

Get together with at least three people and assign roles. Have all the necessary props ready; at least a glass of Mead. Ideally seek out a place that has a labyrinth or make one yourself. Design the rite in three parts; there is the entry into the Otherworld, the marriage with the soul, and the exit. Use your creative mind to construct a rite. Use sections of *Havamal* and other source texts to develop the rite. For instance, define the locale by the entry words of *Havamal*. More hints will be given in the following chapter.

DOOR 8
THE SAYINGS
OF THE ODIN

Havamal is the longest poem of the *Edda*. Scholars claim that the poem has been edited into its current form and distinguish material from different sources. Yet, the arrangement of the stanzas suggests that the original editors composed the text very deliberately.

Textual evidence shows that the poem is divided into two large portions. The division is marked by the interpolation of stanza 111 at which point a narrator introduces the section of Loddfafnir. The same narrator speaks again at the end of *Havamal* (164), where he closes the section. In both stanzas the word *mál* is employed to denote the section in between. When the narrator speaks about the *mál* he means everything between stanza 111 and 164.

Paleographic evidence shows that the editors were aware of three distinct parts. In the Codex Regius manuscript, the sections are marked by an enlarged initial letter. The first section starts with stanza 1. The second section begins with stanza 111. The third enlarged initial is found at stanza 138.

Nowadays, the poem is further divided into smaller sections. The first section is associated with wisdom literature and receives the name *Gestapáttr* or Gnomic Stanzas (1-103). Then the Gunnlod episode follows (104-110). The episode of Billing's daughter is sometimes included in this; in which case we may speak about the Romantic Stanzas (91-110). Next, another set of gnomic wisdom follows, albeit directed to a certain Loddfafnir. The section is therefore called *Loddfáfnismál* (111-137). The last two sections are *Rúnatál* (138-145) and *Ljóðatál* (146-164). In my opinion, these two belong together and form one section (138-163). Clearly, this is how the original editors saw it.

Havamal 111

Mál er at þylja þular stóli á	The speech to chant on the Thul's chair
Urðarbrunni at,	At the Well of Urd
sá ek ok þagðak,	I saw and I kept silent
sá ek ok hugðak,	I saw and I pondered
hlydda ek á manna mál;	I listened to human speech
of rúnar heyrða ek dæma,	Of runes I heard deem,
né um ráðum þögðu	Nor were they silent about their interpretation
Háva höllu at, Háva höllu í,	At High One's Hall, in High One's Hall

Havamal 164

Nú eru Háva mál kveðin	Now has High One's speech been spoken
Háva höllu í,	In the hall of the High One
allþörf ýta sonum,	Very necessary for the sons of man
óþörf jötna sonum.	Unnecessary for the sons of Jotun giants
Heill sá, er kvað, heill sá, er kann,	Hail he, who spoke. Hail he, who knew.
njóti sá, er nam,	An application for him who took it
heilir, þeirs hlýddu.	Hail them who listened

The narrator identifies himself as a Thul at the Well of Urd. We therefore identify him as Odin. Urd's Well and Odin's Hall place the song in a mythical setting.

According to stanza 111, the song was recited in the vicinity of Valhalla, which is called the Hall of the High One (*háva höllu í*). Stanza 164 corroborates this, saying that the song has been uttered in the Hall of the

High One (*háva höllu í*). From a cultic point of view, the Hall signified the secret location where the initiates gathered.

The large section between stanza 111 and 164 may have been the original *Havamal*. Stanzas 111 and 164 reveal the poem's inner structure. A similar interpolation appears almost at the end of *Havamal*. Stanza 162 mixes the *Ljodatal* section with a reference to Loddfafnir. The stanza links the latter part of the poem with *Loddfafnismal*. It must be regarded as a whole.

Havamal 162b

Ljóða þessa mun þú, Loddfáfnir,	These songs shall you, Loddfafnir,
lengi vanr vera;	Long be without
þó sé þér góð, ef þú getr,	Though good for you if you get them
nýt ef þú nemr,	Applicable if you take them
þörf ef þú þiggr.	Necessary if you accept

Opinions disagree on the meaning of the name Loddfafnir. Fafnir appears as the name of a dragon and of a giant. Simek translates the name as Embracer. It possibly derives from the verb *fá* meaning to catch and is related to *fanga*, to fetch. Usually, *lodd* is translated as 'rags'. If this is correct, then it may refer to the costume of the initiand. He would be dressed in rags, reminiscent of the early harlequin, to represent an Underworld creature. In stanza 162, Loddfafnir is associated with *ljóð*, by which the *Ljodatal* spells are meant. In stanza 146, these spells where introduced as *ljóð*. Would Loddfafnir's name originally have been Ljodfafnir? If the name derives from *ljóð*, then he would be the One who Grasps the Spells. In any case, Loddfafnir represents the candidate for initiation.

The first half of *Havamal* must also be regarded as one unit (1-110). Scholars reason that the Gunnlod section is separate from the Gnomic Stanzas, but in reality it belongs to one and the same narrative. The episode is introduced by Odin's love affair with Billing's daughter. The Gunnlod myth seamlessly follows after this and its subsequent aphorisms. The adventure of Odin and Billing's daughter is itself an elucidation of the preceding stanzas on the nature of love and faithfulness (91-95). Stanza 96 functions as the connecting stanza. However, the same topics already appear in earlier stanzas (79-90) where they are mixed with others.

The Gunnlod story is linked with the earlier stanzas by *Havamal* 103. This particular stanza summarizes the aphorisms of *Gestathattr* and can rightly be interpreted as the end of the gnomic section. However, the Gunnlod story is a culmination of the totality of advice given in the Gnomic Stanzas. The main themes of the gnomic section deal with 1) wisdom gained by travelling, 2) the dangers of drinking, 3) friendship or the art of gift-giving and lastly 4) love affairs. Every one of these subjects has a place in the Gunnlod story.

Let us explore this thesis in more detail. 1) According to *Havamal*, a person becomes wise when he travels a lot. He meets many people and sees many things. He will also be a guest in many different households. Hence the section's name, the *páttr* of the Guest. In the Gunnlod story, Odin travels to Jotunheim and is a guest of Suttung. 2) In the hall of the giant, he drinks a portion of the Mead, which is remembered in *Havamal* 13-14. The advice on drinking has bearing on the story. The stanzas unmistakably link the Gunnlod passage with *Gestathattr*. 3) The subjects of friendship and gift-giving must be seen in its wider context. Gifts were exchanged for diplomatic reasons. It therefore refers to Odin's oath and his reception of the Mead in a very immediate way. 4) The advice on love and faithfulness are equally applicable to the story of Gunnlod. When the sayings of the High One are read in the light of the myth of the Mead of Poetry, it becomes clear that many a word relates to this or that detail of the story.

Kvilhaug suggests that the love affair of Odin with Billing's daughter and subsequently with Suttung's daughter must be considered in tandem. The daughter of Billing rejects Odin. It means the god was unable to stand the tests to be married to the maiden. He fails. The Gunnlod episode relates how the story goes when the god succeeds. She accepts the suitor. Originally, the Billing episode may have formed part of the Gunnlod story.

Kvilhaug also suggests that the three last spells of *Ljodatal* refer to the hero winning the otherworldly girl for sacred marriage. I am inclined to suppose that the spells directly concern the Gunnlod myth.

Last but not least, there is one stanza out of place in the first half of *Havamal* and that is stanza 80. The stanza must be read as a further interpolation by the original editors of the poem. It contains similar themes as stanzas 111, 162 and 164. However, its placing is odd. Perhaps it breaks the first half in two further large sections. The first subdivision would coincide with the *Gestathattr* proper. The second would correspond to the Romantic Stanzas. If this is the case, then *Havamal* has been intended to have three portions: the Gnomic Stanzas, the story of Gunnlod, and the song of Loddfafnir. Yet, all three form one whole. Their unity is implied by the various cross-references.

In conclusion, I am of the opinion that the entire poem pertains to the Gunnlod myth. The story of the Mead frames the whole poem. Gunnlod is mentioned in a flashforward in *Havamal* 13-14. The main myth is related in stanzas 107-110. Finally, Odrerir is mentioned again in *Havamal* 139 where the drink is given more consequence. Therefore, the Mead of poetry appears at the beginning, in the middle and at the end of the poem. Since the Mead is supposed to offer wisdom, *Gestathattr* and *Loddfafnismal* symbolically relate to the content of Odrerir. The Mead is supposed to proffer wisdom. It also bestows magical abilities, inferred from *Runatal* and *Ljodatal*.

The Sayings as Ritual

The Song of the High One opens with an account of how a guest enters a hall. Given the cultic context of the poem, the guest is identified as the candidate for initiation and the hall represents the Underworld. More specifically, the guest is Odin and the hall matches either Hnitbjorg or Valhalla. Valhalla originally referred to the world of the dead and must have been symbolically the place where the ancient initiations took place. If *Havamal* is interpreted in this fashion, then Odin's visit to Suttung's court suddenly becomes more palpable.

Snorri interprets the opening stanza of *Havamal* as the entry of Gylfi into Valhalla. The story curiously follows the same line. Kvilhaug interprets Gylfi as a hypostasis of Odin. The guest seeking knowledge at a wise man's court was well known in Ancient Scandinavia. It is also found in *Vafthrudnismal*.

From the opening section of *Havamal* (1-7) we imagine how Odin arrives at Suttung's court. He is eager to receive instructions, but nervous about his place in the bigger picture. We imagine how Suttung and Gunnlod are seated on the dais. Odin enters and is offered the guest's chair opposite the high seats. Then a symbel ceremony would have been organized to welcome the guest.

In his book *The Mead Hall*, Stephen Pollington gives the sequence of events of the symbel ceremony. A horn is blown to summon the court. Everyone enters. They wash their hands. The lord enters and directs everyone to their places. A person's place in the hall reflected his ranking. Then everyone is seated. The lord sits down on the high seat and the lady enters. She brings the Mead or ale with her. She greets the gathering. She offers the drink to the lord first. Then a blessing is said. Maybe special guests are introduced at this stage, such as Bolverk in our story. This is done by the lady, who we identify as Gunnlod. The guest of honour gives thanks and states his business. This often involves an oath or promise. Then, according to Pollington, the *þyle* challenges the guest's oath. I suppose that the challenging corresponds to the Old Norse verb *freista* (*Havamal* 26). The Old English *þyle* corresponds to Old Norse *þulr*. He functions as the lord's assistant.

The rite continues with the lady introducing a horn of Mead to be passed around in the hall. The main picture is clear. Odin states his business to lord Suttung. Baugi, the Spirit of the Oath Ring, challenges his oath. Gunnlod serves the Mead. From this perspective, the words of *Havamal* 104-110 become more meaningful.

The Context of Havamal

Havamal is a cultic text from start to finish. As such, it does not stand alone. The poem must be studied in league with *Sigrdrifumal* and *Rigsthula*. These three poems share a similar structure reflecting the Lesser and Greater Mysteries of the North. All three centre on the theme of initiation.

The recurring elements consist of 1) good advice, 2) initiation, and 3) rune lore. *Havamal* starts with a long section of advice. *Sigrdrifumal* ends with a series of stanzas on guidance. *Rigsthula* opens with Heimdal's visit to three couples, each of which he gives advice (*ráð at segja*). Then, *Havamal* describes Odin's complex initiation of the Mead and the hanging, after which a short section on rune lore and magical spells follows. *Sigrdrifumal* begins with the initiation of the Mead, after which the section on rune lore and magical spells follows. In *Rigsthula*, initiation is implied (35, 44). Equally so, the teaching of the runes is immediately associated with the initiation event, after which follow magical spells corresponding to those of *Havamal* and *Sigrdrifumal*.

Rigsthula is a little different from the other two poems, because the purpose is of a different nature. The story of Rig is only an introduction to a larger saga relating the origins of a royal dynasty. The complete text has been lost to us, but it explains why the inner teachings are only referred to. The poem consequently puts less emphasis on the details. Nonetheless, all the stages are present. In contrast, the lore in *Havamal* and *Sigrdrifumal* is quite explicit.

The elements dictate the different stages of initiatic teaching. Firstly, worldly advice is dispensed. This corresponds to the teachings of the

Lesser Mysteries. The student is asked to build character and discipline in preparation of initiation. He must first learn wisdom and common sense. This section coincides with the passage in the Sumerian epic of Gilgamesh in which the alewife Siduri gives Gilgamesh advice before he embarks for the plant of life. Analogous in the Celtic tradition, the advice-giving of Lady Sovereignty expresses the Lady's hope for a wise king. Then the initiation takes place. Both *Havamal* and *Sigrdrifumal* associate the initiation with the ritual of the Precious Mead. Lastly, a short section on magic follows. In each of the three poems, this last stage is associated with the runes. *Havamal* distinguishes between rune lore and the magical spells, but *Sigrdrifumal* does not. This stage comprises the Greater Mysteries.

Havamal	Sigrdrifumal	Rigsthula
Wisdom	Initiation	Wisdom
Initiation	Magic	Initiation
Rune Lore	Rune Lore	Rune Lore
Magic	Wisdom	Magic

In *Havamal*, Odin is the candidate for initiation. At the same time he is dedicated to himself. Thor Ewing theorizes that members of a magical society became an Odin. I suppose that an initiate had the right to call himself by that name. The same tradition is reflected in *Rigsthula*. Throughout the poem, Heimdal goes by the name of Rig, but when his candidates finish school, they equally adopt the name Rig. In stanza 35, Jarl receives the Rig title; in stanza 44, Kon becomes Rig.

Before initiation the candidate would bear another name and have another function in the school. In *Havamal*, the candidate's name is Loddfafnir. Loddfafnir becomes Odin after the hanging. Then, the Odin confronts his *anima* and she serves him the Mead of Wisdom. In *Sigrdrifumal*, Sigurd is initiated by Sigrdrifa. She is a Valkyrie and serves him the Mead. Sigurd is asked to take an oath (21). Moreover, the Valkyrie and the candidate pledge to marry each other. This confirms that Odin's oath involved wedding Gunnlod.

The much briefer *Sigrdrifumal* might reflect the outline of a true ritual. The text opens with a mythical setting and then begins with an invocative prayer. Interestingly, the Valkyrie only shares advice after Sigurd takes his oath. In a ceremony, this possibly comes before drinking the Mead.

The differences between the poems may reflect the existence of independent mystery schools. Possibly, the *Sigrdrifumal* tradition was originally taught only in the Volsung family. It is interesting to note that the corresponding chapter in the *Volsungasaga* deviates from *Sigrdrifumal* in some respects. *Havamal* may represent a more generic type of school. In *Rigsthula*, the teachings are imbedded in a ballad on a royal family. Presumably, the teachings stayed within the family, but any initiate would recognize the allusions made.

In *Havamal*, the initiation is recorded in stanzas 138-140. Three events are alluded to, two of which are elaborated in the poem, namely the Mead drinking and the Yggdrasil ordeal. The third event centres on learning magic from Bolthorn's son. Three different initiatic moments seem apparent, but they form one whole.

Kvilhaug is of the opinion that the hanging ritual immediately precedes the drinking ritual. She reasons that Odin's hanging would transport him to the World of the Dead. In this place he would be offered the Mead. Also, there is no coincidence in mentioning "nine powerful lays" and a drink from "the precious Mead" immediately after Odin's appropriation of the runes. The lays are a reference to the magical spells appended after the initiation.

The sequence of events is comparable to *Sigrdrifumal*. In *Sigrdrifumal* no actual death seems mentioned, but the hero climbs a hill and passes through a wall of shields. This is slightly reminiscent of the Troy Towns and certainly expresses the road to the Otherworld as discussed in the previous chapter. In *Sigrdrifumal*, the Mead is mixed with songs and runes. *Havamal* 139 associates the runes with ritual death. Havamal 140 associates the magical spells (*ljóð*) with the Mead. *Sigrdrifumal* connects the Mead with runes and *ljóð*. The spells number nine in *Sigrdifumal* and eighteen in *Havamal*. Clearly, rune lore, magic and initiation comprise one complex.

Indeed, the whole *Havamal* poem suddenly contains a lot more information on magic, Galdr, Seidr, and astral travel. Stanzas such as *Havamal* 105 clearly indicate that the text was used in a cultic context. Such stanzas are written in Galdralag, the Magic Metre. With a little imagination, the modern magician would be able to reconstruct the ancient rite of *Havamal* in its entirety.

In conclusion, *Havamal* is a relic of a genuine Northern mystery school tradition. Such schools must have existed already in the Bronze Age. In the Iron Age they presumably developed the Runic Alphabet. In the Viking Age they developed the Younger Futhark and cast their teachings in poems such as found in the Edda. Ewing conjectures that magical societies existed which operated outside of mainstream society. He bases his theory on source material surrounding the Norns, Valkyries, Einherjar and werewolves. I would go so far as to see a reflection of the original mystery schools in those dedicated men and women.

DOOR 9
LORD OF LOVE
AND WISDOM

Havamal incarnates Odin's wisdom. The poem relates how the god becomes wise. At the same time, the words inspire the applicant to take the same road. But drinking from Odrerir and the Yggdrasil ordeal are not the only sources of Odin's gnosis. The myths abound with his thirst after knowledge.

Voluspa mentions how Odin sacrifices his eye in exchange for a drink from the Well of Mimir. *Grimnismal* 7 says that Odin drinks with Saga. At the same time, Odin's adventure related in the *Grimnismal* poem exhibits a journey into the Underworld. The poem has been discussed earlier. Lastly, *Vafthrudnismal* covers all the same themes.

The Mimir myth is rather complex, because the sources have quite a bit to say about it. What we mainly remember from it, however, is that the protagonist drinks from the well. This ties in with the Odrerir theme except that no lady is mentioned. Nevertheless, Mimir is a giant whose name means memory. Here we have a strong parallel with the Mead of Poetry. The concept of the Mead is frequently associated with a Drink of Memory. And, again, Odin must travel to the world of the giants to gain the Wisdom. The myth is complex because *Voluspa* states that Mimir drinks from Odin's eye. I assume the eye represents the well. Moreover, the well is a metaphor for the cauldron (*ker*).

In *Grimnismal* 7, it is said how Odin and Saga drink from golden cups (*ker*) every day. The golden colour refers to Mead. Saga means 'what is said' and she is a goddess of history. Her name refers to knowledge, and to drink with her means to learn. She lives in Sokkvabekk, which means Sunken Bank, and therefore refers to the Underworld. The mythologem is easily linked with Mimir, since Odin visits both on a daily basis.

Vafthrudnismal relates how Odin travels to the world of the giants to meet Vafthrudnir. He wants to meet the giant in order to learn about the distant past. Frigg tells him it is dangerous, but Odin goes anyway. At Vafthrudnir's, Odin remains on the threshold, and is challenged (*freista*) to a word game. We observe that Odin travels to the Underworld to retrieve arcane knowledge.

The Odinic wisdom is invariably situated in the realm of the giants. They possess knowledge that the gods do not have access to because the Jotun giants existed before the gods and still exist outside of their world. On a psychological level, Jotunheim represents our subconscious. When a person wishes to learn about himself, he must face the elements in his subconscious. Meditation is the method to reach that place. In each of the stories, the travelling symbolizes the movement of the mind up and down the levels of reality. Odin represents the mind in meditation to register information which is otherwise inaccessible.

The travelling is done mentally. This is demonstrated by the Hildskjalf motif. When the King of Asgard seats himself on Valhalla's throne, he is suddenly able to see into every world. The throne might be identical with the high seat of the Volva, from which the seeress contacts the spirits. In *Sigrdrifumal*, this very seat is called Vilisessi, the Seat of the Will; in the *Volsungasaga* it is Völusessi, the Seat of the Volva. The interesting fact about this is that Frey, too, is said to take place on the throne. His gaze is inevitably drawn to the beings of Jotunheim. This is no coincidence. The seat opens a door to the spirit world associated with Jotunheim. In a very general way, travelling symbolizes the deepening of the mind.

The etymology of the word Hlidskjalf is uncertain. Usually, *hlið* is taken to mean gate or door. This fits in well with the trance technique to contact the spirits. The word is cognate with English 'lid'. However, the morpheme might derive from *hljóð*, which means hearing. The word is cognate with 'loud' and is used in skaldic poetry to signal the beginning of a performance. The *Voluspa* poem starts with this word. Maybe the same context applies to Hlidskjalf. The name means either lid-shelf or loud-shelf.

From myth and saga, we know that Odin presided over the faculty of altered states of consciousness. His very name means rage. The name originally referred to the storm of battle but later implied the ecstasy of the poet. It equally referred to the ecstasy of the members of the Wild Hunt. And so we see that many of Odin's attributes as a War God have been transferred to his being a God of Consciousness. As a god of war, Odin rules death, and is death not just another state of consciousness?

The two ravens associated with Odin originally belonged to the battle scene. They, too, gradually began to represent aspects of consciousness. Their names Hugin and Munin mean mind and memory. Every day, they are sent into the world. Every night, they return and whisper what they have seen in Odin's ears. The birds signify mental activity. Maybe they are linked with the energy of the ear chakras. They certainly underline the element of Air associated with Odin.

The ravens express Odin's insatiable thirst for knowledge. The is linked with the saying "a little bird told me", and in *Volsungasaga*, the "language of birds" means intuition. The phrase is found throughout the corpus of Scandinavian folktales.

In a very concrete way, the ravens represent Odin's thoughts. When you think of a place or a person faraway, the mind reaches out to its destination as if an airborne bird. Energy follows thought. We imagine how Memory flies through time and Thought through space to spy and retrieve information. The birds are possibly linked with Metis and Mnemosyne. Both ladies are wives of Zeus, but their names also mean Thought and Memory.

Every day, Odin fears his ravens will not return. I interpret this as being afraid of losing focus. It happens, when we think hard about a certain memory or subject, that we start to daydream. We lose our train of thought. The concentration falters.

God of Love

The key characteristics of Odin are well illustrated in *Harbardsljod*. The poem features a dialogue between Odin and Thor in which they boast about their exploits. At some point, Odin says he went out with the giant Fjolvar and they "fought a lot and slew warriors; challenged many (*freista*); and seduced ladies". The first means that Odin is a god of war. The second relates to his mental abilities. 'Trying' women makes up his next most important aspect: that of love.

The poem contains rather a lot of the same. Odin boasts of having had many affairs, all of them with the daughters of giants. Thor prides himself on bashing trolls. In passing, Odin tells Thor that he sleeps with his wife Sif.

Harbardsljod 16

Var ek með Fjölvari fimm vetr alla	I was with Fjolvar five winters in all
í ey þeiri, er Algroen heitir;	On that island, which is called Algroen.
vega vér þar knáttum ok val fella,	Fight we did there–they know–and fell the slain
margs at freista, mans at kosta.	Challenge many, kiss girls

Again in stanza 20, Odin boasts of luring away witches from their husbands. He uses love spells to accomplish this, reminding us of the *Ljodatal* charms 16 and 17. The Master of Asgard is not afraid to use magic in order to gain a maiden's love. Saxo confirms this when he writes that Odin resorts to magic when he needs Rind to bear him a son.

Harbardsljod 20 gives slightly more context when Odin says he deceived the Jotun Hlebard. Odin works it so that Hlebard hands him a magic wand, and then he leaves. The wand is called *gambanteinn*. What happens here resembles the episode of Odin stealing the Mead from Suttung, meaning that the giant will have explained Odin how to use the magic stick.

Gambanteinn means mighty wand. There is some debate as to the interpretation of this word. In my opinion, it may be a corruption of an original *gaman-teinn*, because *gaman* means pleasure. In the Eddic lays, the word is particularly associated with sexual pleasure. Skirnir uses the same *gambanteinn* to forcefully woo Gerd. *Gaman*-runes are mentioned in *Havamal* 120, and especially in *Havamal* 130: "If you want a good woman, speak runes of pleasure."

Havamal further elaborates on two of Odin's love adventures. In stanzas 96-102 Odin boasts of having seduced the daughter of Billing. Little is known about the story, but Billing is understood as the name of a giant. After this passage, we read about Gunnlod. The Gunnlod story incorporates two of Odin's key characteristics. On the one hand Odin travels to Suttung's hall to gain wisdom; on the other hand he beds Gunnlod. In this way, Odin truly becomes a Lord of Wisdom and Love.

Havamal 96-101

This I found when I sat in the reed
And waited for my beloved
The flesh and my heart was to me the shrewd girl
Though I had her not to hold

Billing's maiden I found in bed
White as the Sun sleeping
The thought of a Jarl's joy is nothing to me
Except to live with that body
"And near evening shall you, Odin, come
If you wish to speak to the girl"

All are ill fated except when (only) one person knows
Such fault together

Afterwards I turned back and, methinks, the favour
Of my desire I asked the leader
It would happen, I thought, that I would have
All of her mind and pleasure

So I came next time, but in need were
The fighting folk all awake
With burning lights and bearing timber
So was to me the stride of misery proven

And near morning when I was still coming
Then the hall folk were asleep
A single greyhound I then found, of the good woman,
Bound to the bed

Possibly, the affair with Billing's daughter is referred to in *Harbardsljod*. We cannot identify it with certainty, but it might coincide with stanzas 30-35. When Odin asks Thor what he was doing in the meantime, Thor sincerely responds that he was killing giants. Odin/Harbard replies he was also in Jotunheim, which is traditionally situated in the east, but making love to a pretty girl. Odin admits he could have used Thor's help. Again in all honesty, Thor says he would have helped him if he was there. I am supposing Odin is referring to his affair with Billing's daughter.

The kenning *billings-full* or Cup of Billing refers to poetry. It reveals that the giant originally formed part of the Mead of Poetry story. In that case, Billing probably refers to Suttung.

Harbardsljod 30-35
Harbard said:

"I was in the east and with a single lady I chattered
I played with that linen white one. And a lone thing we had.
I gladdened this gold-bright one. The maiden favoured pleasure."

Thor said:
"Good you had it there, a girl-affair there, then."

Harbard said:
"Your assistance I then needed, Thor,
When I held this one, the linen white maiden."

Thor said:
"I would have granted you that then, if I had come along."

Harbard said:
"I would have trusted you then, except if you would trick me in trust."

Thor said:
"I am not that kind of heel-biter, the same as an old hide-shoe in spring."

From an occult point of view, we interpret romantic love as a symbol of universal love. In the myths, romantic love is love on a higher level. The magnetic power of love works out as the attraction of two opposites. Therefore, the quality of love is inclusive. This facilitates understanding, which in turn leads to wisdom. Consequently, Odin's numerous love affairs are explained as an aspect of the Ageless Wisdom. Divinity is expressed by Love and Wisdom.

In the system of the Seven Rays, Wisdom and Love are sides of the same coin. They are Second Ray qualities. Indeed, the Ascended Masters are also known as the Masters of Wisdom and Lords of Compassion. The Second Ray quality dictates inclusiveness. It transcends all separateness and teaches compassion.

The planetary ruler of the Second Ray is Jupiter, with whom Odin shares many attributes. When it comes to courting women, Odin resembles the Olympian Zeus/Jupiter. The Greco-Roman supreme deity is known for his many brides, whom he chooses among mortals and immortals alike. The planet's main energy is that of inclusiveness. Jupiter rules two signs in the Zodiac; in Sagittarius, he is a Lord of Wisdom, and in Pisces, he is a Lord of Love. We can only conclude one thing. Odin is a Lord of Love and Wisdom.

Valkyries

The qualities of Love and Wisdom are combined in the initiation ritual of the Mead of Poetry. In the myth, Odin loves Gunnlod and receives the wisdom. In the saga, Sigurd promises his love to Sigrdrifa and receives the wisdom.

Sigrdrifa belongs to a special category of women associated with Odin. She introduces herself as a Valkyrie. We have already established that they are paired with the Norns and form a counterweight to the Odinic triad. The Valkyries are best known for their role of choosing the warriors slain in combat. They lead the warriors to Valhalla where they become sons of Odin and are christened Einherjar. The slain heroes are being given immortality.

Grimnismal 36 is very specific about it. "The Valkyries serve ale to the Einherjar." *Grimnismal* 25 claims that a cauldron of Mead is always present in Valhalla. The drink is called *mjöðr* and *veig*. Both concepts are synonymous with *öl* 'ale' of *Alvissmal* 34. According to legend, the Einherjar fight each other in training day after day. They kill each other but wake up again in the morning. Such is the power of the Ambrosia. The link between the Valkyries and the Einherjar is further established by *Helgakvida Hundingsbana hin fyrri* 38.

Snorri Sturluson regards the Valkyries as a subdivision of the Asynjur. After the list of Asynjur, Snorri continues to enumerate the names of Valkyries. The extension is logical since they complement the function of the earlier goddesses. The difference between the Valkyries and the Asynjur is minimal.

The Asynjur list begins with Frigg. The goddesses that follow are mostly related with Frigg. Possibly, Frigg can be identified with any of the goddesses. The list continues with Saga, Eir, Gefjun and Fulla. Gefjun and Fulla are said to be girls (*mær*), unmarried women.

The most remarkable lesser goddess is Fulla. She is described as a handmaiden of Frigg. Fulla wears her hair free and has a gold band around her head. She carries Frigg's basket and shares in her secrets. The name of the goddess refers to the drinking horn, and means full. The Old Norse root word refers to a ceremonial toast to the gods. It is found in compounds such as *Óðins-full*, *Njarðar-full*, and *Freys-full*.

Fulla's name alone is enough to consider her a Valkyrie. She is defined as a *mær* and wears her hair like an unmarried girl. Fulla furthermore takes on attributes of Freyja. The golden band (*gullband*) may be identified with the Brisingamen.

Gefjun, too, is interpreted as a hypostasis of Freyja, since Gefn is a heiti of Freyja. Not much is said about Saga except that she lives in Sokkvabekk. The name of her abode is synonymous with Frigg's house. According to *Grimnismal* 7, Odin drinks with Saga every day. They drink from golden cups, which is a reference to the Sacred Mead. Therefore, Saga seems to be associated with both Frigg and Freyja. Eir is an obscure goddess associated with healing. Her name appears among the Valkyrie names of the Thulur in the *Snorra Edda*. In *Fjolsvinnsmal*, she is one of the nine maidens waiting on Menglod.

After Freyja, Sjöfn and Lofn are mentioned. Sjöfn means affection and she is clearly an aspect of Freyja. She inspires love in both men and women. The goddess Lofn makes it possible for people to unite who otherwise cannot be together. She, too, seems an aspect of Freyja. According to *Gylfaginning*, she works under the command of Odin and Frigg.

Next, three lesser goddesses are mentioned dealing with the Thing. They are Vár, Vör, and Syn. The names mean Promise, Wariness, and Denial. In my opinion, they have bearing on the story of Odin visiting Suttung's court. Syn is a heiti of Sunna in the *Nafnathulur*.

Then, Hlin, Snotra, and Gna are mentioned. Both Hlin and Gna serve Frigg. Hlin means Lee or Protection and her name is a heiti for Frigg in *Voluspa* 53. Snotra means Wisdom. She reminds us of the Gnostic Sophia. The Old Norse concept *snotr* occurs many times in *Havamal*.

Therefore, Saga, Fulla, Lofn, Hlin and Gna are hypostases of Frigg. Fulla, Eir, Gefjun, Sjöfn and Lofn are hypostases of Freyja. The overlap between the two greater goddesses is significant.

After the actual Asynjur, Snorri cites a verse from *Grimnismal*. Thirteen Valkyrie women are named. *Voluspa* contains a list of six Valkyries. Snorri lists a further three after the quotation. In addition, these sources are checked against the *Nafnathulur*.

Grimnismal 36

Hrist and Mist do I want to bear me a horn

Skeggjold and Skogul

Hild and Thrud, Hlokk and Herfjötur

Göll and Geirahod

Randgrid and Radgrid and Reginleif

They bear the Einherjar ale

Voluspa 30

She saw Valkyries come from afar

Ready to ride to the god people

> Skuld held the shield, but Skogul is the other
> Gunn, Hild, Gondul and Geirskogul
> Now are listed the women of Herjan
> Ready to ride over the earth are the Valkyries

In the *Voluspa* stanza, the Valkyries are described as *nönnur herjans*. Herjan is a heiti of Odin, but *nönnur* is the plural of Nanna, which is the name of a goddess. We can therefore include her in the list. Her name is a kenning for 'woman' in poetry. According to the *Gesta Danorum*, Balder falls in love with Nanna when he sees her bathing.

In general, many of the Valkyrie names are kennings for 'woman' in poetry. Examples are Hild, Thrud, Leif and Hrund. In the same way, *dís* is a synonym for 'woman' in poetry. Moreover, the Disir are supernatural women closely associated with the magic of war-fetters. And remember that Freyja is called the Dís of the Vanir. Valkyries are also called *óðins meyjar*.

Most of the Valkyrie names refer to battle. Some names refer directly to battle, others refer to weapons. Both Hild and Gunn mean battle, war. Skogul refers to something that sticks out, like a tusk, possibly a spear. The name means Spear-Wielder. Geirskogul means Skogul of the Spear. The name Geirahod means Spear-Battle, but Hod is also the name of a god, Hoder. Hrist derives from a word meaning to shake. Metaphorically, war gear was shaken in combat. The shaking is said of spears, helmets and shields. For example, the spear name Gungnir is derived from a word meaning to shake. Skeggjold means Age of the Halberd, which is a reference to battle. Randgrid means Obsession (*grið*) of the Shield, but Grid is also the name of a giantess. Her name refers to a place of truce (*grið*).

There is a Valkyrie named Hrund in the Thulur. Her name means ruin, suggestive of the Greek Ate. Thrud is the name of a Valkyrie, but it is also the name of Thor's daughter. Her name appears to mean Strength.

There is one Valkyrie named Hlokk. The name is cognate with English 'lank'. Metaphorically, it may refer to the slender spear.

Some Valkyrie names specifically refer to battle magic. There is Herjafjotur. She is the Fetterer of the Army. The war-fetter refers to the paralysis of fear that comes over a person when he faces the advancing enemy. There is a Valkyrie named Goll. The name is derived from *galdr* and refers to magic. Her name can be translated as Yell, a reference to the battle cry. Another one is called Gondul. The name derives from *gandr*, which word refers to something that is spirit possessed. Possibly *gandr* refers to magically endowed spirits. Then Gondul would mean Wielder of Spirits. In *Sorla Thattr*, Freyja calls herself Gondul when she enters the human world. In the story, the meeting of Hedin and Gondul resembles that of the hero and a foster-mother except that Gondul wishes evil on the hero. There is also Mist, whose name means mist, fog. I am supposing we are talking about mist brought about by Seidr. This kind of battle magic is attested in the sources.

Lastly, there are Radgrid and Reginleif. These are interesting names. The first means Grid of Counsel. The name possibly refers to the good advice which the Valkyrie is thought to give. Reginleif means Patrimony of the Gods. This, too, may refer to the ceremony of initiation and the Mead of Poetry.

Darradarljod mentions Hild, Hjorthrimul, Sanngrid, Svipul, Gunn and Gondul. Hild, Gunn or Gud, and Gondul, we have already discussed. Hjorthrimul means Sword-Clamour. Svipul reminds us of the Odinsheiti Svipal and means Sweeping One. The morpheme *sannr* in Sanngrid reminds us of the Odin names Sann, Sad, and Sanngetall. The Valkyrie's name means Giantess of the Justice, or Truth-Grid.

All of the above are the names of mythical beings. In the heroic poems also exist human Valkyries such as Sigrdrifa, Olrun, Svava, Sigrun and so on. It would lead us too far to discuss these as well. The names contain similar elements and tie in with the archetypical Valkyrie who serves the Mead of Wisdom. Sigrdrifa means Driver of Victory. The name reminds us of the Valkyrie name Rota, which means Sleet Storm. Old Norse *drífa* means snow storm, a common circumlocution for battle. Olrun means Mystery of Mead and Sigrun means Victory Magic; names that refer to magic. Svava refers to sleeping magic, which is used on Sigrdrifa. According to Kvilhaug they fulfill the same roles as their mythical counterparts.

And last but not least, there is Skuld. She is a Valkyrie in *Voluspa* and in the Thulur. Her name means debt and she represents what is bound to happen. Therefore, Skuld embodies the fatality of battle.

Although most of the Valkyrie names refer to battle, they seem to be linked with the Mead of Poetry story. Serving the Einherjar is compared to the role of the drink-offering initiatrix. And the warrior must die before he is taken to Valhalla. It makes Gunnlod a plausible Valkyrie. Gunnlod may be a giantess but she also performs the Valkyrie role. Let us not forget that Snorri's list of goddesses contains rather a lot of giantesses. Svava Jakobsdottir says "the women who were the spiritual channels for souls between the worlds in Norse mythology were either giantesses or valkyries".

We assume that Gunnlod belongs to the Order of the Valkyries. Her name *gunnlöð* means Battle-Invitation. The name sounds like that of a Valkyrie. Symbolically, combat implies the inner struggles which the individual faces on the path of soul alignment. However, the morpheme *löð* on its own can be interpreted as 'invitation to drink'. The older rendering *laþu* is frequently used in Ancient Germanic inscriptions. In *Fjolsvinnsmal* stanza 3, *löð* is used in a cultic sense. We therefore argue that Gunnlod is named after the drink.

Something similar is seen in the Celtic tradition. The Sovereignty of Tara was called Medb Lethderg. The morpheme *derg* means red and refers to the red colour of the Mead. The name Medb is a cognate of 'Mead'.

Another hint is found in the Celtic tradition. Possibly the name

Derga from the story *The Destruction of the Hostel of Da Derga* (*Togail Bruidne Dá Derga*) is taken from the same cultic meaning. The hostel in the story is one of five or six in Ancient Ireland and termed *bruidne*. These hostels are interpreted as Otherworldly places. Each possesses a cauldron. According to legend, the cauldron never grows empty. This is possibly founded on the magical cauldron of the Dagda but it coincides with the Eldhrimnir cauldron of Valhalla. The Dagda corresponds to Odin, since he too is called Allfather (*eochaidh ollathair*). Da Derga is named after the colour of the Sacred Mead but literally means Red God. Interestingly, one particular rendering of the story, the *Orgain Bruidne Uí Dergae*, speaks about Ua Derga instead of Da Derga. Ua Derga means 'cousin of the red goddess'. The red goddess can be no other than Sovereignty or the Lady of the Mead. The Old Irish word for cousin implies kinship but specifically means a spiritual descendant. This completes the initiate and the Mead-offering Otherworld Lady motif.

In the Northern tradition, too, the Mead is associated with a golden colour. This is deduced from a name such as Gullveig. Her name means Golden Drink. *Veig* literally means intoxication. In *Voluspa*, Gullveig is nicknamed *heiðr*, which means clear. In its turn, this morpheme points to the bright colour of the Mead. We find the morpheme again in the name of the goat which provides the Mead for the Einherjar. She is called Heidrun, the Mystery of Clarity. Kvilhaug goes so far as to consider Heidrun as a hypostasis of Freyja.

Interpreting the Gullveig name as a reference to the Sacred Mead elucidates the passage in *Voluspa*. Her stabbing and burning suddenly represent a ritual of initiation. Maybe we find here a vestige of a ritual with a female candidate. Gullveig enters the Hall of the male gods led by Odin. She is ritually sacrificed. This possibly refers to the *són* ritual, but it certainly marks her descent into the Underworld. The triple death might correspond to the three draughts of the Mead or the three nights of Odin with Gunnlod.

In the story of *Fjolsvinnsmal*, the Lady is called Menglod. Jakobsdottir suggests it means Invitation to the Mixed Drink.

The Ancient Germanic Matronae names are usually interpreted as Valkyries names. Examples are Alagabiae, Gabiae, Gabinae, Garmangabis. The exemplar name complexes contain a morpheme for 'giving' which alludes to the Mead serving. The morpheme *gab-* is also found in Viking Age goddess names such as Gefjon and Gefn. The latter is a heiti of Freyja and the former is glossed Diana in the manuscript tradition. There can be no coincidence that Freyja is associated with the Valkyries and the Mead-offering. She is usually regarded as their Queen. She claims half of the Einherjar in battle; the other half goes to Odin. She serves Mead to the giant Hrungnir. And she is associated with gold and rites of fertility. The match is perfect.

There is a particular theme of the sagas in which the hero meets a giantess who symbolically takes the role of Valkyrie. She falls in love with him and promises him her help. She is usually magically gifted and said to be very strong. When they part, she bestows magical gifts on the hero. More often than not, there is an erotic subtext present, especially in the Fornaldursogur.

The theme has been thoroughly discussed in Lorenzo Gallo's article *The Giantess as Foster-Mother in Old Norse Literature*. Typically, the hero lands with his ship and band of warriors. They take shelter for the night. Then the hero goes into the woods to explore the country. He tells his companions to wait three nights. If he is not back by then, they can sail off without him. In the woods, he meets a giantess. She takes him in and becomes his foster-mother (*fóstra*).

The relationship is similar to that of the Valkyrie and the hero. The seclusion expresses the ritual isolation of the candidate. The giantesses are associated with magic. The hero therefore enters an Otherworld. The sexual undertone symbolizes the divine union and the hero is afterwards able to always call upon the help of the giantess, his own soul. The only thing missing is the drinking of the Mead. The magical gifts which the hero receives are reminiscent of the esoteric knowledge acquired through initiation. They are analogous to the list of spells and advice in the Eddic poems.

Some of the foster-mother giantesses bear names that remind us of beings that we encounter in similar contexts. Egil Skallagrimsson's foster-mother was called Thorbjerg. She is strong and knows magic. Thurid is the foster-mother of Thorbjorn in *Grettissaga*. She is old and versed in magic. Grid is a foster-mother in *Illugasaga Gridarfostra* and in *Thorsdrapa*; Heid in *Halfdanar Thattr Svarta*; Hrafnhild in *Ketilssaga Haengs*; Menglod in *Orms Thattr Storolfssonar*; Arinnefja in *Egilssaga Einhenda ok Asmundar Berserkjabana*; and Hildigunn in *Örvar Oddssaga*. Thorbjerg, Thurid and Heid are Volvas. Grid is the name of a giantess but her name appears among the Valkyries. Moreover, a woman named Grid supplies Thor with magical gifts at a critical moment. Might she be his foster-mother? She possesses a *völr* which is a kind of magic staff. It is the emblem of the Volva. Hrafnhild and Hildigunn sound like Valkyrie names. Hild is both the name of a Valkyrie and of a giantess. Arinnefja means eagle beak. The name is associated with magic in *Sigrdrifumal* 16; *á arnar nefi*. Menglod is the name of a Mead-dispensing initiatrix.

Einherjar

In Norse mythology, the Einherjar are warriors brought to Valhalla by the Valkyries. They stay there until Ragnarok. At that time they are awakened from their slumber by Gullinkambi, when they ride forth. The host is led by Odin.

The myth is reminiscent of the Wild Hunt and the Wild Host. According to Farwerck, the legend reflected a genuine cult tradition. A group of people dressed as creatures of the Underworld held a procession along the villages of the community. The procession was wild and noisy.

They painted their faces black, wore white clothes and used masks. Those are the colours of the dead.

It seems reasonable to assume that membership of a magical society involved a sacrificial death. Only the dead enter Valhalla. Ritual death made the person a member of the Underworld while he was still alive. That is what it meant to be initiated. Therefore, when a band of masked initiates raged through the villages, the people said: "Those are the dead." Here is the link with the Einherjar. From his symbolic death on the battlefield, the candidate was transported to the sacred Underworld. The Einherjar formed a secret society of the mock dead.

Thor Ewing hypothesizes that the existence of magical societies was represented in mythology. He says that "the line between people and gods was certainly blurred". Initiates bridged the gap between everyday life and the world of the gods. The female workers were known as *völur*, *valkyrjur* and *nornir*. The male magicians were representatives of Odin, who I associate with the Einherjar. Farwerck defines groups like these as Männerbunde.

According to Ewing, initiates wandered from farm to farm to dispense their wisdom according to need. In the sagas, we often read how a stranger enters somebody's house. He looks like Odin, but he is never recognized as such. The stranger wears a hood, has a staff, beard, and sometimes only one eye. Only afterwards do people realize who he was. The *Grimnismal* story is in fact a good example. The same is found in *Reginsmal*, *Nornagests Thattr*, *Hrolfssaga Kraka*, and the *Gesta Danorum*, among other tales. A similar motif is found in the Greek myth about Philemon and Baukis; and in the Book of Tobit when the protagonist meets Raphael in disguise. Ewing states that those visitors were real people representing the god.

Ewing argues that the collection of sayings in *Havamal* belonged to the arsenal of advice owned by those initiates. He explains the title of the poem not as the 'words of Odin' but as the 'words of the High Ones', interpreting *háva-* as a genitive plural. The compound would refer to initiates dedicated to the wisdom of Odin. This explains why Odin would talk about himself in the third person in for instance *Havamal* 110. The discrepancy of perspective reflects the original cultic use of the text.

Ewing also observes that Odin says in *Grimnismal* that he adopted his many names when he "went among the people". He means to say that Odin literally walked among mankind, albeit in the guise of men of flesh and bone. It means that all the Einherjar are Odin.

The theory presupposes an initiatory school in which the candidate was made an Odin. He was then given the lore of the High One and thereafter operated in his name. This is very close to the opening of *Gylfaginning*. Gangleri visits the court of the High One to seek knowledge. Gangleri reminds us of an Odin figure and the name is an Odinsheiti. It may reflect an actual memory of an initiatory rite. As a leader of the Wild Hunt and of the Einherjar, Odin represents at the same time initiate and hierophant.

The candidate for initiation is singled out in some of the rites associated with the Wild Hunt. Sometimes he limps. Sometimes he is beaten, often with a club. Sometimes he is touched with a spear. Sometimes he is blindfolded, sometimes bound by the hands. In Germanic tradition, hands were bound to seal a contract. The contract could be of any nature, such as claiming land, to marry, and so on. The divine appellations Hapt and Bönd possibly derive from this custom. The custom is retained in Masonic ceremonies. Ewing furthermore remarks that Viking Age iconography shows many male cult images which have one eye marked. He associates this with the myth of Odin's one-eyedness. The candidate was somehow marked in imitation of Odin.

In French folklore, the candidate for initiation was often called 'harlequin'. Sometimes the Wild Hunt was named after the character. In Old French, the terms *hellekin* or *herlequin* first appeared in the 11th century with reference to the Wild Hunt.

The name is of Germanic origin and came into the French language via either Dutch or German. It would derive from an original Dutch *harleken*, which is the diminutive of *harel*, *haerle*, *herle*. The word derives from the same root as Heruli or Erilaz of Ancient Germanic times. The Heruli are attested as the name of a tribe, but they are well known from runic inscriptions and seem to consist of a band of so-called runemasters. The fact that the word survived into late medieval times in a ceremonial context suggests that the original Heruli were indeed a society of initiates. In later times the candidate for initiation was called by the name of that ancient tribe. In English folklore, one of the names for the Wild Hunt is *herla-þing*, the Assembly of Erilaz.

The harlequin of the commedia dell'arte inherited some of the candidate's traits. The chequered costume reminds us of the animal skins and patchwork worn by the participants of the Wild Hunt. Incidentally, the design is still found in the floor pattern of Masonic lodges. Farwerck interprets the chequering as an earth symbol. In my opinion, the alternation of the colours in the design represents life and death. I associate the alternation with the description of Hella, goddess of the Underworld, who is half alive half dead. The symbolism fits the candidate's situation.

There is one more clue. Charles Leadbeater makes an interesting remark when he describes the energy building during a Christian celebration in his *Science of the Sacraments*. According to his vision, the Angel of the Eucharist helps shape the energy of human devotion during a service. At some point he describes the floor design on an energy level. He says that the design coinciding with the church floor looks like "a mosaic of blue and crimson blocks set diagonally, so as to present the appearance of lozenges or diamonds". Crimson is always one of the harlequin's colours.

The character was later equated with the Fool. As a symbol, the fool stands for the ignorance of the candidate. After his initiation, he will no longer be a fool.

In the Lowlands, the character is identified with the so-called *wildeman*. In English, he is known as 'wild man' or woodwose. He appears in heraldic weapons from Germany and Britain, but also in place names in Belgium and Holland. He is usually depicted naked, bearing a club.

Farwerck points out that the initiate or candidate often bears a club. He is also depicted naked most of the time. This fits the description of the berserker, who goes naked into battle and wields a club. It makes sense to consider the berserkers as members of a magical society.

The animal skin must have been an emblem of its members. Terms such as *berserkr* and *úlfheðinn* imply that initiates wore bear or wolf skins. The bear skin recurs in the *Volundarkvida* poem. Volund unconsciously prepares for initiation when he hunts a bear and sits on its skin when he comes home. He has a sword, not a club. The animal skin reminds us of the shapeshifting abilities of Germanic initiates.

In Ancient Greece, the initiate archetype bears the same insignia. Herakles is famed for his club and lion skin. At some point, Herakles, too, descends into the Underworld. Before he does, he sees Eumolpos of Eleusis and takes initiation in the Mysteries. Metaphorically, the twelve labours of Herakles are symbolic of the initiatic tests the individual has to take.

In Sumerian myth, Gilgamesh is also depicted with a lion skin. In his famous epic, he is naked but for the skin and undergoes different trials.

In Norse myth, the god Thor fits the description best. According to Saxo, Thor wields a club. Thor's hammer Mjolnir sometimes appears as an axe or a club. The initiand is identified as Thor.

From the folk traditions listed by Farwerck we remember that initiates wore three kinds of skin; wolf first and foremost, then goat and lastly bear. Horses were mimicked in one way or another, but they more represented the means of entering the Underworld. The goat shape was especially used during Yule time and is associated with the myth of how

Thor sacrificed his goats. The myth features a death and rebirth theme. In the folk ceremonies, too, the goat was always revived after the death trial. On the whole, the goat skin seems to have been used most in the practice of Seidr.

Secret Societies

Farwerck explains how the works of the original sacred societies were watered down in Christian times. The original fraternities were oppressed by advancing Christianity. Nevertheless, they handed down their lore and traditions through the formation of guilds. At first these guilds were associated with towns and villages, close to the original functioning of the Männerbunde. Later, they became the guilds of craftsmen and merchants. At some point, particularly the society of builders increased in importance. They formed lodges and from them the Masonic tradition stems.

Later still, the meaning behind folk traditions was forgotten and some of the songs and plays came into the hands of children, such as the gift-giving on Saint Nicholas Day or the door-to-door singing at Epiphany in Belgium. Hopscotch would be another such vestige. The hopping is reminiscent of the candidate's limping. Farwerck remarks that the secularized folk traditions are still held at times of ancient heathen import, such as Yule Tide. The Wild Host heralds the winter season.

The reality of the Wild Hunt seems to reflect the reality of the Valkyries as well. Both troupes are well attested in both mythology and the real world. Volvas and Valkyries are both well known from myth and saga. The sources make it clear that both offices were practiced in the real world while a mythological framework supported it. The distinction between mythological and factual beings is even less tangible when dealing with the female magicians.

According to the poem *Helgakvida Hundingsbana onnur*, Valkyries ride through air and sea. This, too, is reminiscent of the Wild Hunt and later derivatives, such as the witches' Sabbath or Freemason gatherings. In folklore, eyewitnesses claim to see them flying through the air. But when the witness comes home and tells his neighbours, he says he was happy to lie flat on the floor because they flew so low that their feet almost touched him. Obviously, real ceremonies were mythologized.

The myths highlight the symbolic content of the ceremonies. As a modern symbol, Valhalla represents the School of the Northern Mysteries. Situating Valhalla in Asgard turns the World of the Gods into a Gnostic Kingdom of Souls. The hall becomes the archetypal place of brotherhood. The Einherjar have found their way into the kingdom of the soul. It has proven a long way with lots of battles.

If the Valkyrie is the soul; then Odrerir symbolizes the Wisdom made liquid. To become one of the Einherjar, the warrior was presented the Buddhic Mead by his personal Valkyrie. This explains the multitude of Valkyries in the Halls of the High One. They are the souls or guides of the initiates. It also explains the word *einheri*, because *ein-* signifies an individual.

The Sacred Marriage enacts the communion with his Holy Guardian, and the Mead makes him privy to his innate wisdom. Then the gates swing open and the initiate enters the Doors of Valhalla.

In time, every member of humanity will face those doors. Your Valkyrie is waiting.

Odin's Spouse

The archetypal initiate is no other than Odin. Conversely, Freyja embodies the archetypal Bride found in initiation. The sources seem to back up the hypothesis.

According to legend, the Wild Hunt is led by the Wild Hunter, who is sometimes named after a famous king of history, although more often than not he is named after Od or Odin. Dialect variations include Wode, Gode, Oden, Woden, and Wodan. Alternately, the host is led by a woman, usually Holda or Perchta. Again, variations appear. Variations on Frigg's name also appear, such as Frie and Fuik. Sometimes the Wild Hunter and Holda were seen together.

Holda is cognate with Hel, who I usually call Hella. Her name means Hidden One. Perchta is cognate with 'bright' and Bjarkan. In fairy tales and folklore, Hel or Frau Holle are regarded as a kind person. She is also said to be Odin's wife. The Continental appellation Frau is cognate with Freyja and is used as a title. It means lady.

We identify the female leader with Freyja. *Grimnismal* stanza 14 explains the connection. Freyja claims the initiated dead. This puts her on a par with Odin. Again, in *Gylfaginning* 20, Odin seats some of the Einherjar in Valhalla and some of them in Vingolf. The latter is the hall of the Asynjur. The Edda gives no information as to whom the hall belongs. The hall may be synonymous to Sessrumnir and Folkvang.

In addition, Freyja is married to Od. And is he not the Lord of the Hunt? The intimate relation between Odin and Freyja follows from their shared role as battle deities and gods of the dead.

In *Sorla Thattr*, Freyja is called Odin's mistress (*friðla*). The story tells of how Freyja got the Brisingamen necklace. When Odin makes Loki steal it, Freyja gets angry. Odin says she cannot regain the necklace unless she promotes war between two particular kings. This is interesting, since it pictures Freyja as a war goddess.

There is much evidence in favour of pairing Freyja with Odin. Yet the sources make us believe that Odin is married to Frigg. Are Frigg and Freyja one and the same person? In *Oddrunargrattr*, the goddesses are mentioned closely together. They are both associated with birth and marriage. Frigg is profiled as a domestic goddess but a housewife is called *hús-freyja*. Etymologically, the names Freyja and Frigg derive from the same root. The relation is significant.

But they have more in common. The main connecting mythologem is that of the weeping goddess. Both Frigg and Freyja weep. Freyja weeps when she realizes that Od is gone. She weeps tears of amber and gold. Frigg weeps for the loss of her son (*Voluspa* 33) and her husband (*Voluspa* 51).

The second distinctive feature is that of the falcon dress. Both Frigg and Freyja are said to own one. It means that they can shapeshift into a falcon. It must have been the goddess' power animal. The falcon shirt is mentioned in two or three myths and each time very similar. Loki borrows it to fly into Jotunheim. Thor is coaxed to go with him, albeit without his hammer.

For example, in *Thrymskvida* we read that Mjolnir is stolen. Loki borrows a shirt of feathers (*fjaðr-hamr*) from Freyja, but the kind of bird is not specified. In the prose Edda, Loki borrows the falcon shirt (*vals-hamr*) from Frigg and is asked to bring Thor without his hammer. The same feather shirt is intended. In *Skaldskaparmal*, Loki borrows the falcon shape (*vals-hamr*) from Freyja to save Idun; this time without Thor's help.

Last but not least, Frigg heads the circle of goddesses and many are identified with her. Freyja is second in command but as many goddesses are associated with her, as well as the Valkyries; we could posit that Freyja is a Valkyrie and Frigg one of the Norns. The identification of Freyja with the Valkyrie archetype incidentally explains her teaching Seidr to Odin.

All the above explains the perceived confusion over Freyja and Frigg. In our interpretation we follow in the footsteps of many other authors, such as Ellis-Davidson and Näsström.

Things become even more interesting when we equate Odin with Frey and study where their attributes overlap. This does not mean that they are always the same god. It only means that one takes the role of the other occasionally.

Lord Frey

It may come as no surprise that Odin is identified with Frey. Freyja's twin brother is a leader of hosts and Frey's name, too, is a title. It means lord. In times past, there may have been confusion between Odin and Frey. After all, Frey, too, is an incarnation of Love and Wisdom.

The most curious confusion is the possession of Skidbladnir. The ship traditionally belongs to Frey. *Grimnismal* and *Gylfaginning* say so. But in *Ynglingasaga*, it is an attribute of Odin.

Likewise, the myth of Frey and Gerd resembles the story of Odin and Gunnlod. The details of Gerd's Wooing are interesting in the present discussion. According to *Skirnismal*, Frey first spotted Gerd in Jotunheim from Hlidskjalf. The throne is traditionally Odin's seat. Moreover, Odin travels to Jotunheim to seduce women.

According to *Ynglingasaga*, the son of Frey and Gerd is Fjölnir. The latter is a common heiti of Odin, which makes Allfather a son of Frey. Behind this we see a representation of the vegetation myth, where the son is an incarnation of the father. The vegetation myths are particularly associated with the Vanir, because they are gods of fertility. The loop of those myths explains the incest stories of the Vanic deities and increases the possibility of Odin being a son of Frey as much as Frey being a son of Odin.

Similarly, Odin marries Jord, Mother Earth. As a metaphor, Gerd represents the Earth. She is therefore a hypostasis of Jord. When Gerd is equated with Jord, Frey becomes a mask of Odin.

Freyja might just as well be identified with Gerd. The giantess is a daughter of Gymir, who is Aegir, a sea deity. Freyja's father Njord also rules the sea. He lives near the sea and is prayed to for voyages and fishing. The 'glove of Njord' is a kenning for sponge. And Freyja, too, is associated with Earth's fertility.

Factually, the identification of Frey with Odin becomes all the more plausible when Freyja is in the equation. She is Frey's sister, but she is also his lover. From a Vanic point of view, it was customary for brother and sister to marry.

Both gods are tribal ancestors as well as leaders. According to legend, Frey was a Swedish king. He is the divine ancestor of the Ynglingar, the Swedish royal line, much the same as Odin for other dynasties. Furthermore, Frey's own ancestral lineage might mirror that of Odin. Tacitus traces three of the Germanic tribes to a god Mannus, son of Tuisto/Tuisco. The tribes are the Ingaevones, Irminones and Istaevones. The first tribe descends from Yngvi, which is Frey's original name. Yngvi-Frey might have been the eldest of three brothers. The family unit somewhat corresponds to Odin's own.

Ulf Uggason says: "Frey rides in front … and governs hosts." Frey is called *fólkvaldi goða* in *Skirnismal*. Moreover, Frey is Lord of Elves and ruler of Alfheim, much as Odin rules Asgard and the Aesir. Let us not forget that the expression *æsir ok álfar* is a common designation for the gods as a collective. The words may be synonyms.

Once a year, the Elves were commemorated. The feast was called Alfablot and happened late in autumn. The timing coincides with the Wild Hunt tradition, which is led by Odin. Moreover, *Heimskringla* dedicates the feast to Odin.

Both gods are horse deities. Odin rides Sleipnir, but the 'slayer of Beli' rides Blodughofi. The kenning denotes Frey while the horse's name means Bloody Hoof. In another list, Blodughofi carries Atridi. However, Atriðr and Atriði are heiti of Odin.

Both gods are associated with the boar. It is foremost Frey's sacred animal. The boar frequently appeared as a crest on top of helmets. The custom was linked with a type of warrior known as *jöfurr*, meaning boar. Interestingly, it forms part of a kenning for Odin, *ásgarðs jöfurr*. In addition, Odin is also attributed the invention of the *svinfylking*, the military Boar Formation. The boar is furthermore associated with Yuletide, which is sacred to Odin. Additionally, another one of Odin's names is Thror, which is also a boar name.

In his own respect, Frey is considered a god of love and wisdom.

First and foremost, his position as a vegetation god makes Frey a Lord of Love. The wisdom of Frey is reflected in the 11th century Rällinge figurine from Sweden. He is shown seated cross-legged as a shaman. His hand rests on his chin, and he has a beard, which is a mark of wisdom. Frey is also associated with King Frodi, whose name means wisdom. Snorri identifies Frodi with Frey in *Ynglingasaga* 10.

There is plenty of circumstantial evidence to identify Frey with Odin. We can therefore say that the leaders of the Wild Hunt are Frey-Odin and Freyja-Hel.

Lord and Lady of Love and Wisdom

From Odin's feats of arms, we conclude that he is a Lord of Love and Wisdom. The Gunnlod story powerfully combines the two esoteric qualities of the Second Ray. The Odinic Mysteries are further externalised by such stories as *Grimnismal* and *Gylfaginning*.

In the stories, Odin always hides his true identity. As Grimnir, Odin enters the court of Geirrod incognito, revealing himself afterwards. King Gylfi introduces himself as Gangleri when he enters Odin's court. In the Gunnlod story, Odin introduces himself as Bolverk. At Vafthrudnir's he calls himself Gagnrad.

Even his common nicknames reveal gnosis. Many names describe him as a god of war and death. But mythology teaches that death was a means to gain wisdom. Similarly, battle refers to the tests and trials of the Path. We conclude that Odin's names directly relate to the Mystery tradition.

Likewise, the Valkyrie names refer to the same Mysteries. They look like Odinsheiti and frequently refer to battle, magic and wisdom. Pairing the Valkyries with Odin's nature mirrors the collaboration between Odin and Freyja. Indeed, every Einheri is Odin; every Valkyrie is Freyja.

In the Wild Hunt, the masculine and feminine forces are relatively balanced. Moreover, Freyja is associated with Frigg and Hella. The three of them remind us of the Matron worship known from Continental Europe. The goddesses are associated with Norns and Valkyries alike. The triad of women is cleverly mirrored by the Odinic triad Odin, Vili and Vé. All of this suggests a clean balance between the pairs of opposites in Germanic magical thinking.

We imagine how Odins and Freyjas walked among us in ancient times. Odin's visits on the earth plane are explained by Thor Ewing as the professional work of initiates. These so-called Odins visit farms and give advice or test people as to their spiritual strength. The same is found in *Rigsthula*, where Heimdal changes his name and travels incognito among the people.

Initiates of Odin and Heimdal travelled about dispensing their wisdom and do the god's work wherever they visited. We imagine how these initiates channelled the Wisdom of Odin when they assumed his lofty name. And again, the custom is mirrored by the travelling Volvas. Freyjas and Hellas travel from farm to farm and from town to town to foretell the future and give women support through the feminine Mysteries.

DOOR 10
THE LABOURS OF THOR

What is initiation? Initiation marks an expansion of consciousness. By means of ceremony, the degree of spiritual development attained by the individual through effort and perseverance is permanently fixed. From an esoteric perspective, it secures the presence of the soul in the personality of the individual. He enters the spiritual life.

Initiation is preceded by the Path of Probation. The seeker enters this path when the phenomenal side of life no longer satisfies. He recognizes something that is more real and beautiful. Then he enters the Hall of Learning. The seeker learns to know himself. He starts to clearly see his strengths and weaknesses; he recognizes the difference between the lasting and the transient. In this Hall, the aspirant builds his character. He consequently builds his own Valhalla "in the quarry of the personality".

At some point, the individual dedicates his every effort to the advancement of his spiritual development and he enters the Path of Discipleship. More and more, he sets himself apart from mainstream society. Consequently, the Path of Discipleship marks a stage of transition tinged with difficulty and suffering. The disciple's lower self naturally rebels at being transmuted because it loses control. In the Northern tradition, this stage is well described by the *Lokasenna* poem. The events of *Lokasenna* precede that of Ragnarok.

Personality and soul are unified by transmuting the lower self. The individual foregoes the glamour of the material world through sacrifice and purification. This prepares him to carry the voltage of the higher energies that go together with initiation. According to *A Treatise on Cosmic Fire*, "the fires of the mind and spirit burn up matter." At initiation, the inner fire burns away the web that separates the deep physical from the deep emotional. Again, "This etheric web ... forms a barrier between the physical and astral planes... When a man has, through meditation and concentration, expanded his consciousness to a certain point he is enabled to include the subtler planes, and to escape beyond the limits of the dividing web." The web operates as a sort of Ring Pass Not.

The purifying fires of initiation correspond to the advent of Surt and the sons of Muspell at the onset of Ragnarok. They burn away the earth, which represents the deep physical counterpart of the individual. The initiand "bathes in the fires of purification". Afterwards, Jormungand, representing the Ring Pass Not, is slain by Thor.

The qualities of the disciple include a sense of service to humanity and a comprehension of group work. He consequently seeks contact with the Aesir. Furthermore, the disciple finds that friends and family feel somewhat discomfited by his being different. His dispassion resembles the silence of Vidar. He guards his words and slowly recognizes the power of speech. He ultimately aims to speak only "with altruistic purposes in order to convey the energy of love". Thus he puts into practice the valuable lessons of Odin, the Lord of the Voice and the God of Sound.

After a longer or shorter period of time the disciple stands at the Doors of Valhalla and graduates from the Hall of Learning into the Hall of Wisdom. Now the person walks the Path of Initiation.

Whereas in the Hall of Learning, the lower and the Higher Self competed, in the Hall of Wisdom only the Higher Self is seated.

The ceremony of initiation takes place in Valhalla and is administered by Odin and witnessed by the Aesir. Odin wields his Spear of Power, Gungnir, to transmit the subtle energies to the candidate.

In Bailey's book *Initiation, Human and Solar* an interesting link is made between the three main stages of self-realization and three of the external senses. Hearing is associated with normal life where no effort is made to look behind the phenomenal world. This represents the Wheel of Life. Hearing symbolizes the inner voice of conscience. In the Norse myths, it is associated with Heimdal, who sacrificed his ear. Touch is associated with the Path of Probation and the Path of Discipleship. The individual responds to control and vibration. He recognizes all that exists outside himself. He becomes sensitive to the touch of the Aesir. In Norse mythology, it is associated with Tyr, who sacrificed his hand. Last but not least, sight symbolizes the recognition of truth, of what is real. It corresponds to the Path of Initiation. Odin is identified with sight. He sacrificed his eye.

The myths conceal a lot of information about initiation and the way that leads there. Esoterically, Odin's life reveals much about initiation. But the candidate is represented by Thor. His exploits teach us how to achieve; they resemble the labours of Herakles.

Thor's Twelve Labours

In Alice Bailey's work *The Labours of Hercules*, the idea is put forward that Herakles embodies the disciple. The twelve labours symbolize the tasks, tests and trials that the disciple faces on the Path but which bring him to the Portal of Initiation. Each of the tests corresponds to one of the signs of the zodiac. Herakles matches Thor.

The notion of linking the labours to the signs of the zodiac is old indeed. In his lemma on Belenos, Harry Mountain points out that "The 12 Labors of Heracles were symbolic of the 12 signs of the Zodiac during a sun cycle." Graham Robb, in his book *The Ancient Paths*, when discussing the *Via Heraklea* of Celtic Europe, says: "His (Herakles) twelve labours were equated with the twelve constellations of the zodiac through which the sun passes in the course of the year." According to Continental Celtic thinking, Herakles represented the Sun.

The outstanding characteristic of Herakles is his power to act. He is never afraid and sometimes rushes blindly into an enterprise. The same is true of Thor. But they share more.

In Greek myth, Herakles is the son of the god Zeus begotten on a mortal woman. Esoterically, this symbolizes the duality of the soul in the body. The same duality is pictured in the parentage of Thor, who is the son of Odin and Jord. His parents are Heaven and Earth, spirit and matter. It is said that Herakles married and got three children. They represent his soul and its three developing qualities. Likewise, Thor is married to Sif and has three children, Modi, Magni, and Thrud.

According to legend, Herakles was well educated and accomplished. When he came of age, he killed his teachers (Gemini), which symbolizes the disciple's decision to take life into his own hands. He no longer needs a teacher to tell him what to do. He can think and act independently and responsibly. That is why we always hear how Thor relies on his own might and main. The Old Norse expression *trúa á matt ok megin* appears quite often in the sagas.

The same symbolism extends into Thor's wading of the Kerlaug rivers in order to reach Urd's Well. Every one of the other gods rides their horses over the bridge but Thor follows on foot. The twin Kerlaug rivers also represent duality and Thor's resolution to transcend it. Greek legend pictures the same duality as the two serpents which Herakles slew when he was just a kid.

At the same age, Herakles killed the Nemean lion. It was the first of many monsters that he subdued and esoterically symbolizes his service to humanity. In the same way, Thor goes out alone and fights the giants of Jotunheim. One of Thor's opponents is Hlebard, whose name means Leopard.

The stories about Thor mainly focus on his deeds. Similarly, the legends of Herakles remember his feats but not his words. This marks the Path of the disciple. Later, as the initiate becomes Odin, more emphasis will be laid on words.

The labours of Herakles are traditionally listed as follows: 1) slaying the Nemean lion, 2) slaying the Lernean hydra, 3) binding the Ceryneian hind, 4) binding the Erymanthian boar, 5) cleaning the Augean stables, 6) slaying the Stymphalian birds, 7) binding the Cretan bull, 8) stealing the horses of Diomedes, 9) gaining the girdle of Hyppolyta, 10) stealing the cattle of Geryon, 11) stealing the apples of the Hesperides, and 12) binding Kerberos. When the labours are related to the signs of the zodiac the order changes a little. Esoterically, the candidate goes through each of the tests according to the heavenly wheel. They will be discussed in this order.

LABOUR ONE

The first labour of Herakles finds place in the first sign of the zodiac. Herakles is asked to bind the mares of Diomedes. According to lore, Diomedes is a giant and a son of Ares, who is equated with the planet Mars.

The horses devastate the surrounding lands and people. In particular the mares are feared, because they eat people and they breed war horses. According to the text of Alice Bailey, the horses are thought-forms created by the individual. The mares symbolize the mental power to create. At their worst, they represent the effect of wrong thinking and wrong speech. The man-eating horses are selfish thoughts resulting in criticism, gossip and words that sound less kind than intended. Consequently, the individual learns to check his motives and feelings towards others and attempts to delete any harmful thought or word.

Herakles easily drives the mares into a corner, but when he lets his friend Abderos watch them, he makes a mistake. His friend is not strong enough to control them and is eaten. According to Bailey, the friend represents the personality, while Herakles represents the soul itself.

The legend corresponds to Thor's journey into Jotunheim. Every day, Thor travels to the realm of the giants with the intent of lessening their number. In the Norse myth, the giants represent those same harmful thought-forms as the horses of Diomedes. In folklore, the giants of Scandinavia are known to be man-eaters. Thor's constant battle shows the effort necessary to control the mind and avoid regressing to a more primitive way of life.

One particular day, Thor travels to Utgard in the company of Loki. In the story, Utgard symbolizes a world of illusion. It represents the lure of matter in which the individual finds himself. This world appeals to the lower self, represented by Loki, who also happens to be the king of this land.

Thor and Loki set out in the goat driven chariot of the Thunder God. Before they reach Utgard, they spend the night at a human farm. As a gesture of thanks, Thor sacrifices his goats to contribute to the evening meal. The farmer and his wife have two children, Thjalfi and Roskva. At some point, Thjalfi sucks the marrow of bone without Thor's knowledge. The next day, Thor ritually resurrects his team of goats, but one of them limps. The farmer compensates the god by leaving his children in his care. This corresponds with the inability of Abderos to control the horses. Thor leaves behind his goats and takes Thjalfi with him.

Incidentally, the goats in the story indicate the sign Aries. Among other things, the star sign represents commencement and resurrection. Both are found in the myth of Thor and Loki. At the end of the myth, Thor returns to Thrudvangar, the Fields of Strength. The land symbolizes the realm of the soul.

LABOUR TWO

The second labour is set in the sign of Taurus. This time, Herakles is asked to catch the Cretan bull and bring it to the mainland. Thus he sails to Crete and stalks the beast until he finds opportunity to wrestle it down. He takes the bull to Athens where it is to be sacrificed. However, the sacrifice was dedicated to Hera who refuses it.

Bailey interprets the story as a twofold test. On the one hand, Herakles subdues his animal nature, represented by the bull; on the other, the hero is faced with glamour and the problem of sex. According to Bailey, the sign of Taurus teaches the Law of Attraction. The Law works out in all layers of reality. Spiritually, it explains the urge to unite with the divine. On the lower planes, it manifests in romantic love. The world of glamour is represented by the sea which Herakles has to cross. On the island, it is the labyrinth of Crete. The maze symbolizes confusion. Therefore, the Cretan bull embodies the pull of the lower self.

The Greek story coincides with the next stage of Thor's journey. He sails to Utgard, the world of illusion. There, they meet a giant called Skrymir. Circumstance forces Thor to travel with him. In the night, Thor attempts three times to slay the sleeping giant, but every time Skrymir wakes from the blow unharmed. In this we recognize the attempts of Herakles to catch the bull. At the end of the story, Skrymir explains that he used glamour and deceived Thor at the time. He would have been dead otherwise.

Star lore adds to the story. In the constellation, the eye of the bull is Aldebaran. It symbolizes illumination and heralds the light of the Seven Sisters or Pleiades. Only by means of light will illusion be dissipated. In my opinion, the star is the same as the Toe of Aurvandil from Northern mythology. As the story goes, Thor carried Aurvandil on his back when he traversed the Elivagar river system after visiting the giant realm. Unfortunately, frost bit one of Aurvandil's toes. Thor broke off the toe and cast it into the night sky. This became Aurvandil's Toe.

The Norse myth is lost, but it appears that Aurvandil was once a well known character. Saxo Grammaticus mentions Horwendill in his *Gesta Danorum*. His name appears as Earendel in Old English, for example in *Crist I*. It is glossed *iubar* in Latin, a word for light, specifically in an astronomical sense. In medieval Germany, a hero Orendel was known.

The German Orendel poem gives a little background information. Orendel is a king's son. The king rules over twelve kingdoms, and has three sons, of which Orendel is the youngest. The hero receives a sword as a gift on Saint Stephan's day. The context looks very Germanic, since the twelve kingdoms compare with Snorri's twelve kingdoms of Troy. The three sons are likened to the Odinic Trinity. Saint Stephan's day occurs during Yuletide.

When Orendel comes of age, he seeks a queen to marry and sails out. Three times he is overwhelmed by a storm, and the first time he is caught in the so-called Klebermeer. The sea is sticky, and that is why they cannot move. According to legend, the Sticky Sea lies at the end of the world. The second storm loosens the ships, but the third storm annihilates the entire fleet. Only Orendel survives. After a while, a fisherman finds the castaway and helps him. I suppose the poem sketches what happened to Aurvandil before Thor found him. Groa must have thought him lost, but Thor saved him from the waves of the Elivagar in Niflheim. It goes without saying that the Klebermeer and the Elivagar are symbols of the sea of glamour.

According to the Bailey text, the Cretan bull is accompanied by seven sisters. They correspond to the Pleiades but from the Northern point of view are identified as a group of *völur*. Aurvandil's wife Groa is a Volva and a healer. She possibly corresponds to Alcyone, the most prominent star of the Pleiades.

Beneath the Bull constellation lies Eridanus. In Greek mythology, the river runs in the Underworld. According to the Bailey text, the heavenly river is termed the River of the Judge. This is the River of Life which carries souls into incarnation. The river corresponds to the Elivagar, since it matches the Norse myth. The Elivagar likewise carry souls into incarnation. The streams leave the Well of Hvergelmir but congeal. The coagulation symbolizes incarnation, which is a theme that belongs to Taurus. The form-building aspect moreover coincides with the frozen toe. This train of thought identifies the Well of Hvergelmir as the Rigel star, where the celestial river starts.

Crist I, 8: 104-108

éala éarendel engla beorhtast	Hail Aurvandil, brightest angel
ofer middangeard monnum sended	Over Midgard sent to men
and sodfasta sunnan leoma,	And steadfast the Sun's light
tohrt ofer tunglas þu tida gehvane	Bright over moons that in each season
of sylfum þe symle inlihtes.	You of yourself always enlighten

LABOUR THREE

The third labour is an interesting one because it is composed of different tasks. Herakles is asked to gather the apples of the Hesperides. He is not told where he can find either the garden or the Tree. Therefore he first searches for The Old Man of the Sea. The sea god tells Herakles where the golden apples are to be found. Still, Herakles meets trouble on the way. The giant Antaios challenges him. When the giant is overcome, Herakles continues his journey. Before he reaches the garden, he chances to see Prometheus bound and suffering. Herakles comes to the rescue and releases him. In exchange, the giant tells Herakles how to obtain the apples.

Herakles follows the advice of Prometheus and finds Atlas. At the sight of the mighty giant, Herakles recognizes the burden that Atlas carries. He offers to take the weight off his shoulders for a minute and Atlas happily concedes. In return, the giant goes into the garden of the Hesperides and obtains the apples.

The golden apple symbolizes the object of the spiritual seeker. It represents the fulfillment of self-realization. The meaning especially surfaces in the Norse myths because the apples of Idun equal immortality, or either the consummation of soul life.

In Greek mythology, the Old Man of the Sea is traditionally thought to be Nereus. He embodies the teachers on the Path. But Nereus' shapeshifting nature makes it difficult for the student to recognize the truths behind the forms that he is given. Nonetheless, if rightly interpreted, Nereus' counsel leads to soul life. On the other hand, Antaios represents the lure of the material world. As long as he touches the earth, he is invincible. Only when Herakles lifts him in the air, is he overcome.

When the individual enters soul life, he becomes active in the field of service. He recognizes both the need of Prometheus and Atlas and does not hesitate to relieve them. Moreover, in helping Atlas, Herakles foregoes his own mission. Yet, by his act of kindness the labour is completed. That lesson is important to remember. Selfishness in regard to one's own spiritual growth makes attainment hardly possible.

The myth resembles the *Hymiskvida* poem in which Thor is challenged to fetch a cauldron for Aegir. Thor gets help from Tyr. According to the poem, the cauldron is hidden in the land of Tyr's ancestors. When the two gods arrive at Hymir's hall, the giant takes Thor out fishing. At sea, Thor faces Jormungand for the first time.

Tyr takes the role of Nereus. He informs Thunder God about where and how the cauldron can be obtained. Evidently, the cauldron represents the spiritual attainment similar to the golden apples. But Thor's antagonist emerges as Jormungand. The monster represents the lower nature. According to the Bailey text, Antaios represents "the serpent of astral glamour". He corresponds to Jormungand.

It is interesting to note that Thor cannot find the cauldron in Hymir's house. The giant possesses many containers, but only one is the real one. Analogous to Herakles' story, Thor obtains the object indirectly. He hurls vessels until he finds the right one. Aegir's cauldron is the one that does not break. Hymir might be equated with Atlas, since the Norse giant indirectly helps Thor. The god uses Hymir's unbreakable skull to test the vessels. On top of that, Thor is told by Hymir's wife to hit the giant's head. She takes Prometheus' role.

Gemini rules this labour. The star sign represents duality. In the story, this is expressed by the good words of Tyr and Nereus on the one hand and on the other hand the struggle with Jormungand and Antaios. The duality is also expressed by the apples of immortality, which resembles the cauldron of initiation. The individual as a mortal being makes an effort to transcend that mortality and enter the kingdom of the soul. As an air sign, Gemini rules the mind.

The two stars of Gemini are Castor and Pollux. They represent the lower self and the Higher Self, or either transiency and immortality, matter and spirit. They are the feminine and masculine poles of duality. In Norse mythology, the stars might well be associated with Embla and Ask.

LABOUR FOUR

In Cancer, Herakles performs the fourth labour. He is sent on his way to capture the hind of Artemis. The hind symbolizes intuition, seen but difficult to grasp. The star sign offers the opportunity to transmute instinct into intuition, since Cancer is the instinct.

It is unclear to what myth of Thor the story corresponds but the astrological background gives a clue. Cancer and its opposite sign Capricorn represent the gates of Earth and Heaven. Cancer is the sign in which souls take incarnation. The constellation consequently signifies the human family, mass consciousness and herd instinct. In Capricorn, the individual is able to pass through the portal of initiation. Thus he enters the universal life of the Spiritual Hierarchy.

The times of the year correspond to the summer and winter solstice. In Scandinavia, the death of Balder is commemorated at the summer solstice. He is the dying light of the Sun. Balder represents one half of the year, his twin Hoder the other half. As Balder matches the Greek Sun god Apollo, the god's lunar sister Artemis must correspond to Hoder.

The astrological relation brings to mind the circumstances of Balder's slaying, because the event is associated with the summer solstice. In the story, all the gods gather around Balder and throw spears and other gear at him. Yet he remains unhurt. No-one can touch him. This corresponds with the elusiveness of the Ceryneian doe. The gathered Aesir represent the masses, as expected from Cancer. But Hoder also takes a shot. The god is blind, but his hand is led by Loki and when Hoder casts his arrow he strikes Balder. The scene neatly explains the workings of the intuitive faculty. The individual feels blind, but is guided. He trusts his intuition. Therefore, the myth of killing Balder corresponds to capturing the hind. In some version of the myth, Herakles hits the doe with an arrow.

Between the zodiacal signs of Cancer and Capricorn, but closer to Cancer, is found the old constellation Argo. Today, the constellation is split into five, to wit Carina, Puppis, Vela, Pyxis and Antlia. The first four literally mean Keel, Stern, Sails and Compass, though the latter originally denoted the mast. The constellation sails the Milky Way. Taking Balder's story as a source of inspiration the celestial ship becomes Hringhorni.

LABOUR FIVE

In Leo, Herakles defeats the Nemean lion. The monster is a pest. Many warriors try their strength against it but fail. When Herakles hunts the lion, he traps the beast in its lair. The lion's cave has two entrances. Herakles shuts one and enters through the other. Then he wrestles down the beast.

In Norse mythology, monsters usually take the shape of giants. In this case, we are dealing with Hrungnir. The Aesir sound a cry of distress when they find Hrungnir suddenly among them. Thor immediately responds. Like in the Greek myth, the people rejoice in his proffered assistance. And just as the lion is reputed to be invulnerable to weapons, it is said of Hrungnir that every part of him is made of stone.

Hrungnir made his way into Asgard and unnerves the gods and goddesses. When Thor arrives, he challenges the giant. Thjalfi comes along and helps the god. Hrungnir holds his shield in front of him as one would expect, but Thjalfi tells him that Thor will strike from below. And so, Hrungnir moves his shield and stands on it. Thor slays the giant.

The interpolation of Thjalfi is very interesting. It reflects the story about the lair with two openings. Herakles shuts one. Similarly, Thjalfi makes sure that one end is shut and the other open. Besides, Thjalfi's remark may relate to the natural phenomenon of lightning. A discharge of lightning seeks earth. Standing on the shield might symbolize disconnection from the earth.

The cave represents the pituitary gland according to Alice Bailey. The gland is protected by bone, which represents the cave's shape. The gland consists of three lobes, two of which are better developed in humans, namely the posterior and the anterior, each of which represents an opening of the cave.

Symbolically, the lion rampant represents the dominance of the personality. The importance of the ego increases with the development of individuality, but at some point it becomes an obstacle to further progress on the Path. The individual learns to eliminate the power of the ego and to live from the perspective of the soul. The person becomes less and less selfish.

The symbol of the lion occultly represents the power to dare. Herakles understands the nature of his task and faces it bravely. At first, he uses arrows to hunt the beast, but those are ineffective. In the end, he even throws aside his trustworthy club and uses his bare hands to strangle the lion. In the story of Thor, the power of daring is expressed in a different way. It is told that Hrungnir's helper Mokkurkalfi trembles with fear when he sees Thor. Neither Herakles nor Thor ever backs out when a challenge is met. That is the mark of the disciple.

LABOUR SIX

The labour associated with Virgo is that of obtaining the girdle of the Amazon queen. According to legend, Queen Hippolyta was so impressed with Herakles that she decided to freely offer him her girdle. But then Hera caused discord amongst the Amazons and they thought Herakles planned to abduct their queen. Consequently, they ventured to the hero's ship and a battle followed in which Hippolyta was killed. Herakles sailed away with the girdle.

Connected with this myth is another. On his way back, Herakles rescues the maiden Hesione from the appetites of a sea monster sent by Poseidon. So, while he killed Hippolyta in confusion he saved the life of Hesione.

The girdle of Hippolyta symbolizes unity. First and foremost, it expresses the quality of synthesis esoterically associated with the zodiacal sign Virgo. Secondly, it stands for universal brotherhood. Next, it symbolizes the alignment of soul and personality. But it also stands for the union of man and woman. The object corresponds to Freyja's famous Brisingamen necklace. The Norse goddess of love happens to be a manifestation of Virgo while the Amazons correspond to the Valkyries.

The closest parallel to the Greek legend that I can find is the story of how Thor retrieves his hammer from Jotunheim. The story is described in the *Thrymskvida* poem. The giant Thrym has stolen the hammer, which Loki discovers. In return, the giant expects to marry Freyja. Enough mythological elements agree to match both stories. Thor needs to retrieve his hammer. In the process, Freyja is insulted when first asked to visit Thrym as a decoy bride. Here is an interesting clue. According to the poem, Freyja is so upset that her necklace shatters.

Retrieving the hammer corresponds to obtaining the girdle. Killing Hippolyta corresponds to the breaking of Brisingamen. The maiden theme is very much present in both myths. There is Hyppolyta and Hesione in the Greek story and Freyja in the Norse story. What is more, Thor dresses like Freyja, with the necklace about his body, and visits Thrym in disguise. The theme somewhat corresponds to saving Hesione. Unity means cooperation, and both myths have much to say about that. The myths particularly display the forces between the sexes.

What is so important about the *Thrymskvida* story is that Thor identifies himself with his polar opposite. At that time, he embodies the Virgo energy. According to *Esoteric Astrology*, "the symbology of Virgo concerns the whole evolutionary process, which is to shield, nurture and finally reveal the hidden spiritual reality." When Thor is seated in his bridal seat, Thrym reveals the hammer.

LABOUR SEVEN

The seventh labour of Herakles is twofold, which is to be expected from the star sign Libra. Herakles' labour of binding the boar of mount Erymanthos is connected with his revel with the Centaurs. In the myth, Herakles meets his Centaur friend Pholos and is served food. When Herakles asks for wine, his friend tells him that the cask belongs to all the Centaurs in common. Herakles drinks anyway, but when the other Centaurs arrive, they get angry. A fight ensues and Pholos is slain accidentally.

Afterwards Herakles proceeds to the mountain. He easily finds the roaming boar and takes his time to trap it. He uses a net to catch the animal.

The myth corresponds to *Lokasenna* and the story that immediately follows, which is the binding of Loki. Thor takes a particular role in the Norse diptych. *Lokasenna* relates how all the gods assemble in Aegir's hall and drink. Loki has been cast out but returns, angry that he may no longer share a table with Odin. A fight ensues, though not with weapons but with words, in which each and every one of the gods is wounded. Thor only emerges at the end to remove Loki.

Afterwards, the gods run after Loki to sentence him. Loki flees to a mountain top but when he suspects the approach of the gods he takes flight. He changes himself into a salmon and hides in a river. When the gods arrive, Kvasir finds the remains of a net in Loki's old fireplace and understands that Loki tried to burn the means to catch him. Despite many attempts, no-one is able to catch the fish. Then Thor wades through the river and captures the fish with his bare hands.

Loki evidently matches the Greek boar, the individual's desire nature. The changing nature of Loki represents the fluidity of emotions. On the mountain top he builds a house with four doors, the material world. The water in which he hides is the emotional world. The fish and the boar are the animal nature.

The difficulty of bringing the emotional world under the control of the overall personality appears from two things. First of all, the banquet of the gods represents their indulgence in pleasure. It corresponds neatly to the Centaur revel. Secondly, all of the gods work together, but they still have trouble catching the salmon. Eventually Thor succeeds. This shows the changeability of the emotional nature. Often enough, emotions rule our rational thinking without our noticing. The whole episode points out the discrepancy between what people say and what they think or feel.

In Greek lore, the mountain of Erymanthos was dedicated to Artemis, protectress of all animals. She is Skadi in Norse myth. According to *Lokasenna*, it is Skadi who eventually binds Loki on the mountain top. Loki's mountain is called Franang, from which the water falls.

Libra balances the pairs of opposites. At this stage, personality and soul are in equilibrium. Both aspects have equal power. The star sign channels the energies of the careful weighing of options. Always both points of view are seen. The sign relates to the heated discussion at Aegir's hall and the earlier indecisiveness to bind Loki.

LABOUR EIGHT

In Scorpio, Jormungand is faced again. Herakles must now slay the nine-headed hydra. The monster represents the serpent of illusion. The lesson is essentially the same as lifting Antaios in the air.

The aspirant is tested as to whether he can distinguish between reality and illusion, between what really matters and what does not. In *Esoteric Astrology*, we read "in Scorpio ... the disciple undergoes those tests which will enable him to take the second initiation and demonstrate that the desire nature is subdued and conquered ... Hercules, the Sun-God ... overcomes the nine-headed Hydra or serpent of desire by being forced to his knees and from that position of humility lifts up the serpent into the air, and then deliverance comes."

The labour corresponds to the time when Thor found himself with his comrades in the halls of Utgard. At some point, Thor is challenged to lift the domestic cat of the giants. Thor thinks this a little feat, but he can barely manage to have the cat lift one paw off the floor. Later, it is explained that the cat was an illusion, like everything else he saw in Utgard. The cat was really Jormungand, embodying the serpent of illusion. The act of lifting the snake in the air is reminiscent of Antaios' challenge and the esoteric interpretation of Scorpio.

In the same myth, Thor is challenged to wrestle with an old lady. Again, he thinks this below himself, but in the end he is forced onto one knee. Later, he is told that the lady represented Old Age. In his defeat, Thor adopts the position of humility which is key in overcoming the Serpent. Humility means "to see your plight objectively and recognize your shortcomings". In addition, lady Old Age is a manifestation of Death, which is a theme strongly associated with the Scorpion sign.

According to the Bailey text, "each head of the hydra represents one of the problems that beset the courageous person who seeks to achieve mastery of himself". The problems are presented in threes. The first three represent the appetites of the lower self; sex, money, and comfort. The second three represent the inhibiting passions; fear, hatred, and desire for power. And the last three represent the vices of the unillumined mind; pride, separativeness and cruelty. The triad corresponds to the three energies of the personality. In Norse myth, the nine heads return as the three times that Thor faces the Midgard Serpent; first at Hymir's, a second time at Utgarda-Loki's, and lastly during Ragnarok.

The symbols are also found in the heavens. The constellation Ophiuchus represents the hero who wrestles with the serpent of illusion, the constellation Serpens.

LABOUR NINE

The next labour in the zodiac comprises the chasing away of the birds of Lake Stymphalis. When Herakles first arrives he has no clue how to go about it, but he eventually uses the clamour of a rattle (*krotala*). In many cultures, loud noise is used to drive away evil spirits at New Year's Eve or any such important day. I believe, in Norse mythology, the sound symbolically corresponds to the thunder that claps when Thor swings his weapon.

There are no birds to fight in the myths of Ancient Scandinavia, but they may be represented by flocks of giants and trolls. When Thor and Tyr return from Hymir with the cauldron, they are mercilessly pursued by a mass of angry giants (*Hymiskvida* 35-36). Thor pauses, swings his hammer (*veifði hann mjöllni*), and kills the entire host. According to the poem, this adventure happens before he journeys to Utgard with Loki. Again, at the end of *Thrymskvida*, when Thor reclaims his hammer, he rises and kills every giant within reach.

According to Bailey, the birds symbolize wrong thought and wrong speech. Cultivating right thinking and right speech will clear the last stage on the Path of Initiation. Gossip at the one hand and talking about yourself on the other hand engross the ego. It impedes true inner growth. Gradually, the individual realizes the impact of his words and starts to weigh them more carefully. The symbolism reminds me of Thor's duel with Hrungnir. The giant casts his whetstone as a weapon and Thor hits it midair with his hammer. The stone shatters, but a piece gets stuck in his head, which is a symbol of the mental world, where words and thoughts are shaped. Later, Thor is helped by Groa to remove the splinter, but Thor's words decide whether the sting stays or goes. Halfway through, Thor tells her that he brought home her husband Aurvandil. Groa becomes so excited by the news that she is unable to continue her magic. As a result, the splinter stays in Thor's head. The image of a stone arrow flying from a person towards you is a very accurate description of what actually happens when someone thinks angrily of you.

LABOUR TEN

In Capricorn, Herakles is asked to bind Kerberos. The dog guards the Underworld gates. Therefore Herakles must first ritually prepare himself. He is consequently initiated in the Eleusinian Mysteries and is thus able to enter Hades. In the Underworld, he meets Theseus and the Centaur Peirithous. This time, Herakles resolves to help. He attempts to rescue Theseus and Peirithous from the World of the Dead. In doing that, he would restore the Centaur to life, which somehow balances his earlier act of accidentally killing his Centaur friend.

Eventually, Herakles comes to Hades and asks permission to take Kerberos. Hades grants permission on condition that Herakles does not use weapons. The hero subdues the dog with his bare hands.

In Norse mythology, the dog guarding the Underworld is known as Garm. At Ragnarok, the animal fights Tyr, which makes it plausible to see a manifestation of Fenrir in the beast - all the more so because Tyr is the person who binds Fenrir. In Greek mythology, Kerberos is a blood relative of the Hydra. Analogously, Fenrir and Jormungand are brothers. The Tyrian myth explains the binding of Kerberos.

Thus, the dog and the wolf are one symbol. They represent fear, while the Underworld represents the Jungian shadow, ignorance, and the great illusion. This all transforms Fenrir into an image of the Dweller on the Threshold.

As in Cancer, we do not find a correspondence in the Cycle of Thor, but in other tales from the North. The part where Herakles attempts to free Theseus and Peirithous matches Hermod's ride to Hel. In the Norse myth, Hermod tries to rescue Balder and Nanna. The story ties in with the Cancer one. This descent into the Underworld represents the descent into the material world. In that way, the hero faces the noble task of introducing his fellow humans to the truth of the spiritual world.

LABOUR ELEVEN

The sign of Aquarius is linked with the labour of cleaning the stables of Augeas. The story represents an act of service. The individual no longer regards himself as the main object to develop. He now goes into the world and tries to clear humanity of as much Karma as he can bear.

Herakles cleanses the stables by redirecting two nearby rivers. He breaks the back end of the stable and allows the streams to enter the building. The rivers symbolize forces. By an effort of Will, Herakles consciously directs those forces and applies them purposefully. Bailey says: "Hercules had to aid in the cleansing of the world by the right direction of the forces…" Clearing the stables is a powerful symbol of purification.

One of the rivers is the Alpheios. The name is related to Germanic *alba-* and Old Norse *álfr*, originally meaning white. In addition, the name of king Augeas or Augeias etymologically means bright, dawn, daylight. Both names refer to the Sun and hence to light and enlightenment.

In Norse mythology, Thor is associated with many rivers, but his closest encounter is that with the river Vimur. Owing to a promise by Loki, Thor travels to the halls of the giant Geirrod. On the way, he wades through the Vimur River. In the middle of it, the waters start to rise, which makes it difficult to progress. One of Geirrod's daughters stands on the shore and causes the swell. In a reply, Thor states his initial intention: "Do you not wax now, Vimur, for I intend to wade you into the giant's yard." The words reflect the same idea as that of the Greek myth.

According to the Bailey text, breaking out the back end symbolizes the breaking down of barriers. In particular, it nullifies separativeness; like the breach in the wall of Asgard during the Vanic War. The two rivers represent the two divine races. Esoterically, the rivers symbolize the waters of life and the streams of love. Both concepts apply to the Aesir and Vanir respectively.

Skaldskaparmal 26 stanza 65

Vax-at-tu nú, Vimur,	Do you not wax now, Vimur,
alls mik þik vaða tíðir	For I intend to wade you
jötna garða í	Into the giant's yard

LABOUR TWELVE

The last labour of the zodiac requires that Herakles steals the cattle of Geryon. The latter is a giant who lives on an island in the West. According to legend, Herakles is gifted with a golden cup by Helios. The hero sails to the island in that cup. In his attempt to steal the cattle he kills Geryon. At last, he sails back with the cattle, but has trouble keeping them together once he steers them overland.

The story matches Thor's journey to Geirrod's court. He is gifted a magical pole and other gear by Grid. He uses the pole to traverse the river Vimur, which is a kenning for sea. Geirrod resembles the Greek giant by homonymity. The giant is killed by Thor.

According to the Bailey text, the cattle represent the animal nature or the lower desires. Then, the shepherd symbolizes the mind taking control. In this interpretation, Geryon becomes the symbol of humanity.

The shepherd is found in Norse myth, but unlinked to Thor. When Skirnir journeys to Jotunheim on Frey's command, he is halted by a shepherd of giant kin. Hounds guard the sheep. They also guard the gates to the sea hall of the giant Gymir. Dogs also feature in the Heraklean myth.

In my opinion, the herd of cattle represents humanity. Consequently, Herakles becomes the Good Shepherd in Pisces. In the Norse myth, the cattle to be controlled are represented by Loki. He causes the labour and accompanies Thor. The god ventures into Jotunheim because Loki promised this to Geirrod. The god of thunder knows it is a trap but he goes anyway. It ties in with the energy of Pisces, which is the sign of obedience. If the myth is read aright, then we learn that Thor saves Loki. The trickster represents erring humanity, blind and submerged in the world of glamour. Thor helps him out.

Many of the Herculean myths specifically relate to Thor's journey into Utgard, which is preceded by the *Thrymskvida* poem. After visiting Utgard, the story says that Thor returns home. He returns on the Path of Evolution. Some other episodes are grouped around *Lokasenna*, which is preceded by *Hymiskvida*, and before that the Death of Balder. And last but not least, parallels are found in the Geirrod tale.

The Life of Odin

Five great episodes lace the life of Christ. They are his birth at Bethlehem, the baptism in the Jordan River, the transfiguration on Mount Carmel, his crucifixion on Mount Golgotha, and his resurrection. Each of these events expresses initiation, each time on a different level. Each also contains a crisis by which opportunity for the expansion of consciousness is made possible. Since these five initiations constitute a universal law on our planet, they might just as well be found in the Norse tales. Indeed, by interpreting the life of Christ as a metaphor for the life of Odin we are rediscovering the universal truth of mythical stories.

Initiation relates to the soul and only through his own soul does a person achieve initiation. Therefore, the life of Odin pertains to the soul which becomes an Odin once esoterically initiated into the Kingdom of Asgard.

FIRST INITIATION

The first initiation marks the individual's entrance into the world of the soul. It signifies the dedication of the physical plane life to the soul. From then on, a permanent link between personality and soul exists, however tenuous in the beginning. It is symbolized by the birth of Christ, but in the Norse myths it is expressed by the creation story.

In her work *From Bethlehem to Calvary*, Alice Bailey says about the first initiation, whether individual or collective: "And out from the darkness of the womb of matter the Christ child can enter into the light of the kingdom of God." The dark womb of matter is represented in Norse myth by the primal sea out of which Odin and his two brothers heave the earth and so inaugurate a new era. The myth symbolizes a transition from one stage of consciousness to another.

The primal sea was formed by the blood of Ymir. Odin and his two brothers slew the giant and made the earth from it. Ymir's blood filled the Gap and drowned his numerous offspring. This relates to the Massacre of the Innocent.

No stories about the birth of Odin are known. Yet we have this myth about Bur, his ancestor. He was licked from the primeval ice by the cow Audumla. The ice symbolizes the world of matter. Audumla corresponds to the Virgin Mary from whom the boy Jesus was born. By a feminine force only is the human mind freed from the bounds of matter. As first the head of Bur appears, the mental aspect.

Mary, and consequently Audumla, is associated with the constellation of Virgo, which rises on the horizon at the time of Midwinter. At this time, every solar god is born, whether he is called Christ, Odin, Balder or Bur. Midwinter eve was traditionally dedicated to the Mother Goddess.

In addition, the winter night sky shows Sirius as the Star of Bethlehem in the East. At that time, Orion is also present. His Belt was called The Three Kings in earlier times. They are Odin and his two brothers.

SECOND INITIATION

The second initiation signifies the consecration of the desire nature. It corresponds to the baptism in the River Jordan. Jesus comes to John the Baptist at the River Jordan and asks him to baptize him. The ritual signifies purification. According to tradition, John baptizes with water, but later Christ will baptize with fire, which is a symbol of spirit. The former is a preparation for the latter, since the cleansing with water represents the sanctification of the sentient feeling nature and the emotional life but purification by fire relates to the mental world. Interestingly, after the baptism, Christ goes through a period of trial and temptation.

Do we find this in Norse myth? The Ancient Scandinavian people knew a name giving ceremony which involved sprinkling water over the baby. A similar action is found among the charms in *Havamal* (158), where Odin is said to know how to sprinkle a hero with water so that he will not fall in battle. However, no myth has been recorded in which Odin undergoes such a sprinkling.

In a more abstract sense, we remember how the Norns are said to rub Yggdrasil with clay from the well. The act is mentioned in *Gylfaginning* 16 and alluded to in *Voluspa* 19. This mud prevents the tree from decaying. It makes holy, and leaves a white 'shell', like an aura. The Norns administer the sprinkling. They ultimately decide what kind of life the person will have. Yggdrasil can be identified as a manifestation of Odin. The tree certainly symbolizes Ask, the first man. Overall, it corresponds with the baptism.

The three temptations that come after the baptism are found in the Norse myths as the offspring of Loki. At some point, the gods are faced with the evil which Loki spawns into the world. The goddess Hel is cast into the Netherworld, the serpent Jormungand is cast into the wide sea, but the wolf Fenrir is kept among the gods. Those three express how Odin deals with tests and trials.

THIRD INITIATION

The third initiation corresponds to the transfiguration of Jesus. The Greek word is *metamorphosis*. The core of the myth involves climbing the mountain. At the top, Jesus radiates. Light is the keyword. Important to the story is the fact that the voice of the Father in the heavens is heard. After the event, Jesus Christ begins his life of service towards humanity.

There is a curious episode in the life of Odin that might correspond to the Christian story. The episode is related in *Sigrdrifumal* 14. "On the mountain he stood with the Brimir sword. He had on his head a helmet. There said Mimir's head wisely the first word." After this, four stanzas follow containing very mystical sayings, but they end with an affirmation of the dissemination of wisdom. "And they (the Mysteries) were sent on the wide ways. They are with the Aesir. They are with the Elves. Some are with the wise Vanir. Some do the human people have."

No context is given to the *Sigrdrifumal* episode except that we know from stanza 13 that we are dealing with Odin. Yet, the appearance of Mimir offers a clue. The event is probably linked with the sacrifice of Odin's eye. In exchange for his eye, Odin was imparted the Ageless Wisdom.

The Norse mountain experience is an exact match. The words of the Christian God are mirrored by the pronunciation of the Runes or Mysteries by Mimir. Odin's eye represents light. And the dissemination of the Runes reflects a life of teaching and service. Moreover, the Transfiguration applies to the mental body. That is why the head is emphasized in the Eddic stanzas.

FOURTH INITIATION

The Crucifixion is a complex story. There are three main episodes. On the night before, there is the Last Supper. Jesus installs the ritual communion of bread and wine. Later, Jesus travels with three of his disciples to the garden of Gethsemane but feels misunderstood by them. He asks them to stay awake with them, but they fall asleep. This happens three times. Then he is arrested. The next day, Jesus is crucified on Golgotha.

The story corresponds to a complex Odinic narrative centred around his self-sacrifice on the Tree. The story is told in *Havamal* 138-141. Odin's Yggdrasil ordeal is closely associated with the Mead of Poetry myth. Therefore, the episode of Odin and Gunnlod corresponds to the Last Supper and the subsequent retirement in the garden of Gethsemane. The number of times the disciples fall asleep matches the three nights that Odin spends with Gunnlod. The arrest corresponds to Odin's oath breaking. Suttung means to seize Odin, but the god escapes.

The crucifixion obviously corresponds to Odin's hanging. On the cross, Jesus uttered the words: "My El, my El, why have you forsaken me." The Hebrew word El means God and is probably cognate with Old Norse *álfr*. The saying expresses a sense of loneliness. The same feeling is experienced by Odin, who declares that no-one offered him food or drink. This feeling implies the ultimate sacrifice; the individual can no longer rely on anything that he regarded as true. Jesus understands that his reliance upon his innate divinity was also based upon sentiment. Now he must become completely independent and at that point even sacrifice his soul. Only then will the Breath of Life surge through him. This is the spirit, or the concept of *önd* or Andi in the Northern tradition. Herein lies the secret of the fourth initiation. It is also called the Renunciation.

It is doubtful whether the Yggdrasil event happens after the Gunnlod episode in the life of Odin, but the symbolism matches the Christian myth perfectly.

Included in the stanzas is a reference to magic spells that Odin learned from the son of Bolthorn. This may actually allude to the Mimir episode.

Stanza 141 concludes with the words: "Word led me from word to word. Work led me from work to work." In the saying, Odin pronounces his life of service. The words are reminiscent of an occult catechism mentioned in Alice Bailey's books. I will give the words below; they can be used in a reenactment of the Gunnlod story. Replace Cross with Tree.

> I play my part with stern resolve, with earnest aspiration
> I look above, I help below
> I dream not, nor I rest
> I toil, I serve
> I reap, I pray
> I am the Cross, I am the Way
> I tread upon the work I do,
> I mount upon my slain self
> I kill desire, and I strive, forgetting all reward.
> I forego peace, I forfeit rest
> And, in the stress of pain,
> I lose myself and find Myself
> And enter into peace.
> To all this I solemnly pledge myself,
> Invoking my Higher Self.

FIFTH INITIATION

The last recorded episode in the Life of Christ is that of his resurrection. The event is associated with his ascension. His life after death symbolizes the continuity of consciousness. In the Norse myths, this is depicted by the story of Balder's death. He fares on the ship of initiation towards Hel where he awaits his time. When the Great Conflict of Ragnarok finally subsides, a new earth rises. At the same time, Balder returns from the Underworld. He is a manifestation of Odin.

In Odin's own life, the resurrection and ascension are found in the twin myth of Yggdrasil and the Mead of Wisdom. After nine nights, Odin is released from the Tree and comes back from the world of the dead. By going through that process he learned the Mystery of Life. The ascension is symbolized by his transformation into an eagle when he leaves Gunnlod and ascends to Asgard. In the process, he learned the Mystery of Consciousness.

Briefly put, the birth of Jesus is like the emergence of Bur from the ice. The Baptism to that of Yggdrasil by the Norns. The Transfiguration is the dialogue of Odin and Mimir on the mountain top. Odin sacrifices his eye. The Crucifixion relates to the Gunnlod story and the Yggdrasil experience. The resurrection relates to Odin's changing into an eagle.

Conclusion

The Labours of Herakles and the Life of Christ spell out the spiritual carreer of the one who seeks enlightenment. To these two great lives, one other should be added and that is Buddha, but it would take us too far to discuss his life and work in detail. Yet he can be identified. As Herakles corresponds to Thor and Christ to Odin, so Buddha matches Heimdal, the Norse god of light. Buddha attains enlightenment under the Tree, but Heimdal watches at Yggdrasil. Buddha journeys around the country to teach, but Heimdal descends to Midgard to teach and initiate the people.

DOOR 11
GODS
AND GODDESSES

In religion, gods are real beings that people worship. In stories, gods are likely to be archetypes. From a cultural perspective, we can say that the gods dwell in the group soul of a nation. From an individual's standpoint the gods are archetypes within one's own psyche.

Working with Gods

A clear distinction must be made between working with the god as a real entity or as an archetype. Gods are real beings. But sometimes it is easier to access their power when you regard them as archetypes. When the magician would like to work with the gods he must be aware of this twofold truth. A god represents a force outside of himself, but an archetype resides within his own mind. It is therefore important to distinguish between an invocation of a god and an evocation of an archetype. They are two very different approaches. As such, the practice is reflected in cultic worship on the one hand and mythmaking on the other hand. Offerings of food and drink attract the intelligence behind the image of a god, which is real enough and can be communicated with, but working with myths activates the archetypes, whether it is in meditation or in ceremony. Evidently, when the gods are interpreted as mere archetypes, then the real entities are still watching in the background. They lend their energy to an active archetype since they are that energy.

One way of looking at the gods of the North as archetypes is to see them as potential powers of the Self. Someone who is in tune with the

Northern mysteries current will have access to all of the gods and goddesses of that pantheon. Then, it is only a matter of activating the god pattern within the Self.

The nature of the contact depends on the purpose. Remember that the gods are real. If the magician utters a prayer, he supplicates primarily a force outside of himself. Furthermore, he appeals to the god with a specific intent. In most cases, the energy will touch the corresponding archetype in the magician's mind. Energy flows in the path of least resistance. If the magician is unable to contact the god directly, the energy will be channeled to his Higher Self. In order to appeal to the god, the magician will either visualize the god or use its symbols.

When the person visualizes the deity, he works through the Astral Plane. He recognizes a force working out in his life as the doings of a god, then he contacts the god's energy on the Mental Plane. On the Physical Plane, the act of worship with offerings of food and drink establishes contact with incorporeal beings on the Etheric Plane. The essence of the offerings is absorbed by the god or goddess.

So, how do you evoke a god archetype from the psyche? The most direct way to activate an archetype is to identify with the god's personality. Imagine yourself as the god. Sit down and have in your mind's eye all the attributes of the god with you. Sense the god's energy while you imagine being that god. When you have the visualization firmly in place, verbally identify with the god. Say: "I am Odin;" or "I am Frigg." Say things that the god would do. Do things that the god would do.

This technique can be used as a preliminary exercise for learning to channel a deity. The technique can also be used as an empowerment. Still, you invoke the real god behind the force to draw on its energy.

A Society of Divine Beings

Not just the gods but the tribes of the gods and the different classes of supernatural beings represent archetypes. In Norse mythology, the great polar opposites in the kingdom of the divine are the Aesir and the Vanir. Therefore, before discussing particular gods, an overview of the different classes is due.

Traditionally, the gods are collectively known as the Aesir. In poetry, they appear as *æsir ok álfar*. They are teamed because of the alliteration of the expression but they also connect semantically. Both concepts ultimately relate to ancestor veneration. The Alfar are closely related to the Vanir. Vana-Frey rules Alfheim.

Symbolically, the Aesir are juxtaposed to the Vanir. The Aesir are associated with the mental realm. They are strict and stern and intellectual and correspond to Mars and the Kabbalistic Pillar of Severity. They represent the thinker. The Vanir are associated with the emotional. They are soft-hearted and in tune with their body and correspond to Venus and the Pillar of Mercy. They represent the feeler. The Aesir are associated with a male-oriented society while the Vanir are linked with women, goddesses, and male gods who are in touch with their feminine side.

From *Voluspa* and *Lokasenna*, we gather that groups of gods existed under the names Regin and Tivar. Although typically male gods are listed among the Aesir, Alfar, Regin and Tivar, we should remain open-minded and consider the appellation as referring to a global idea that transcends gender.

The Regin gods represent an institution of government. They therefore represent the manager. The Tivar are in particular mentioned in the context of war. They rule victory and death. It is difficult to assign any particular archetype to the Tivar except perhaps the winner and the loser. But the drive of the Tivar gods is found in every aspect of a person's life. They may best be described as the doer. The Elves correspond to the watcher type.

Twelve Gods

There are twelve Aesir. In ancient times, the number had more significance than the composition of the group. Worldwide the number signifies the chosen, the elect. Twelve are the number of apostles. Twelve are the knights of King Arthur. The Greek pantheon counts twelve Olympians. All of them are a reflection of a band of initiates and disciples. Esoterically, the number stands for completed work.

In the Viking Age, the number occurs as the chief's personal guard. For example, there is Hrolf Kraki and his twelve berserkers. An elite warrior band consisted of twelve men. In the sagas we often hear about twelve brothers who form a band. Furthermore, the Germanic Thing consisted of twelve judges. The myth about the Aesir especially refers to this legal assembly. Last but not least, Snorri states in his introduction that the world was divided in twelve kingdoms and ruled by a High King.

Only later the need was felt to name each of the twelve gods. From the sources, we can tell that traditional lists must have circulated. This was especially true in skaldic schools. A similar evolution is found in the Greek tradition. The number twelve was fixed in antiquity. Later, the individual gods were named, which resulted in variations in the lists of the Olympian gods.

The twelve Aesir are headed by Odin. He does not partake of the twelve. The same is true of King Arthur and his knights and of Jesus of Nazareth and his disciples. Therefore, the number totals thirteen. In the Norse tradition, Loki is listed, too, totaling the list to fourteen gods.

The major association of the number twelve is that of the zodiac. Possibly, each of the signs correlates to one of the Aesir. In the least, each of the signs represents an aspect of Odin. Since the Sun stands at the centre of the zodiac, the celestial body corresponds to Odin. In the Ageless Wisdom, the number also refers to the twelve creative Hierarchies, of which humanity and the Ascended Masters are two.

The Creative Hierarchies

In the works of Alice Bailey, the human evolution is called the Fourth Creative Hierarchy. This implies two things. It means firstly that the human family treads the path of evolution as a collective effort. It inspires the individual to work together with his brothers and sisters. Secondly, it means that the human family is a member of a still larger group.

The larger group consists of twelve Creative Hierarchies. The sum makes up the life of our Planetary Logos, Mother Earth. Five of these Hierarchies have attained such a high degree of development that they have liberated themselves from the seven planes of human experience. The other seven evolutions walk alongside each other on this planet. Of these seven, the fourth equals the human kingdom. As a collective, we are only a part of Mother Earth's body.

The Hierarchies are called creative because they are builders of form. The members of these families are creative in one way or another. For instance, the material world is the work of the Deva evolution, in cooperation with Elementals. The human evolution is creative on another plane and works with thought-forms.

7.1.	Ray I	Divine Flames	Logoic Plane	Muspelli
		Divine Lives		
6.2.	Ray II	Divine Builders	Monadic Plane	Light Elves
5.3.	Ray III	Lesser Builders	Atmic Plane	Vanir
4.4.	Ray IV	Human Hierarchy	Solar Angels	Aesir
		Initiates	Buddhic Plane	
		Lords of Sacrifice		
3.5.	Ray V	Human Personalities	Mental Plane	Mankind
2.6.	Ray VI	Lunar Lords	Astral Plane	Giants
1.7.	Ray VII	Elemental Lives	Earth	Dwarves

Curiously, but not surprisingly, the seven Creative Hierarchies are related to the seven Rays. Moreover, their existence seems to coincide with the different races of Norse mythology.

The data in the table are taken from Bailey's *Esoteric Astrology*. The tabulation shows only the seven Hierarchies. If all twelve were listed, the numbers would be different. Sometimes synonyms of a Hierarchy are given.

There is little information available on the first of the seven Creative Hierarchies. The members of the second Hierarchy are, according to Bailey, "too sinless and holy to find opportunity in that very material and intellectual evolution". These beings are higher than human Monads. I therefore link them with the Alfar, Ljosalfar, or Light Elves. The beings of the third Hierarchy are called Lords of Sacrifice and Love. Their nature prevents them from incarnating in the three lower worlds. I associate them with the Vanir. Together, the second and third Hierarchies form the Deva evolution. In Western occultism, they are likened to Angels. In Norse myth, the Vanir and the Alfar are connected by Frey, a Lord of Love and Freedom.

The fourth and fifth hierarchies relate to the human evolution. The fourth Creative Hierarchy is the kingdom of the soul. Every human being is connected with this Hierarchy through his soul, but only so-called initiates work consciously from this plane. They are esoterically seated in Valhalla. The fifth Creative Hierarchy expresses the downflow of the fourth. On this plane, the individual aligns his personality. He endeavours to be conscious of his etheric, emotional and mental vehicle. Once they are on one line, they start transmitting the force of the human soul into the three lower worlds. The fifth Hierarchy is in particular related to the human mental body. As such we know the inhabitants of Midgard.

The last two Hierarchies are personified by the dwarves. The beings of these collectives are elementals and nature spirits. They are represented by the many sorts of wights collectively associated with the dwarven race. Both Hierarchies are a lower plane reflection of the two higher

Deva kingdoms. This is hinted at in Norse mythology. The dwarves are alternatively known as Dokkalfar or Svartalfar. They are the Dark counterpart of their higher brothers. The terms Dark and Black refer to the denseness of the plane on which they operate. Their lives underlie every aspect of physical existence. The Deva evolution works through the Elemental evolution, which means that the Ljosalfar and the Svartalfar work together.

The Jotun race is included in the Elemental evolution, because they relate to the emotional plane. Yet some of them possibly belong to the Deva evolution. The Jotun giants have more intelligence and a higher degree of consciousness than the dwarves. They might well be evolving Devas. Their race is linked with the Spirit World.

Greater Builders	Deva Evolution	Alfheim	Light Elves
Lesser Builders		Vanaheim	
Human Initiates	Human Evolution	Asgard	Midgard
Human Personalities		Midgard	
Lunar Lords	Elemental Evolution	Jotunheim	Dark Elves
Elementals		Svartalfheim	

In concluding, it must be pointed out that a human incarnation in the three worlds necessarily adopts substance ensouled by the dwarves and the giants in addition to its particular mental vehicle. Therefore, an individual who has attained soul contact automatically interacts with the Fourth, Fifth, Sixth and Seventh Hierarchy. A person without soul contact might at times experience the overpowering urges of his physical body or of his emotions. He might not be strong enough of mind to go against the power of either. Even in a later stage, when the person is mentally oriented, he might be torn between what he feels and what he thinks. Such is the choice of the human being – and the world that he lives in.

The Gods

In late times, the names of the twelve Aesir were given. They appeared in a given order, but the beginning of the list is more reliable than its end. This is due to the fact that the actual listing is a late invention.

In his Edda, Snorri Sturluson gives a list of the twelve Aesir in different places. He lists them in the beginning of *Gylfaginning* and again in the beginning of *Skaldskaparmal*. A second time he lists the gods when they visit Aegir. In the Thulur, he gives two separate stanzas each containing a list of gods; at one time as sons of Odin. The verses are reminiscent of such short works as the *Abecedarium Nordmannicum* which were designed to memorize information. I assume that the surviving stanzas are remnants of existing god lists, either skaldic or cultic.

When Snorri gives the kennings for each of the gods in *Skaldskaparmal*, he maintains the order of the Aesir as he knows it. This amounts to about five lists, four of which are Snorri's learned construction. Interestingly, when he lists the gods in *Gylfaginning*, he starts with actually numbering the Aesir. He says that the sons of Odin are first Thor, secondly Balder, thirdly Njord. After Njord he stops counting. I suspect he was not feeling sure about the numbers. This is specifically so because he lists Frey as a son of Njord and not of Odin. Frey is otherwise always listed fourth after Odin. Tyr always comes after Frey. The second half of the lists shows discrepancies. Then again, the skaldic stanzas do not take order into account.

Further information is found in the Poetic Edda. Snorri's lists must be compared with those of *Lokasenna* and *Grimnismal*. What is so interesting about those poems is that the gods as well as the goddesses are mentioned, which is comparable to Greek mythology. The twelve Olympians usually divide into six gods and six goddesses.

The *Gylfaginning* list has 1) Thor, 2) Balder, 3) Njord, Frey, Tyr, Bragi, Heimdal, Hoder, Vidar, Ali/Vali, Ull, Forseti and Loki. Then he lists the Asynjur; he counts fourteen goddesses. The first *Skaldskaparmal* god list has Thor, Njord, Frey, Tyr, Heimdal, Bragi, Vidar, Vali, Ull, Hoenir, Forseti and Loki. Balder is not included because he has already died in the story line. The second *Skaldskaparmal* list has first Odin, and then Njord, Frey, Tyr, Bragi, Vidar and Loki; this listing introduces the *Lokasenna* story. We know from the story that Balder had already died and that Thor was out fighting giants. All three lists are complemented by a list of goddesses, which will be discussed later.

When Snorri enumerates the heiti and kennings of the gods, he maintains the following order: Odin, Thor, Balder, Njord, Frey, Heimdal, Tyr, Bragi, Vidar, Vali, Hoder, Ull, Hoenir and Loki. In the list, the position of Heimdal seems out of place. Then Snorri gives the Thulur. One stanza reads: "Odin's sons are Balder and Meili, Vidar and Nep, Vali, Ali, Thor and Hildolf, Hermod, Sigi, Skjold, Yngvi-Frey, Itreksjod, Heimdal, Saeming." Another stanza reads: "There is Ygg, Thor, Yngvi-Frey, Vidar and Balder, Vali and Heimdal. Then there is Tyr and Njord, Bragi I name as the next one, Hoder, Forseti. Here Loki is last." Again, Heimdal is more in front of the list.

	Gylfaginning	Skaldskaparmal	Skaldskaparmal	Kenningar	Thulur
1.	Thor	Thor		Thor	Thor
2.	Balder			Balder	Frey
3.	Njord	Njord	Njord	Njord	Vidar
4.	Frey	Frey	Frey	Frey	Balder
5.	Tyr	Tyr	Tyr	Heimdal	Vali
6.	Bragi	Heimdal	Bragi	Tyr	Heimdal
7.	Heimdal	Bragi		Bragi	Tyr
8.	Hoder	Vidar	Vidar	Vidar	Njord
9.	Vidar	Vali		Vali	Bragi
10.	Vali	Ull		Hoder	Hoder
11.	Ull	Hoenir		Ull	Forseti
12.	Forseti	Forseti		Hoenir	

The prose *Skaldskaparmal* lists should be compared with the *Lokasenna* since this must have been Snorri's main source. The male gods in *Lokasenna* are introduced as Odin, Thor, Bragi, Tyr, Njord, Frey, Vidar and Loki. They roughly correspond to the *Skaldskaparmal* list. The list is mixed with the names of the goddesses. The actual poem gives the gods in the following order: Bragi, Njord, Tyr, Frey, Heimdal, Thor, apart from Loki, Odin, the goddesses and lesser divinities.

The *Grimnismal* poem starts with a list of mythical locations. They belong to twelve of the gods and goddesses. The list has Thor, Ull, Vali, Saga, Odin, Skadi, Balder, Heimdal, Freyja, Forseti, Njord, and Vidar. The list differs from the others and names eight of the twelve Aesir.

	Lokasenna	Skaldskaparmal	Grimnismal
1.	Odin	Odin	Thor
2.	Frigg	Njord	Ull
3.	Thor	Frey	Vali
4.	Sif	Tyr	Saga
5.	Bragi	Bragi	Odin
6.	Idun	Vidar	Skadi
7.	Tyr	Frigg	Balder
8.	Njord	Freyja	Heimdal
9.	Skadi	Gefjun	Freyja
10.	Frey	Skadi	Forseti
11.	Freyja	Idun	Njord
12.	Vidar	Sif	Vidar

Snorri lists the same male gods as *Lokasenna*. He changes two things. He separates the gods from the goddesses and he rearranges the list of Aesir according to his knowledge of the traditional order of gods.

In establishing traditional lore, we usually depend more on the poetic sources. However, we have only one stanza quoted by Snorri in his Thulur. Snorri Sturluson must have had other knowledge which was common at the time. In his prose Edda, the lists from *Skaldskaparmal* are the most traditional while that from *Gylfaginnnig* and the enumeration of the kennings derive from his own genius.

Still, a few things can be deduced. Thor is always named first. Forseti is always last; reflecting his late inclusion in the Viking pantheon. Balder is always second. Tyr, Njord and Bragi form one group. They are grouped together in the Thulur stanza and in *Lokasenna*. Snorri has the habit of mentioning Frey right after Njord because they are father and son. This is not necessarily true traditionally. Remember that this is where Snorri falters in his numbering. In *Lokasenna* and the *Nafnathulur*, Frey seems paired with Vidar. Heimdal does not seem to have a particular place, but

Snorri associates him with Tyr and Bragi. Snorri likes to include Ull, but the god never occurs in skaldic lists. Hoder and Hoenir are equally uncertain and appear toward the end, but Vali appears in almost every list. Snorri associates him with Vidar.

Loki is always mentioned and closes every list.

The beginning of a traditional list may have looked like this: Odin, Thor, Balder, Njord, and Frey. Then Tyr, Bragi, and Heimdal would follow in my opinion. Then Vidar, Vali and Ull would plausibly follow. Position eleven would be assigned to either Hermod, Hoenir or Hoder. The list ends with Forseti and Loki.

The Goddesses

Let us not forget the ladies. Most of Snorri's god lists are complemented by the goddesses. Likewise, in his Thulur, he includes stanzas on the Asynjur. I suspect that he had access to existing goddess as well as god lists. From the Thulur it is clear that no-one ever worried about an exact number of twelve goddesses.

The stanzas have the following: "Now shall all the Asynjur be named. Frigg and Freyja, Fulla and Snotra, Gerd and Gefjon, Gna, Lofn, Skadi, Jord and Idun, Ilm, Bil, Njorun." And: "Hlin and Nanna, Hnoss, Rind and Sjofn, Sol and Saga, Sigyn and Vör. There is Vár, and Syn is named, but Thrud and Ran are summed up next." That is a long list and Snorri reiterates them in his *Gylfaginning* overview of the gods and goddesses. The goddesses are grouped by alliteration.

The first *Skaldskaparmal* list gives Frigg, Freyja, Gefjun, Idun, Gerd, Sigyn, Fulla and Nanna. The second time in *Skaldskaparmal* they are Frigg, Freyja, Gefjun, Skadi, Idun and Sif. Later in *Skaldskaparmal*, Snorri enumerates the kennings of the goddesses. The order in which they appear is as follows: Frigg, Freyja, Sif and Idun. Then he quotes the complete

Gylfaginning	Skaldskaparmal	Skaldskaparmal	Kenningar	Thulur
Frigg	Frigg	Frigg	Frigg	Frigg
Saga	Freyja	Freyja	Freyja	Freyja
Eir	Gefjun	Gefjun	Sif	Fulla
Gefjun	Idun	Skadi	Idun	Snotra
Fulla	Gerd	Idun		Gerd
Freyja	Sigyn	Sif		Gefjon
Sjofn	Fulla			Gna
Lofn	Nanna			Lofn
Vár				Skadi
Vör				Jord
Syn				Idun
Hlin				Ilm
Snotra				Bil
Gna				Njorun
Sol				Hlin
Bil				Nanna
Jord				Hnoss
Rind				Rind
			Sjofn &	Sol
			Saga &	Sigyn
			Vör &	Vár
			Syn &	Thrud
				Ran

Haustlong story to illustrate the myth of Idun's disappearance. After the digression, he forgets to continue with the Asynjur kennings.

Some bits and pieces can be gleaned from the synopsis on the goddesses. Frigg and Freyja are mentioned first. Idun and Sif are paired. Gefjun or Gefjon comes early in the list. Fulla frequently appears, but she has no given place.

Again, the mixed list from *Lokasenna* is an interesting clue to traditional lore. *Lokasenna* pairs the goddesses with the gods. The goddesses appear as Frigg, Sif, Idun, Skadi and Freyja in the introduction and Idun, Gefjon, Frigg, Freyja, Skadi and Sif in the actual poem.

	Lokasenna intro	Lokasenna poem	Skaldskaparmal
1.	Frigg	Idun	Frigg
2.	Sif	Gefjun	Freyja
3.	Idun	Frigg	Gefjun
4.	Skadi	Freyja	Skadi
5.	Freyja	Skadi	Idun
6.		Sif	Sif

They correspond exactly to Snorri's prose rendering. As expected, Snorri lists the gods according to his knowledge of traditional lore. The beginning of a traditional arrangement may have been Frigg, Freyja, Gefjun, Idun, and Sif.

DOOR 12
THE SAYINGS OF LOKI

The story of *Lokasenna* gives a good overview of the gods as archetypes. In the story, Aegir invites the gods for a drink. The invitees are listed in the prose introduction to the poem. Later, Loki addresses each of the Aesir and Asynjur one by one. He accuses them of all kinds of lowly things, but the gods always defend themselves.

Although the gods are portrayed as caricatures, much may still be deduced from the text. The list of gods is not all encompassing, but it gives a good insight in the nature of the gods of the North.

In the tabulation below we give the order of the gods as they are mentioned in the introduction. Almost every god is paired with a goddess.

1. Odin   Frigg
2. Thor   Sif
3. Bragi   Idun
4. Tyr   Fenrir
5. Njord   Skadi
6. Frey   Freyja
7. Vidar

I believe the pairs represent opposite poles which therefore complement each other. Insight is gained by looking at the partners. It deepens the understanding of the male gods, but it is of particular interest for interpreting the female deities, since less is known about them. For instance, it is interesting to see that Frey and Freyja are paired as if they were husband and wife.

Tyr and Vidar are exceptions. Tyr has no wife. He is paired with Fenrir although the wolf is not present in the story. Vidar is not married either. He is called "the son of Odin" therefore pairing him with the Master of Asgard. Vidar is significantly mentioned last. He plays no role in the history of the gods until Ragnarok.

What is so interesting about the poem's list is that it adds up to twelve although they constitute a mixed company. They are 1) Odin, 2) Frigg, 3) Thor, 4) Sif, 5) Bragi, 6) Idun, 7) Tyr, 8) Njord, 9) Skadi, 10) Frey, 11) Freyja and 12) Vidar.

The question remains whether Aegir must be included in the tabulation. He is mentioned first of all. The text says of him that he is also known as Gymir, therefore pairing him with himself. Clearly, the editor was thinking in pairs. It is a common strategy in skaldic poetry known as Tvideilur.

In the *Skaldskaparmal* version of this event, Snorri separates the names of Aesir and Asynjur. If we pair the lists, we obtain the following.

1. Odin Frigg
2. Njord Freyja
3. Frey Gefjun
4. Tyr Skadi
5. Bragi Idun
6. Vidar Sif

It appears that Snorri had no regard for the original pairings. He retains his own traditional order. Furthermore, he omits Thor, because he is not present. He includes Gefjun. In *Lokasenna*, Thor is honourably mentioned in the introduction. Gefjun plays a role in the actual *senna*.

Of course, the story is about Loki. He is mentioned in all the sources. With him the list continues.

Three more pairs follow. The text mentions Frey's servants as well as the servants of Aegir. In between, the editor claims that many Aesir and Elves were present as well. Significantly, they are mentioned together. The concept is used in a very general sense. It therefore includes gods and goddesses of all kinds.

The editor maintains his habit of pairing names. The three pairs are in fact triads. Frey's name is mentioned to introduce Byggvir and Beyla. Aegir's name is mentioned to present Fimafeng and Eldir. Loki is juxtaposed to the Aesir and Alfar.

Of Aegir's wife Ran, nothing is said. In *Skaldskaparmal*, Snorri mentions her afterwards. Similarly, Loki's wife Sigyn is not mentioned, though she features in the epilogue of *Lokasenna*. In the sources, Loki appears as a solitary god. He takes full responsibility for his actions.

The full list of the *Lokasenna* prose introduction looks like this.

1.	Aegir	Gymir
2.	Odin	Frigg
3.	Thor	Sif
4.	Bragi	Idun
5.	Tyr	Fenrir
6.	Njord	Skadi
7.	Frey	Freyja
8.	Vidar	Odin
9.	Loki	Frey
10.	Byggvir	Beyla
11.	Aesir	Alfar
12.	Aegir	
13.	Fimafeng	Eldir

The list differs somewhat from the guests who actually partake in the discussion of the *senna*. It is therefore worthwhile to consider the gods and goddesses mentioned in the poem proper. The tabulation below shows the appearance of each of the gods so that a second line-up is created.

Eldir denies Loki entry
- Eldir (1-5)

Loki enters
- Loki (6-7)

Vidar makes room for Loki
- Bragi (11-15)
- Idun (16-18)
- Gefjun (19-20)
- Odin (21-24)
- Frigg (25-28)
- Freyja (29-32)
- Njord (33-36)
- Tyr (37-40)
- Frey (41-42)
- Byggvir (43-46)
- Heimdal (47-48)
- Skadi (49-52)

Sif challenges Loki
- Sif (53-54)
- Beyla (55-56)

Thor enters
- Thor (57-63)

The poem is divided in different sections which are marked by a line of prose. These demarcations are shown in the tabulation above. However, the main structure is threefold. First of all, Loki is stopped at the door and Eldir declares him a *persona non grata*. The second portion constitutes the bulk of the poem and consists of the actual *senna* or insult. Lastly, Thor enters and ends Loki's offensive words.

Vidar does not partake in the discussion. As the Silent God, he cannot. But he plays a role in the poem. All the other gods in the introduction say something. Two more gods appear on stage: Heimdal and Gefjun. Balder is honourably mentioned by Frigg but he is not present.

The whole is fired off by Loki's dealing with Fimafeng. Aegir is not included in the conversation. He only provides the setting.

If all the beings mentioned in *Lokasenna* are listed in their order of appearance, we obtain the following series: Aegir, Odin, Frigg, Thor, Sif, Bragi, Idun, Tyr, Fenrir, Njord, Skadi, Frey, Freyja, Vidar, Loki, Byggvir, Beyla, Fimafeng, Eldir, Gefjun, Balder, Heimdal, Nari, Narfi, Sigyn. It totals 25 names. If we single out the male gods we obtain fifteen names: Aegir, Odin, Thor, Bragi, Tyr, Njord, Frey, Loki, Byggvir, Fimafeng, Eldir, Balder, Heimdal, Nari and Narfi. If we remove Aegir's court, we are left with twelve names. It gives us a hint as to who the twelve Aesir are. The goddesses number eight.

The Archetypes

An interpretation of *Lokasenna* tends to divide the characters in separate categories. Each of these categories has its own function and represents a separate archetypal energy. The first class centres on Aegir. He hosts the party but does not participate. The next category features the gods and goddesses. They support each other and team up to counter Loki's intentions. They will be discussed in three classes; firstly individually; then, collectively as a separate class; finally as the collective of Aesir and Alfar. As a separate category, Loki and his family will be studied. He is the antagonist of the Aesir and Alfar.

First Class: Aegir and his Servants

AEGIR

Aegir is introduced as the host of a great banquet. He has invited every one of the gods and deploys two serving boys especially for the occasion. Snorri explains that he organizes the feast in return for the gods' hospitality when he was received in Asgard. For the event, Aegir ordered an enormous cauldron (*ketil*) to be brought. He has brewed beer (*öl*) and ladles it from the cauldron. How the kettle came into Aegir's possession is told in the Eddic *Hymiskvida* poem.

Aegir's realm is a special place. The prose section informs us that Aegir was also known as Gymir. Both names mean sea. Therefore, the scene takes place at or in the sea. Such a mythical ruler of the sea is remembered in many European folk stories. A Russian story from the Sadko Cycle may here be of interest.

One day, the musician and merchant Sadko sails his merchant ships on the wide sea. A storm comes up and the sailors fear for their lives. Sadko suddenly confesses that he has never paid tribute to the King of the Sea. He decides to offer the Sea King silver and gold, but to no avail. He realizes that a human sacrifice is demanded, and lots are drawn, much in the same tradition of the sagas and hagiographies of the Germanic heathens. Eventually Sadko sacrifices himself willingly. But when he sinks to the bottom of the sea, he does not drown. He arrives at the ocean floor and sees a palace. He enters and meets the King and Queen of the Sea. The scene is reminiscent of many Scandinavian myths.

In the hall, Sadko angers the King for some reason, but Sadko takes out his musical instrument and starts to play. Immediately, the Sea King starts to dance. Neither of them can stop. The text explains that the king's dance causes the seas to whirl and storm. Much damage is done on the surface, of which Sadko is oblivious. As some sort of *deus ex machina*, an old man comes in and counsels Sadko. The man is defined as Saint

Nicholas, the patron of sailors, and with his help, Sadko is able to leave the Sea Palace.

The Sea King corresponds to Aegir, who is king of the sea. Aegir is usually paired with Ran, who matches the Sea Queen. Ran is the power at sea that takes the lives of sailors. In the story of Sadko, the Sea King offers the merchant a bride, and many wonderful maidens show up. I interpret these as the daughters of Aegir, who are the waves. The many maidens are presented to Sadko in three waves; each time three hundred women show up. The number reminds us of the nine daughters of Aegir. And the image evokes the endless waves rolling over beach and rock.

The Saint possibly corresponds to Thor, who is the patron of sailors, and comes to immediate help when invoked. The Saint's presence in the hall of the Sea King reminds us of the sudden appearance of Thor in Aegir's hall, when Loki goes out of control. Conversely, Saint Nicholas is traditionally a mask of Odin, who is the patron deity of merchants. He, however, has no special connection with the sea.

The Sadko story is interpreted as a variation of the Biblical story of Jonah. Many elements from the Biblical story are found, such as the attempt to throw overboard cargo to appease the storm, the drawing of lots, and the main character as the one who is to blame. But once Sadko sinks into the sea, things change to a European heathen setting.

The choosing of a bride is a trick of the Sea King to keep Sadko in the Underworld. If he would kiss his bride, he would never be able to leave the sea. Similarly, in Greek mythology Persephone is presented the pomegranate before she leaves the Underworld. Because she eats it, she must stay a third of the year in the Underworld.

The ocean floor is Aegir's true abode. The surface may be swept by the wind and cause waves and storms but the depths of the sea remain calm and dark. As a symbol, the hall transcends the superficial emotions that sway us this way and that. Rather, it reflects the depth of the soul.

Aegir furnishes his hall with gold. He uses the substance as a source of light. If we interpret his abode as the deep emotional mind, the light becomes meaningful in a truly esoteric sense. Furthermore, the name of Aegir's servant Eldir means fire. In kennings, gold and amber are frequently termed the 'fire of the sea'. Gold represents purity, perfection and divinity. Fire suggests light, enlightenment and purification. Fire and gold become symbols of the soul. The hall is illumined by the light of the soul. No torches are needed. No transient material is needed to light the world of the soul. Instead, the spiritual substance of the soul itself is used.

In its most basic sense, gold is wealth. In this, Aegir resembles his Greco-Roman cousins. Underworld gods such as Pluto are associated with wealth. The link is readily made. The earth's depths hide gold and silver and all kinds of minerals. Similarly, riches wash ashore from the ocean's depths.

From the sources we gather that Aegir is a giant, yet the gods visit him often. He seems friendly towards the gods. When the gods visit Aegir, it means that the mind contacts the deep Self. The Aesir embody qualities of the soul clothed in mental substance. As they dive into the deep they are able to reflect the intuition of the Buddhic world. The gods represent the activity of the mind.

The descent of the Aesir into the depths of Aegir's world symbolizes meditation. While the individual shuts his external sensors, the gods plunge deep into the Self. Whether the person is able to maintain a deep state of mind or not depends on his training and experience. Eldir makes an attempt to keep Loki out, but at long last the pressure becomes too much. When Loki enters, one loses concentration. Loki distracts the mind. In the poem, the male deities respond differently to his presence than the female deities, but no one is truly capable of removing him on the spot.

All in all, his connection with water makes Aegir a sensitive and empathic person. His depth of calm makes him a balanced person. He does not take sides, invites gods and Elves alike, Loki included. He remains impartial at all times, indifferent to difference, as a soul-contacted person is. He does not judge nor is he judged. This somewhat explains why Aegir does not participate in the *senna*. At the same time, it makes it impossible to touch him. Loki can only harm him via his servants.

He is a fine host and manages his business well. Aegir has a sense of perfection and leaves nothing to chance. He comes about as a man of honour and keeps his word. After a splendid reception at Asgard, he promises to organize a banquet for the gods in return. He seems like a social person. Aegir is a jovial and generous man.

Fimafeng and Eldir help out Aegir at the banquet. Since they appear in no other tale, they must be regarded as aspects of Aegir.

FIMAFENG

The quarrel between Loki and the gods comes to pass when the gods praise Aegir's servants. Loki cannot stomach the sweet talk and eventually kills Fimafeng. By doing that he shows disrespect for Aegir's hospitality. Moreover, it draws out the gods. To Loki's taste, the gods have lost their sincerity.

Fimafeng means Quick Fetcher, which refers to the quickness of his service. If he is regarded as an aspect of Aegir, then he represents the inborn urge to come to everybody's help at once. The name implies that he instantly appears where he thinks he is needed. The gods applaud his zeal and thoughtfulness.

After the murder, the gods chase away Loki, but he returns later. This time he is ready to tell off the gods. He never slanders Aegir though. The manslaughter reflects Loki's contempt for the gods.

ELDIR

The harsh conversation between Loki and Eldir that follows on Loki's return equally reflects Loki's contempt. Aegir's servant only carries out his job. Loki acknowledges that.

This time Loki does not slay the errand boy straightaway. He speaks rather nicely to the boy. At the same time, Eldir sides with the gods. Loki is no longer welcome at the party after killing Fimafeng. Consequently, Eldir has been appointed to deny him entry.

Loki asks Eldir many questions. In turn, Eldir is truthful about what happens behind Loki's back. In that way, the servant becomes a source of information. He is an informant. His behaviour reflects Aegir's honesty and correctness.

The conversation happens outside the hall. Eldir acts as a doorkeeper. This reminds us of other myths. When seekers wish to enter a Hall of Wisdom, they are first interrogated by a giant. The entire conversation between Odin and Vafthrudnir takes place on the threshold. Skirnir meets a giant before he can enter; Fjolsvin goes through the same trial. Therefore, Eldir incarnates the doorkeeper archetype.

The doorkeeper's task is to keep out unwanted influences. He expresses an aspect of protection in the aura. When a person sits down and meditates, he tries to shut off the influx of unwanted thoughts as much as possible. Depending on the person's experience the degree of success varies. Eldir realizes that Loki is his superior and accepts that. He pushes as far as his own self-confidence allows him to challenge the intruder, but then he steps down. He refuses to fight, either with weapons or with words. In the practice of meditation, it helps to not fight unwanted thoughts. Register what happens, but do not partake of the stream of thoughts nor go against it with your will. That is how Aegir deals with it. Then, the mind will regulate its own deepening.

Taken together, Aegir and his two servants represent Service. Aegir himself does not act but stays in the background. He organizes the whole event and sees to everyone's needs. He works from behind the scenes. The roles of Fimafeng and Eldir are extensions of this quality. In esoteric terms, Service is expressive of the heart energy. Moreover, Service is for the group and not one's own selfish needs. It is the outstanding quality of the initiate.

Second Class: the Gods and Goddesses

BRAGI

When Loki enters the party, he immediately challenges the gods. He says: "Appoint me a seat in the symbol, or tell me to leave." His words cannot be misunderstood. The gods are baffled. After a long silence, Bragi takes the stage. He is angered by Loki's frank behaviour and wishes that he had spoken first.

It is significant to note that none of the gods act when Loki enters. Even Bragi is silent, who is otherwise known for his verbal proficiency. Already, Loki has the gods where he wants them.

In Asgard, Bragi has the honour to welcome the slain warriors in Valhalla. That makes him the right person to respond to Loki's request. But because Bragi's words are out of place, Loki simply ignores him and addresses Odin. Bragi believes he can bribe Loki.

Bragi is the god of speech. He is seated in the middle of the hall which is the place of honour, the Thul's Seat. As such, his role is to act as the spokesperson of the Aesir and Alfar. Bragi would take the lead in any discussion. He is the kind of person who feels confident speaking in public. He always has his arguments ready. Consequently, he has strong opinions about many things. As an archetype, he would be a representative in a trades union.

Bragi sees it as his part to refuse Loki a place at the table. In doing so he passes over the leader of the host, Odin. Bragi feels overconfident. Loki retorts that Bragi is all talk and no action. According to Loki, the god of eloquence avoids confrontations. At home, he feels well and talks big, but on the battlefield he cowers and lacks initiative. Loki means that Bragi cannot be counted on. The accusations remind us of stanzas 5 and 16 of *Havamal*.

Because he sits at home Bragi has no real life experience. He shamefully keeps away from the fight. He boasts of being the best but he never achieves anything. He has no strength of character. Eloquence is his great talent, but he hides away in it. He is unable to develop any other quality. That is why Loki tells him he will never make money or own a horse. He does not have the guts to leave his comfort zone. He sits on the bench.

Evidently, Bragi cringes at Loki's words. He does not want them to be true. This makes Bragi sensitive to criticism. It is very difficult for Bragi to see another person's point of view.

Then, his wife stands up. But what Idun says just makes it worse. She says that Bragi has had too much to drink. She knows that Bragi becomes aggressive when he is drunk. It suits Bragi's personality. Drinking is a practice strongly associated with the god. The *braga-full* cup is named after him. This ties in with *Havamal* 12.

When he loses his inhibition, Bragi becomes a fighter, showing his hidden potential. Metaphorically, a warrior is someone who is ready to face his dark side.

IDUN

Idun asks Bragi to stop. Her main concern is to prevent an escalation. It is however curious that she scolds him. As his wife, she feels having power over him. She is concerned about his well-being and his reputation. She does not really care about Loki and says nothing to him, which is a smart move, but Loki slanders her nonetheless. Again, Idun claims to have behaved properly in the situation. She remains calm and polite. She keeps from fighting Loki knowing it to be a lost cause. She is very resolute.

When she explains her reasoning, it appears that she puts the well-being of her family before all else. She is the person in the family who endlessly tries to reconcile parties. She likes a family to be happy. The truth is often very different. Every family has its problems. That was already recognized in the Viking Age. As a mediator, Idun aims for peace.

Loki taunts Idun anyway. He says that she slept with the person who killed her brother. We have no knowledge of a brother of Idun. Moreover, Loki typically accuses every one of the goddesses of infidelity. He says she is *ver-gjörn* which means man-willing, but Bragi may just as well be meant by it. In that case, Bragi would have slain Idun's brother. On the other hand, Loki may be talking about himself. Then, Thjazi would be Idun's brother. According to the myth, Thjazi wants Idun as his wife.

The point Loki wants to get across is that Idun disregards her family despite what she claims on the surface. The fact that the topic comes up means that it is one of Idun's attributes. From the sources we know that she cares about the Aesir.

From the text, it seems that Idun's lover killed her brother while she was bathing. This incidentally associates Idun with hygiene. It ties in with her basket of maple wood, since maple was used because of its hygienic qualities. The wood is durable. It withstands insect damage better than any other wood.

The bathing reminds us of the bathing Valkyries, which is a recurring theme in saga and legend. Idun is *ítr-þveginn*. The word means 'extremely well washed' and is an epithet for a lady's beauty. The verb also refers to *þvátt-dagr*, which is a synonym of *laugar-dagr*. Washing day nowadays corresponds to Saturday, which is Njord's day. From an occult point of view, the bathing refers to a rite of purification.

What does her choice of husband tell about her? She likes to marry someone with standing. A good reputation is important to her. She likes to stay in control. She therefore refrains from drinking. She takes household affairs into her own hands and keeps her husband under the thumb.

GEFJON

After Idun bites back at Loki, Gefjon takes the floor and scoffs at Loki. She is a little too eager to scorn Loki. There is no direct reason why she should, but she does. What is more, she only repeats what has been said before. All she wants is to have her say. She wants to be heard.

Loki accuses Gefjon of being easy. He relates a story about a boy who gave her a trinket (*sigli*), in return for which she sleeps with him. The boy is called *sveinn inn hvíti* 'the white boy'. The wording implies that a specific person was meant and that the audience would recognize the kenning. Among the Norse gods, 'the white one' is an epithet of Heimdal. It is also a quality ascribed to leek or garlic. The plant denoted virility and possibly represented the phallus. But *sveinn* denotes a young boy, which description better suits Frey.

Since the Old Norse *sigli* can be translated as 'necklace' the story reminds us of the Brisingamen myth. Freyja receives the necklace from a team of four dwarves in return for sexual favours. The word *sveinn* might refer to dwarves. They have a pale skin colour because they live underground, which agrees with the whiteness. Indeed, Gefjon is considered a hypostasis of Freyja.

The text depicts Gefjon as a romantic girl. She likes to receive presents and she likes to be seduced.

Then Odin intervenes. He is afraid of Gefjon's wrath. It suits her personality to be easily irritated. Odin possibly refers to the time when the gods angered Freyja to such a degree that her Brisingamen necklace burst asunder. Gefjon/Freyja explodes when she is angry.

Odin concurrently reveals that Gefjon is clairvoyant. She has psychic abilities. She shares this with many of the goddesses, but Odin particularly claims that Gefjon knows people's Orlog (*örlög hygg ek at hon öll um viti*). The word denotes destiny but refers to the deepest aspect of a person's fate. In esoteric terms, it corresponds to the soul's mission. Moreover, Orlog is associated with the Norns. Orlog explains the meaning behind events.

ODIN

When Loki enters the hall, he significantly turns his attention to Odin. He has good reasons. Odin rules the gods. He therefore manages their business. When Loki enters, he acknowledges Odin as his chief and pays his respects. The decision to allow or deny entry to Loki is Odin's to make. Odin has the right to show either clemency or punish. At the same time, Loki puts himself on an equal level by addressing Odin. He reminds the King of the Aesir that they are sworn brothers. In this way Loki puts pressure on Odin's decision making, because he understands that Odin is a man of his word.

As we have seen in the Gunnlod story, Odin is able to disregard an oath when it suits him. Yet, he admits Loki at the table. Is he being generous? As the patriarch of the gods, Odin is responsible for keeping the peace. He realizes that he can only procure peace when he invites Loki to the table. Odin knows that Loki will be venomous, but he also knows that more harm will come when Loki is shut out. Sometimes it is better to give a person the chance to rant. The energy of anger is thus channeled, if not it would turn destructive. From the Gunnlod story, we also deduce that people are wont to trust Odin's oaths. As an archetype, he therefore represents a reliable person. Whether Odin keeps his oath deliberately or not, the situation still makes him a responsible guy.

Once seated, Loki is quick enough to defame his Lord. He accuses Odin of being arbitrary. As a god of war, Odin deals out victory and defeat. According to Loki, he acts very randomly in granting victories. Loki means that Odin is not an honest guy. He is not trustworthy. He cannot be relied on. Odin clearly has a different set of ideas about who to support or not. According to Loki, Odin often lets the weak conquer the strong. The accusation sounds almost Christian. But I take it to mean that Odin values poets as much as warriors. Not everyone fights in the same way, but as long as someone puts effort into what he does, he is worth supporting. That is the underlying idea.

Odin never contradicts what Loki says. That makes of him an honest person. But people do not understand him. He responds differently in situations because of his ethics. He is less bound to conscience than the average person. That makes him freer to act as he should. To others it seems that he acts as he pleases, but Odin operates from a higher point of view. He works for the good of the community.

Odin owns the power to give success as he grants victory on the battlefield. As such, he is known as the Wish Lord or Granter of Wishes. Everyone knows him, but only those with a pure heart are given what they ask. In magic, sincerity is the key to success. It is a quality that is especially driven by being honest with oneself.

But according to Loki, Odin is unfair with dealing out successes. Indeed, he is unfair when it comes to oaths. He implies that Odin is a little corrupt. If that is the case, then Odin is prone to abuse of power. The King of Asgard is known to be an aristocrat. That may make him biased against the populace. Power makes it more difficult to remain humble. Corruption and power abuse rise from an aggrandisement of the ego. However, the lower self is not able to sustain a sense of happiness for long. Always it needs more. Always it seeks new thrills. Only through contact with the Higher Self is it possible to gain a constant condition of bliss.

When he stands up for the weak, Odin demonstrates a sense of spiritual knighthood. He emerges as fair when he defends Gefjon. To him, Gefjon is his equal. It bespeaks his humility. Perhaps Odin knows what the weak go through. He himself is an outcast. He therefore helps his fellow man regardless of standing.

Loki underlines Odin's otherness. He accuses him of practicing Seidr and of being a sorcerer. Odin is called a *völva* and a *vitki*. The former is used for sorceresses, but the latter for male magicians. Still, his acts are seen as shameful.

According to the text, Odin is *argr*. In the Viking Age, the word denoted cowardice. However, it is of a wholly different nature than what Loki accuses Bragi of, since *argr* is singularly found in the context of magic. Such sorcerers and sorceresses did not go out and fight. Instead they stayed home and lay down as if going to sleep. But in the act of seemingly sleeping, they worked magic. To most men of that time this looked like cowardice.

The word is cognate with modern Dutch *erg*, and appears in compounds such as *ergernis*, *argwaan*, and *arglist*. The root word means bad, terrible. The compounds respectively translate as irritation, suspicion and cunning. For argument's sake, Dutch *ergernis* denotes the condition of being *argr*. I assume that the state of trance is meant to which the sorcerer induced himself. *Argwaan* reflects the opinion of others towards a person of whom they suspect a condition of *argr*. The Dutch word implies they do not trust such a person. The word *arglist* is used of someone who uses cunning. The association with wizards and cunning men is obvious. The Dutch word *argeloos* means to be without *argr* and denotes innocence.

The same root is found in modern German. The adjective *arg* means bad, terrible, but the substantive *Arg* denotes some innate evil in a person. German also has the word *Ärger*, which corresponds to Dutch *ergernis*, but specifically means annoyance, irritation, resentment, anger. It seems that in late times, *argr* designated a person who intentionally harmed people.

Loki accuses Odin of cross-dressing, of sorcery, and of scheming. He depicts him as someone who intentionally harms people. The cross-dressing accusation is common in connection with Seidr practicing men. Odin says the same of Loki.

An interesting parallel is found in *Helgakvida Hundingsbana hin fyrri* 37-39. Sinfjotli accuses Gudmund of behaving like a woman. He is like a Volva on an island. Odin, too, is said to be like a Volva on an island, Samsø, in *Lokasenna* 24. Later, Sinfjotli prides himself of being a werewolf.

In *Volsungasaga* 8, Sinfjotli and his father Sigmund change into wolves. The connection with the Odinic Mysteries is clear.

VIDAR

Vidar's character evinces from what he does but not from what he says. He is a silent god and although he is present at the symbel, he does not say a word. Consequently, Loki says nothing about him.

Vidar observes. He does not judge. He has no inclination to express his opinion on what goes on. That sort of dispassion or equanimity marks the advanced disciple on the Path.

Vidar comes out as a compliant son of Odin. He does not resist his father's request to make room for Loki. He needs no more motivation than that it is asked of him. On the occult Path, he represents the World Server, always ready to help others. He understands the art of a voluntary sacrifice in the name of the greater good. Vidar does not argue with Odin's greater vision. He knows his place in the scheme of things.

As an archetype, Vidar is aware of his social position and the commitment that it brings. He knows that he is guided from above, either esoterically or exoterically. He is confident and disciplined.

FRIGG

Frigg intervenes when Loki and Odin are fighting. She chides them for talking about the past and treats their ancient deeds as secrets. The words *rök* and *örlög* are mentioned in this context, referring to the deepest happenings in a person's life. They relate to a person's destiny and accomplishments.

She is a woman of secrets. She does not like to stir the past. She is afraid that old deeds will cause unnecessary trouble. On the one hand she teaches letting go of the past. Frigg knows that it cannot be altered. Yet on the other hand she suppresses the trauma. That way the old sores can never heal.

Frigg is a woman who has experienced so much grief that she has become very sensitive. Wherever she goes, she shuts her eyes to the world's suffering to relieve her own pain.

She has a great burden to bear. She knows the future of every being, says Freyja (*örlög Frigg hygg ek at öll viti*). This means she knows how Loki will be bound afterwards. It also means that she knows that Loki is the murderer of her son. Freyja continues saying that Frigg does not reveal the future.

Frigg knows from experience that to know fate is not the same as to alter it. She knows how futile it is to fight what is bound to happen. In the myths, she attempted to warn Balder with all that was in her power, but to no avail. Fate has her ways to fulfill itself. Stories of dark prophecies abound in Greek mythology. Each time, everything is done to escape the evil foretelling, but destiny can never be voided. The tale of Oedipus is one such instance. I know the mechanism personally from working with dreams.

Frigg is wise to keep silent about what she knows. With foreknowledge, people would only worry more. That is why she says nothing. She sympathizes with everyone around her and wants to sustain people's happiness. She knows very well that happiness is oft a fleeting thing and people should cherish the times when they feel untroubled.

That is the burden she carries. In the silence of her heart, Frigg sympathizes with the fate of friends and family. She knows more. She knows what ails people, whether they will make it or not. She likes to live past the suffering which she experiences, for she suffers in the stead of all. She cannot be innocent, because she knows all. At the same time, that makes her understanding and compassionate. She resembles much the angel Gabriel.

All this makes Frigg a woman who can keep a secret, who believes in what must happen, but at the same time remains loving and protecting. Even when the odds are against her she fights for her family. In this respect, her power as a mother shows.

Frigg is very proud of her children. She is particularly fond of Balder. In being a mother, she finds her true power. But mentioning Balder makes her prone to living in the past. Her son is no longer among the living. In this way, Frigg expresses her grief as much as she hearkens back to her days of glory. A person like this cannot let go of the past.

As a Mother Goddess she is associated with the home. Loki alludes to this when he implies that she stays home when her husband travels about. According to Loki, Frigg sees no harm in inviting her husband's brothers into her bed at those times. Loki accuses her of infidelity, but in her own eyes, she is only being practical. She is prepared to undergo the consequences, since she carries the world's suffering already.

All in all, Frigg is not afraid to speak her opinion. She asserts herself and is able to withstand to Loki's taunts.

BALDER

Balder is mentioned as the son of Frigg. Earlier Vidar was called the son of Odin. Here is the difference. Vidar incarnates the promising son of which the father will be proud, but Balder embodies the mother's sweetheart. She overprotects him. The former is disciplined and independent. The latter is soft-hearted and drifting.

If we take Frigg's words at face value, then we surmise that Balder was the best among the Aesir. He would have had the power to kick Loki's butt. He is singularly brave, strong and honourable. A man of action. He would not sit and have Loki spew venom but take action and remove the bastard.

As the missing god, Balder represents the ideal. Frigg would like all her children to be like him. He embodies the promise of a good and dutiful person.

FREYJA

After Odin, Freyja is the second to call Loki by name and to look him in the eye. Freyja defends Frigg from Loki's flyting. By doing that, she defends all the goddesses. Freyja comes about very confident. She has no fear of being Loki's next target. Her words sound vengeful.

The goddess attacks Loki in a direct way. Her words are very clear. Freyja is frank, which makes her open and honest. She will not deceive anyone, but always speak true. Freyja speaks her mind.

Freyja speaks about Frigg's foresight. However, Freyja herself prophesies. She tells Loki that his words in Aegir's hall will mean his end. In turn, Loki calls her a witch. The Old Norse *for-dæða* denotes a woman who intends harm. It is quite possible that Freyja has schemed and plotted but she is not shamed by it. Moreover, her witch aspect inspires fear. That is half the magic. Freyja is aware of that. No one can touch her because she is independent.

Freyja is a free woman. The best that Loki can do is accusing Freyja of promiscuity. According to the story, the Regin gods caught her red-handed in her brother's bed. Frey must be meant. On top of that, Loki claims that Freyja has had sex with all of the gods. The bottom line is that she does what she damn well likes.

NJORD

Njord defends his daughter. In fact, he defends the entire congregation of goddesses. He says that there is nothing wrong with having a lover. He is open-minded. This bespeaks his Vanic nature. As a god of fertility, sexuality is a part of his life. Indeed, according to Loki, Njord begot Frey and Freyja by his sister. Njord means that it is fine to have rules but no one should feel bound by them. Everyone must judge his own situation. His view on the matter completely nullifies Loki's taunts.

Loki depicts Njord as a man without a will. He was sent away as a hostage after the Vanic wars and has since been maltreated. Njord lets people do with him as they like. He is subject to the will of the Aesir. He lets himself be taken without a fight.

During the war, he lost his home. His fate resembles Skadi's, except that he meekly undergoes his fate. That means he feels out of place in Asgard. By having to move, Njord lost his self-respect. He no longer cares about himself.

However, he takes pride in his son. He praises him as the best among the gods. His response mirrors Frigg's. Njord therefore represents the father archetype. His son is what is important to him. Although he disregards his own reputation, he minds his son's. Njord steps aside to make place for the next generation. He is of the opinion that young people should be in the spotlights and manage things. Njord is a person who retires from professional or public life.

Njord appears a somewhat broken man, away from home with his famous son as his only consolation. He tends to nostalgia and loses his desire to express himself. According to *Lokasenna*, he is humiliated by giantesses, but he remains indifferent. Nonetheless, he comes about as a man of principle and his arguments are strong. He admires children. He defends his two children. In fact, he stands up for children and women in general.

FREY

When Frey first came to Asgard, he was a stranger among the Aesir. Yet he stood his ground and grew both famous and loved. He believed in himself and competed with the Aesir of his generation. He shows a drive to be acknowledged. Frey's high position in society is entirely due to his own effort. It follows that Frey is a person of ambition and success.

Everyone likes Frey. He is being praised by Njord, Tyr and Byggvir. The number of people admiring Frey is astonishing. Njord claims that no one dislikes him. This includes Loki.

Njord claims that Frey has no peer among the Aesir. Tyr backs up this claim by saying that Frey is the best rider of all (*beztr allra ballriða*). His bravery is praised. Frey incarnates the knight and the gentleman. Despite all adoration, Loki maintains that Frey will not meet the expectations.

Frey's nature is described by Tyr. He says that Frey never makes a woman cry. The comment reminds us of Odin and Gunnlod. It means that Frey acts responsibly. But first and foremost, he will never give anyone a reason to hate him. He occultly practices harmlessness and right speech.

Tyr continues by saying that Frey frees whoever is bound. His very name is the root of the English word 'freedom'. Now, Frey appears as Prince Charming rescuing the imprisoned princess. Metaphorically, he is a problem solver. He frees people from their troubles. Frey intends to liberate mankind from the fetters that bind it. He will rend the nets of glamour and illusion with his flaming sword wherever he can and set humanity free to realize the truth of the spiritual world.

All qualities are balanced in Frey. He is the perfect gentleman and treats the ladies well. They adore him and he never lets them down. He is unbiased towards who he saves. He is a saviour, acting purely out of goodwill. He shows a sense of altruism. He is a kind person. Byggvir hints at Frey's blessed condition.

Frey demonstrates his Vanic power of foresight. He warns Loki of his pending doom. He has also inherited his father's riches. Loki portrays Frey as a wealthy man and a giver of gifts.

There is one flaw in Frey's character. He easily falls in love. He worships love more than war. When he woos Gerd, he puts aside everything else. No other thought enters his mind. On the one hand it symbolizes Frey's one-pointedness, but on the other hand he will be blind to his duties. Frey's inclination to romantic love distracts him. It undermines his fighting abilities. His mind turns to love easily so that he loses sight of his duties.

The weakness in his character is underlined by the story of his wooing Gerd to which Loki alludes. Frey sacrifices wealth and health in return for Gerd's love. The object of his desire becomes an obsession. He loses energy because of it. In bargaining the love of Gerd, Frey gives away the apples of Idun. They symbolize good health and vitality. Frey pays her gold to convince her. This is his material wealth. As a metaphor, it may be sacrificing ideals to satisfy his lust. Last but not least, Frey gives away his sword, the very thing for which he is praised. It means that he forgets his fundamental nature in exchange for gratification. It also signifies a loss of power.

Frey buys Gerd's love against her will. It means that Frey always gets what he wants, even against the odds. Frey gets what he desires.

Loki says that Frey is defenceless because he lost his sword. As with all the other gods, Frey will fight at Ragnarok. Lacking his good sword, he will not be able to defend himself. He will not be up to the task. In spiritual terms, he prefers the long way around. He chooses material gain over spiritual reward. Since the sword is a symbol of decisiveness, it will put Frey in a position of impotence. He is unable to protect himself, but more importantly, he will not be able to protect his friends and family.

TYR

From the context, we assume that Tyr heads the Tivar. This class of gods is mentioned a number of times in *Lokasenna*. Frey and Njord represent the Alfar and Vanir; Odin the Aesir. Frigg represents the Asynjur.

The Tivar represent the gods who fight at Ragnarok. The frequently added morphemes *sig-* and *val-* typically refer to battle. The compounds Sig-Tivar and Val-Tivar refer to the gods as warriors. At this point in the story, Balder is already safe in Hel. Neither does Loki form part of this group, as he fights against the Aesir, nor Njord, who stays home with the Asynjur. Therefore, the Tivar include Odin, Tyr, Thor, Frey, Heimdal, Vidar, and maybe Modi and Magni.

Loki holds it against Tyr that he is unable to reconcile two disagreeing parties. It is his function as a judge to procure peace. His task is to find a solution that makes everybody happy. He therefore takes on an important position.

We conclude that Tyr is a god of peace. From other evidence, we know he is also a god of war. In that case, we must see war as Tyr's course of action to bring harmony. On the occult path, a crisis always precedes a higher state of harmony.

As a judge, Tyr assumes a halo of transcendence. In order to remain neutral, he puts himself above and outside of society. As such, he signifies unity. He embodies the greater good of the community.

He answers to no-one but himself. His judgment is final. That must be the reason why he remains unmarried. Were he married, he would be prone to taking sides and be more vulnerable to corruption. Yet Loki claims he has a wife.

Loki attempts to upset Tyr by mentioning the episode with Fenrir. The god of war lost his sword hand to the wolf, in exchange of which the threat of Fenrir was sealed forever. Tyr deemed this worth the sacrifice. The sword hand means everything to a warrior. It is synonymous with his skill. Without it, he means little to his fellow men. We therefore interpret the binding of Fenrir as the highest aspiration of the warrior. The wolf evokes themes like greed and fear. He embodies a large portion of the Dweller on the Threshold. Binding the wolf frees the individual from what impedes his further growth.

The event teaches the value of sacrifice. Of all the gods, Tyr was the only one willing to confront the monster. He understood the terms of binding Fenrir. Tyr understands that a true sacrifice is not a sacrifice at all but a plain realization of what must be done.

As a mythical character, the event leaves Tyr handicapped. Loki means to say that Tyr is not untouchable. It humbles the god. All the more so, it shows that Tyr is unafraid of being vulnerable. He demonstrates understanding and compassion.

BYGGVIR

Byggvir is one of the lesser gods. He idealizes his master Frey. He feels small. In defending his master, he is able to speak up but unable to act on his words. As such, he is an expression of the Second and the Sixth Ray. He describes himself of being of a low family. Loki calls him 'little' and compares him with a dog. The latter is an allusion to Fenrir who has been mentioned in the preceding stanza, and the son of Loki.

Byggvir feels very honoured to be at the same table as all the high-ranking gods. One day, he wants to be like them and perform great deeds. He learns how to assert himself. He calls himself *hróðugr*. The word means fame and it expresses his sentiment of being invited among the Great Ones. At the same time, it covers another allusion to Fenrir, since Fenrir is called Hrodvitnir in stanza 39. The element *vitnir* is a kenning for wolf and means Thinker. Self-assertion comprises Byggvir's answer.

As an archetype, he is the average human being. Yet he shows dedication and ambition; two qualities that will take him a long way on the path of self-realization. As a servant, he is the World Server. And in relation to Frey as a Master of the Wisdom, he incarnates the typical disciple.

According to the text, Byggvir works the quern or mill. His very name means Barley. It typifies the god as a worker. The turning of the mill symbolizes Samsara, the Wheel of Life, esoterically corresponding to the zodiac. Byggvir is the aspirant on the occult path who works hard in order to attain spiritual selfhood. In Bailey's book *Esoteric Astrology*, it is said that the mass of humanity goes through the zodiac in one way, but for the disciple and the initiate the wheel turns in the other way. Most people are blind to the hidden workings of the universe. They walk in circles acting out their supposed part in society without realizing the truth behind the phenomenal world. Hence the saying 'to mill around'. Once reoriented towards spiritual attainment, he is able to escape the mindless treading of the mill.

Loki describes Byggvir as a coward. Like Bragi, he stays home when he should be out fighting with everyone else. He hides. He is not ready to face his fears. Loki also accuses Byggvir of being partial. He is liable to favour one above the other. Since everyone is equal in esoteric terms, Byggvir hereby sins against the concept of brotherhood.

Byggvir suffers from low self-esteem. He shows promise, but is not capable yet of expressing his sensed ideals into real service. He needs an idol to look up to. He symbolizes the unrealized person.

HEIMDAL

Not many words are bandied with Heimdal. Loki tells the god that he has been allotted a most ungrateful task. In ancient times, Heimdal has been appointed to watch over the gods. He is forever stationed at Yggdrasil to guard the bridge that leads into the home of the gods. This is hardly an insult, and Heimdal takes it calmly. He is well aware of his place in the scheme of things.

Heimdal has no physical freedom, but he accepts his fate stoically, knowing that he is only a part of a greater mind. He understands that his function is a key function. In a way, he is the Door of Initiation. He decides who goes up to heaven and who does not. In real life, he is a security guy, a gatekeeper, a guardian. As many others among the Aesir, Heimdal understands the Law of Sacrifice.

Heimdal accuses Loki of being drunk. His speech resembles the *Havamal* stanzas on drinking. The god's tendency to lecture reflects his function as an Odinic initiate. In such a disguise he visits three families in *Rigsthula* and gives them advice. He therefore comes about as a responsible person. In a profane sense, he is someone who feels the need to interfere and point out people's weaknesses. He may be a teacher but may well be a little pedantic.

Loki mentions that Heimdal must ever stay awake. Elsewhere it is said that he needs less sleep than a bird. This, too, is a positive aspect. It symbolizes Heimdal's vigilance. He embodies awareness. In an esoteric sense, to be awake means to have a measure of soul contact. He realizes the True, the Beautiful and the Good in the world. Such a person has left ignorance and idleness behind him.

SKADI

Skadi outright threatens Loki. Her threat is based on seeing the future. As many of the goddesses, Skadi possesses foresight. Since she married into the Aesir clan, she also adopted their abilities.

The goddess has a personal reason to see Loki hang. From her speech, we deduce that she is embittered and would like to see nothing better than Loki's defeat.

Skadi plays a particular role after the *senna*. When Loki is bound, she gives in to torturing him with drops of burning venom. Skadi is a vengeful person. She does not easily forget. She is cruel.

SIF

At long last, Sif takes initiative. She speaks on behalf of her husband and praises Loki for sparing Thor, but Loki only taunts those who talk back to him. Loki explains that it is very careless of Sif to mention Thor. First of all, it puts her in the spotlight. Secondly, it brings Thor into the conversation. Now both are vulnerable to Loki's words.

What does this tell us about Sif? She is proud of her husband. She speaks too quickly. She misjudges the situation, since she thought victory was hers. Yet she shows initiative. Loki adds that she is unfaithful. The comment humiliates both her and Thor.

Loki describes Sif as "wary and wroth with a man". Whether any man or her husband is meant is unclear. In any case, it illustrates her attitude towards men in general. She is uncomfortable with men, being touchy, maybe frigid. That may be the reason why she identifies with her husband so much. From Loki's words we assume that Sif is embarrassed. She will not publically talk about her sex life. Loki tries to bring her out of her shell.

BEYLA

Beyla puts an end to things. Her words sound like a premonition, but they can also be interpreted as an invocation. She simply states that Thor is coming and two stanzas later the Defender of Midgard appears. In any case, she functions as a herald, a messenger. Her recognition of Thor's coming symbolizes intuition.

Although Beyla is considered Byggvir's wife, she is very different. Her action shows more self-reliance. In contrast to Byggvir, Beyla needs no-one to defend her. She is sufficiently confident to act on her own. In the order of speakers, she comes at the end. Moreover, she is not paired up with either Byggvir or Frey.

She is very down to earth. She simply states matters as they are. This attitude makes her mentally oriented and less vulnerable to emotional damage.

Loki says she "mixed much with cruelty" but the verb *blanda* hints at mixing Mead. She may therefore rank among the Valkyrjar. He also depicts her as a dairymaid. She is a worker like Byggvir. From the context, we surmise that she does not avoid dirty work nor think it is shameful. That makes her humble and honest.

THOR

Thor's coming changes everything, like a sudden breeze that clears the air. He is the aspect that takes action. Still, Loki is able to delay execution and have his say. Thor needs to repeat his threat to remove Loki from the scene four times. Meanwhile, Loki attempts to embarrass Thor, but the god never takes the bait. He does not allow himself to be sidetracked. Thor is the kind of person that keeps a focus no matter what.

Thor's response to need is immediate. Typically, he appears as a *deus ex machina*. The same happens when Hrungnir drinks excessively in the hall of the gods. Thor's help is invoked and he immediately appears. Thor is reliable, responsible and strong. He acts as a sort of guardian angel. In times of need, he can be relied on. As a matter of fact, the stanza spoken by Beyla may be used as an invocation. Her words precede Thor's presence and therefore function as a summoning. Though maybe closer to the truth, Thor responds to his wife's call. She does not mention his name, but only thinking of him makes him turn up.

The first thing Thor does when he enters is giving Loki an ultimatum. Leave or die. Thor gets down to business. Such a person knows no hesitation. He brings forth his hammer, which is rather curious, since no weapons are allowed in a Hall of Peace (*griða-staðr*). Thor breaks the rules. However, it is tolerated of him. He cannot be bothered with petty rules and regulations. When something needs to be done, it shall be done. He disregards protocol and trespasses social boundaries, but that is a mark of his courage, since he acts with sincerity.

Thor is someone who feels comfortable with being alone. He usually ventures into Jotunheim alone. Loki calls him an Einheri, which is an Individual Warrior. Thor embodies the energy of a person who is single. He works alone. He seldom if ever joins a social event. Since Thor is often portrayed as rough, he may represent a person with low social skills. The fact that he disregards local politics confirms this. However, he is goodhearted and helps out his friends unconditionally.

Furthermore, Thor is depicted as a big guy, strong and sturdy. That is why he is the active defender of the Aesir. He is the strongest among them. But he is still a small man in comparison to the giants. Loki reiterates the story of his adventure with Skrymir. At that time, Thor mistook the giant's glove as a large building. Loki insinuates that Thor still feels awe for the might of the giants. Loki means to say that Thor often makes a fool of himself.

Loki points out that Thor will never be able to help everyone. At Ragnarok, Odin will fight Fenrir; Thor knows that the beast is too much for his Father; yet, Thor has his hands full with fighting Jormungand. He cannot fight both. Odin falls, and that stings Thor.

In passing, Thor's appetite is mentioned. Thor eats a lot, which makes him a healthy person, contextually. This motif also appears in *Thrymskvida*. As a symbol, it can mean a few things. Hunger is related to the instincts and the life of the physical body. That makes Thor a primitive man. Metaphorically, hunger refers to the hunger of the mind. People who never stop reading or gathering information show this kind of hunger. Loki in particular uses the concept of hunger to denote deprivation. Since he refers to Thor's thorny situation, he points out the god's holes in his confidence. The deficiency referred to is on an emotional level. That is Thor's weakest point.

Third Class: The Asynjur

The number of goddesses is well balanced in relation to the male gods. Nonetheless, a very one-sided picture emerges from Loki's flyting. The trickster god accuses all the goddesses of being unfaithful. He strongly emphasizes their sexuality. Curiously, these accusations are never countered. Why Loki brings this knowledge in the open means that this divine attribute is treated as a secret. In a very primitive way, the goddesses' sexuality symbolizes fertility.

Idun and Freyja are accused of being promiscuous. Moreover, Idun loved her brother's murderer. Frigg slept with her husband's brothers. Freyja slept with her brother. Freyja's case is an example of incest, but Frigg's and Idun's equally point to a lack of respect for family relations. Sif and Skadi spent the night with Loki. Sleeping with the enemy comes down to treason. In addition, Skadi's case relates to family, too, since both she and Loki are of giant stock. Beyla is the only goddess in the clear, but Loki describes her as ugly.

It is interesting to note that most of the goddesses have mythological relations with Loki as well. In Freyja's case, Loki steals her Brisingamen necklace. In Skadi's case, Loki steals Idun. In Sif's case, Loki steals her golden hair. Loki claims to have bedded just these goddesses. When he steals Freyja's necklace, he changes into a fly and enters her bedroom.

Moreover, Loki accuses Freyja of having slept with all the Aesir and Alfar.

Loki regards the goddesses as inferior. Through them, he hopes to hurt the gods. By slandering the goddesses he humiliates their husbands, brothers and fathers. This is Loki's way of demonstrating the perceived inferiority of the female line. On the other hand, it means that the gods have no control over their female side.

Other traits are shared among the goddesses. The characteristics appear from their own words and actions. They attempt to procure peace. They either soothe Loki or chide their men. Collectively, they represent diplomatic abilities. They try to avoid fighting at all costs. Their means of defense consist of words instead of weapons. At the same time, they do not want to lose face because of their men. They care about reputation. They hope to gain standing through their husbands. While this makes the women dependent, it also shows their willingness to connect.

One last major trait is shared. Almost every one of the Asynjur possesses the ability to foretell the future. Gefjon and Frigg are explicitly said to know Orlog. Freyja and Skadi prophesy Loki's future. Sif and Beyla announce Thor. While the latter is not a very direct mention of knowing the future, it does suggest premonition. Beyla obviously senses Thor's appearance before everyone else.

To know the fate of all beings is an ability subscribed to the Volva. It relates the goddesses with the feminine mysteries, the matron cult and the mythos of the Norns.

The *Lokasenna* text reveals that Odin's foreknowledge of events stems from the same ability. The same goes for Frey. Loki accuses Odin of being a Volva. He learned it from Freyja. The ability is generally associated with the Vanir.

Fourth Class: Aesir and Alfar

The Aesir are mentioned a number of times in *Lokasenna* as a collective.

Sometimes they are the Aesir, sometimes Aesir and Alfar, sometimes Sig-Tivar, Regin, Bönd or simply 'gods'.

In the beginning of the story, the Aesir are invited into Aegir's hall as a group. After the list of specific participants, the text says that many Aesir and elves are present. The expression *ása ok álfa* implies that there are more gods present than enumerated in the list.

Loki is a member of this divine group. First of all, he is initially invited. Secondly, Gefjon and Frigg explicitly call him one of the Aesir. The goddesses understand the futility of fighting among equals. Conversely, Loki is repeatedly placed in opposition to the collective gods. In the prologue, Loki disagrees with the Aesir when they inappropriately praise Fimafeng and Eldir. From that point onwards, the gods form a cordon against him. They chase off Loki.

When the trickster returns, he understands his position very well and greets the Aesir as a collective. In response, Bragi denies Loki the right to enter and claims to speak in the name of the Aesir. His use of the concept excludes the trickster. The poet god symbolically represents the collective; he is their spokesperson. Similarly, Balder is the power to act. Thor emerges as the impeccable one among the group. He has integrity. Thus, each god has a quality to contribute to the Aesic egregore.

Loki formulates a general accusation towards the male gods as much as he did with the goddesses. As he sees it, they sit back and rely on their past achievements. According to Loki, the gods lack initiative.

Many of the gods are boastful, but their words prove hollow. Bragi claims he wants to fight Loki, as does Byggvir, but they never get up and do something. Odin, Njord, Tyr and Heimdal just sit back. They represent the elder generation. Of all the gods, Thor is the only one who acts.

The Aesir do collectively recognize Loki as a criminal. They use everything in their power to root out this symbol of evil. He criticizes them mercilessly. Loki represents the tendency to mental criticism. This tendency results from an analytical way of thinking, but it undermines cooperation. The energy of criticism separates. The mind, that is the Aesir, tries to rid itself of this bad habit. This sort of personality refinement is what it takes to progress on the spiritual Path.

What is important is that the Aesir act in unison. They all cover each other and aim to exclude Loki. Their united effort expresses group consciousness. They bond. As such they are referred to in the epilogue, where the collective is called Bönd. The name incidentally refers to Loki's binding.

The text further features the expression Aesir and Alfar. This must be interpreted as a concept referring to the collective of all divine beings. It includes Aesir, Vanir, Elves, lesser gods, and the giantesses married into the clans. In the *Voluspa* poem, it is synonymous with Regin, which word also appears in *Lokasenna*. Presumably, the term Alfar covers the Vanic race. They are all one family and regarded as such by all parties.

The expression Aesir and Alfar is particularly mentioned in stanzas 13 and 30. Loki describes the collective as a band of warriors. Symbolically, they represent the spiritual warrior.

Loki further claims that all of the gods have slept with Freyja. She strings Aesir and Elves as beads in a necklace and thus unites them to a common purpose. Freyja embodies the Great Goddess who mystically marries the collective as a unity. The band of Aesir and Alfar are archetypes of Man in all his aspects whereas Freyja represents the full kaleidoscope of Woman.

Lastly, the main trait shared among the male gods is their readiness to sacrifice themselves for the good of the community. First of all, Vidar gives up his seat for Loki. Then, Tyr's story about how he lost his hand is mentioned. Next, we hear about Heimdal. He dedicates his life in guarding the spiritual world. The Aesir demonstrate the Law of Sacrifice and serve the group's well-being.

Fifth Class: Loki and Family

LOKI

Loki is the main character in the poem. Everything that is said and done relates to him. The title of the work cannot be mistaken. In stanza 3, he declares his evil intentions to Eldir. He says he will mix 'harm' in their Mead. The Old Norse *mein* connotes blame. Loki faces the Aesir with the intent of reproach.

Conversely, Loki is a man of honour. He reminds Odin of their oath of bygone times. Odin is bound to seat him.

Loki represents the smooth talker. He is good with words. He embodies the archetype of the merchant who is able to make the unsuspecting customer buy something he does not need. This is inferred from stanza 5. Loki is significantly challenged by Bragi first, since the poet god symbolizes eloquence. They compete in word-power. In passing, Loki praises people of action while he disrespects Bragi for his cowardice.

In stanzas 10, 16, 28, and 29, Loki's words of criticism are termed *lasta-stafir*, *mein-stafir* and *leið-stafir*. The gods retort. Bragi calls Loki a liar. Gefjon calls him playful (*leikinn*). Odin and Heimdal call him *ör-viti*, out of his mind, implying that Loki speaks before he thinks. Freyja seconds this opinion and calls him a liar. But the Aesir simply do not understand him. Frey calls him *bölva-smiðr* which is a bale-smith or Worker of Evil.

Loki is aware of his talents. At the end of the poem, he reveals something about himself. In a reply to Skadi, Loki describes himself as a person who is very good at scheming. This resulted in the deaths of Balder and Thjazi. Later he acknowledges to be *læ-víss* or treacherous. He also boasts that he will live long. He knows how to get in trouble, but he always finds a way to avoid lethal danger.

However, Loki's true intention is revealed in stanza 64. Just before he leaves the scene, he says: "I said to the Aesir that which my mind encouraged me to." Loki speaks his mind. The Old Norse word *hugr* means mind with the notion of desire. *Hugr* also denotes courage. Loki feels a need to articulate his thoughts about the gods. The Old Norse verb *hvetja* means to whet but metaphorically expresses persuasion. Loki's long churning inner reflections whet his words. He burns to speak his opinion. Moreover, Loki has the courage to show up knowing he is unwelcome.

In short, Loki's true motive is to disclose the gods' masquerade. They praise Fimafeng, but it angers Loki because he senses their hypocrisy. Consequently, he makes it his mission to shake the very foundations of Asgard's ethics. The Aesir deem Loki's slaying an injustice to Aegir. In truth, they find Loki's presence unbearable. From Loki's perspective, the gods' behaviour is meaningless. He wants to wake up the gods and point out their demise. While the Aesir become decadent and inactive, Loki incites them to action.

Loki embodies the counterforce of the gods. He is able to penetrate their core, where the gods are most vulnerable. The Aesir are powerless in keeping him out of their system. Despite his initial banishment, he returns. Finally, he decides to speak plainly and force a response from the gods.

The story of *Lokasenna* shows how Loki compels the Aesir to take a position (7). Then he demands answers and next he holds each responsible for their deeds. He points out their every mistake. Esoterically, he has become the Dweller on the Threshold. The individual will have to purify every aspect of his lower self if he wants to bind what Loki represents. Indeed, to clear his own conscience.

Loki's intention to speak plainly is reflected in his words towards Frigg and Skadi. He openly admits to be the killer of Balder and Thjazi. He no longer hides the truth and cares not whether he damages people's feelings by being honest. Loki's slayings are associated with his cunning. In the same way, he tells Njord that he will no longer keep things secret.

Lokasenna will prove the god's doom. The gods are very clear about it. Freyja, Frey and Skadi warn Loki, but he does not listen. Frey and Skadi are very particular about how Loki will be bound. Orlog cannot be avoided. In fact, by cheating the gods, Loki finally gives them an excuse to pursue him.

Odin further divulges that Loki lived in the Underworld for eight winters (23). He literally lived 'under' the earth (*jörð neðan*). Possibly the spirit world is meant since the Nine Worlds are also situated "beneath the earth". It emphasizes Loki's giant nature. At that time, he changed into a milking cow and a woman. The former somehow reminds us of the mysterious Audumla; the latter may be a reference to *Thrymskvida*. Odin goes on and says that Loki bore children into the world. Other myths attest Loki's gender-crossing. He gave birth to Sleipnir, and according to the *Shorter Voluspa*, Loki also birthed the *flögð*, which is a kind of giantess. Later, Njord confirms Odin's accusation.

Loki's gender-crossing can be interpreted in two ways. In a positive way, it expresses his power to manifest. Bearing children does not only denote fertility but also creativity. The gestation period and the actual birthing represent the shaping and implementation of a thought-form. In the *Lokasenna* stanza, the Underworld is the part of the mind which shapes the thought and the eight winters signify the length of time necessary to vitalize it. In a negative way, it expresses instability.

Njord, Frey and Tyr get to Loki by speaking about his offspring. They know how much it hurts to take offence directed to your sons and daughters. Even though Loki only spawned monsters in the eyes of the gods, they are still his children and he cares about them. The gods specifically pick on Fenrir. They foresee that Loki will undergo a similar fate as his wolf son. Finally, Thor says he will cast Loki into the East. The direction is usually associated with the giant kind. Thor means that this is where Loki belongs.

As an archetype, Loki is a person who feels misunderstood. He feels excluded. First and foremost, he wants to be accepted by his kith and kin. But he breaks when the pressure to integrate becomes too much and he realizes he cannot deny the freedom of his inner self. This realization expresses itself in a search for truth. Is he fated to be alone? Does he need others around him? Can he live true?

From his own words (64), we infer that he is bent on unveiling the truth, not just about the gods and goddesses but also about himself. Although he seems harsh toward his companions, he does not spare himself. Ultimately, Loki aims to speak the truth. He is able to admit his own shameful deeds. He has nothing to lose and breaks down his conscience. Yang Jwing Ming, a shaolin teacher that I have met in the past, used to say: "Embarrassment is the seat of enlightenment." One must be prepared to let go of pride. We often feel vulnerable in the face of shame, but it helps destroy the power of the ego and makes further progress on the Path possible. Despite Loki's deconstruction of ego, he is still a proud person. He always has to have the last word.

Loki's grand quality is that he knows everything. He does not possess foresight like the goddesses, but he knows how to stay informed. From his engagements it follows that he has a very good network and always knows things first. He knows people's secrets and uses it for leverage. He is an informant, an undercover agent, a spy. In *Sorla Thattr*, he changes into the shape of a fly to spy on Freyja. At other times, he employs the falcon shirt to spy out Jotunheim.

However, many things betray Loki's weaknesses. First of all, he is presented as a shapeshifter. Although his ability to change *persona* from time to time can help deal with different situations, it also makes Loki a fickle person; it is difficult to trust him. As such he resembles the Greek Proteus. At one time Loki is man enough to face his shadow, the Aesir, and braves their contempt as if he is Thor. At another time he escapes his fate by running from danger, as would Bragi, out of pure self-interest. Loki has no shame in hiding when he has to; at the same time, he boldly defies the gods.

Secondly, Loki is sensitive to ranking. He believes in social standing. That is why he ignores Bragi in the beginning of the flyting and addresses Odin. Loki thinks himself on equal footing with the Lord of Valhalla. When Byggvir speaks up, the trickster god becomes angry, because he deems Frey's servant unworthy of talking to him. Again, when Thor confronts him, Loki recognizes his power. The fault of separativeness plainly shows in his character.

FENRIR

At the end of the story, we hear a little about Loki's family. At the actual event, Loki stands alone, like a true disciple, and defies mainstream society. His son Fenrir is mentioned both in the prologue and in the dialogue; the wolf is dear to Loki. When the binding is mentioned, the gods mean to say that Loki birthed evil into the world while they pride themselves on having defeated it. The wolf represents fear; the crucial thing to overcome in the personality. Fear cannot have a place in the soul life. Now Loki is all that is left of the evil in the world (*böl*). Furthermore, he personifies its very source.

NARI NARFI

In the epilogue, we hear about Loki's wife Sigyn and their sons Nari and Narfi. Both names derive from the same stem **narw-* meaning narrow. According to Snorri Sturluson, the names are synonymous. In *Gylfaginning*, Narfi is the father of Nótt, the goddess of the night. Their names relate to the Jungian shadow concept which Loki represents to the candidate struggling for initiation.

The text says that Nari was killed and Loki bound with the boy's bowels, but Narfi changed into a wolf. According to Snorri, the other son was called Vali and changed into a wolf and killed his brother while in wolf shape. Elsewhere, Vali is Balder's avenger. He slays Hoder.

The shapechanging and the binding are aspects of Loki's life. He is the darkness deep within us. Every time we think we bind our vices, the shadow sneaks out and changes shape ... Until at some point the Dweller of the Threshold is finally overcome and one stands at the Door of Valhalla.

According to the poem, Loki is bound to a sword. It is the sword of reason that keeps us alert. With its blade to Loki's neck, the individual will always be reminded to minimize the pull of the material world.

SIGYN

When Loki's wife Sigyn sees her husband's suffering, she comes to him and supports him. She shows empathy and takes a bowl to collect the poison that drips from a snake's mouth tied above Loki's head. Her actions betray the energy of the heart. She is devoted to her husband and will not part with him. The story is versified in *Voluspa* 34. Sigyn loves Loki unconditionally. Maybe her strength is to see the good in everyone.

Her name gives away her Valkyrie identity; it is the feminine personification of *sigr*.

In order to ease Loki's suffering, she uses a basin meant for washing the hands. It is a symbol of purification. Sigyn thus represents the power to accept every aspect of the personality. She judges not. That is her power. Together, the binding and the washing produce the lasting purification which one attempts to bring about.

Archetypically, Sigyn is the kind of person who helps others but disregards herself. She wishes to help everyone. Ideally, she would bear the world's suffering.

DOOR 13
BEYOND
THE MYTHS

The question arises whether something practical is gained from the myths. Nothing is gained except understanding. The myths are a pathway into the realm of the soul. Its images evoke a deep response and help us understand the mechanisms of the human psyche. Ultimately, to "know thyself" and subsequently understand other people leads to wisdom; a quality very close to the Love and Wisdom of Master Odin.

The process of understanding is often triggered by the recognition of archetypes such as are found in stories and dreams. Further continuation of the process hinges on a day-to-day self-reflection and self-evaluation discipline. Let us assume that this is what it means when the Aesir gather around the Well of Urd day after day and contemplate world affairs. Put briefly, much of that Inner Alchemy goes on internally.

Γυωθι Σεαυτον

Throughout our discourse on Norse mythology, we have frequently touched two aspects of the process. They are purification and soul contact.

Self-development entails refinement. Refinement is achieved through purification which happens on all levels of manifestation. First of all, the occultist will be keen on physical hygiene and express an overall orderliness. Secondly, he looks after his psychological hygiene. The occultist monitors his emotions and controls his thoughts.

Exercises to purify the physical, astral and mental body are found in any handbook on magic. The student will find instructions in the Alice

Bailey books, but also in Aleister Crowley's texts, such as *Liber III vel Jugorum*, and in the works of Annie Besant and Dion Fortune.

A specific ritual in support of clearing the aura and preparing for the download of subtler forces and energies would be the famed Lesser Banishing Ritual of the Pentagram. Since the early 1900s it has become the stock-in-trade of contemporary Magick. Today, the rite has been adapted a hundred times over to suit the magician's personal world view. A Northern Mysteries version of the rite can be found in *Secrets of Asgard*.

Exercises to contact the soul, or causal body, have always been the major aim of the ancient Mystery Schools. Therefore, many of their rites pertain to this purpose. These especially include rites of initiation. We specifically recall the story of the Mead of Poetry, its ritual and its spiritual significance. But there are also the stories of Odin's death, Balder's death, Skirnir's journey, and Svipdag's journey, all of which can be reenacted either as a pathworking or as a ceremony to induce soul contact.

The practicing magician breaks down the myths in its essential elements and constructs or reconstructs a personal myth with specific purposes. He can do that because he knows the meaning behind the images.

But working with myths has an added value to the magician. He works with material that is not exclusively his. Shared symbols and images make it possible for a group of magicians to work together over a distance. Moreover, everyone within the same tradition has access to the thought-forms and energies generated by one particular group. But time, too, can be bridged. Indeed, it is possible to enter the egregore of Mystery Schools of the past by the right use of myths and symbols.

The Fimbulgaldr

The invocation at the very beginning of this book is a very simple means to facilitate soul contact. The prayer is based on the Great Invocation, formulated by Alice Bailey and Djwhal Khul in the first half of the 20th century. I have kept as much of the original text as possible while replacing certain words with images from Norse mythology. In this way, the universal energy of the Ageless Wisdom becomes anchored in the Northern Mysteries current. At the same time, magical work performed within the tradition of the Norse myths will contribute on more a global scale.

The invocation is said out loud and used every day. It is a quick and simple means to draw down Light and Love into the world. The invocation can be easily shaped into a ritual, solitary or in group. Visualizations may be added and the temple built accordingly.

When you say the first stanza, you can visualize Odin and/or Heimdal, their hands aloft. Golden light streams forth from the brow and heart and hands into the minds of men and women. At the same time visualize the Sun. When you say the second stanza, you can visualize Odin and/or Freyja, standing at one of the roots of Yggdrasil, hands aloft. White light with a soft pink touch streams forth from the heart and hands into the hearts of men and women everywhere. When you say the third stanza, see Urd's Well at the Tree of Life, and all the gods around it. All of this is enveloped in an endless sphere of brilliant white light. Those are the main visualisations.

The Pledge of the Einheri

In the works of Alice Bailey, another poem is found that can be used to strengthen one's resolve to tread the Path and work with the Aesir. The text is known as the Affirmation of the Disciple. I call my Northern version the Pledge of the Einheri, or Pledge of the Valkyrie, as the case may be. The formulation is further inspired by one of Amergin's songs.

> In the morning I am the eagle that carries the Sacred Mead aloft.
>
> In the day I am the white horse that pulls the Chariot of the Sun.
>
> In the evening I am the snake that slumbers beneath the roots of Yggdrasil.

In the night I am the fish that circles the Nine Worlds.

I am a Rune of Light spoken in the vastness of Ginnungagap.

I am a bead of amber in the necklace of the goddess Freyja.

I am a hallowed Rune of Fire burned in the hands of Surt.

I walk among the gods.

I am the Rainbow Bridge that leads to the front gates of Valhalla.

I am the Mead of Wisdom shared by the Valkyries.

I am the Sword of Frey that shines throughout the darkness.

I walk among the gods.

And in the great halls of Gladsheim I take my seat.

And for the last battle of the Aesir I prepare.

And all the weavings of the Norns I know.

And thus I walk among the gods.

As with the Fimbulgaldr, the pledge can be done in a ritual setting. Certainly, when you would like to pledge yourself to the Great Work of inner transformation, then the affirmation can be said in a little ceremony. The words encompass an attitude of sincerity, compassion, and purpose. May these three qualities guide you on your Path!

Knock

And it shall be opened unto you

ALU

BIBLIOGRAPHY

- Freya Aswynn, *Northern Mysteries and Magick*, Llewellyn Publications, St. Paul, Minnesota 2002.
- Alice A. Bailey, *Initiation, Human and Solar*, Lucis Publishing Company, New York 1972, first printing 1922.
- Alice A. Bailey, *A Treatise on White Magic*, Lucis Publishing Company, New York 2005, first printing 1934.
- Alice A. Bailey, *Esoteric Psychology*, Volume I, Lucis Publishing Company, New York 2002, first printing 1936.
- Alice A. Bailey, *From Bethlehem to Calvary*, Lucis Publishing Company, New York 1973, first printing 1937.
- Alice A. Bailey, *Telepathy*, Lucis Publishing Company, New York 2001, first printing 1950.
- Alice A. Bailey, *Esoteric Astrology*, Lucis Publishing Company, New York 1997, first printing 1951.
- Alice A. Bailey, *A Treatise on Cosmic Fire*, Lucis Publishing Company, New York 1973, first printing 1952.
- Alice A. Bailey, *The Externalisation of the Hierarchy*, Lucis Publishing Company, New York 2011, first printing 1957.
- Alice A. Bailey, *The Labours of Hercules*, Lucis Publishing Company, New York 1982.
- Annie Besant & Charles Webster Leadbeater, *Thought-Forms*, The Theosophical Publishing House, London 1925.
- Jean Shinoda Bolen, *Goddesses in Everywoman*, Harper 2004.
- Joseph Bosworth & T. Northcote Toller, *An Anglo Saxon Dictionary*, Oxford University Press, London 1898.
- Jean Chevalier & Alain Gheerbrant, *The Penguin Dictionary of Symbols*, Penguin Books, London 1994.
- James Allen Chisholm, *The Eddas*, Houston 2003.
- Richard Cleasby & Gudbrand Vigfusson, *An Icelandic-English Dictionary*,

- Clarendon Press, Oxford 1957.
- Benjamin Creme, *Transmission, a meditation for the New Age*, Tara Press, London 1983.
- Kevin Crossley-Holland, *The Penguin Book of Norse Myths*, Penguin Books, London 1982.
- Aleister Crowley, *Magick*, Red Wheel/Weiser, Boston 2002.
- Stephanie Dalley, *Myths from Mesopotamia*, Oxford University Press, Oxford 1989.
- Ursula Dronke, *The Poetic Edda*, Volume II, Clarendon Press, Oxford 1997.
- Hilda Roderick Ellis-Davidson, *The Road to Hel*, Cambridge University Press, Cambridge 1943.
- Hilda Roderick Ellis-Davidson, *Hostile Magic in Icelandic Sagas*, in *The Witch Figure* pp.20-41, London 1973.
- Hilda Roderick Ellis-Davidson, *Roles of the Northern Goddess*, Routledge, London 1998.
- Michael J. Enright, *Lady with a Mead Cup*, Four Courts Press, 2013.
- Clarissa Pinkola Estés, *Women Who Run With the Wolves*, Ballantine Books, New York 1992.
- Thor Ewing, *Gods and Worshippers in the Viking and Germanic World*, The History Press, Stroud 2008.
- F.E. Farwerck, *Noord-Europese Mysteriën en hun sporen in het heden*, Ankh-Hermes, Deventer 1970.
- Anthony Faulkes, *Edda*, Everyman, Vermont 1987.
- Werner Fiala, *The Tales of Krakonos*, the Spirit of the Mountains, 2001.
- Dion Fortune, *Aspects of Occultism*, Red Wheel Weiser, Boston 2000.
- Dion Fortune, *The Cosmic Doctrine*, Red Wheel Weiser, Boston 2000.
- Dion Fortune, *Esoteric Orders and Their Work*, Samuel Weiser, York Beach 2000.
- Lorenzo Gallo, *The Giantess as Foster-Mother in Old Norse Literature*, in Scandinavian Studies vol.78 no.1, 2006.

- Kveldulfr Gundarsson, *Spae-Craft, Seiðr, and Shamanism*, Our Troth/ Hrafnar, 2001.
- Lee Hollander, *Heimskringla*, University of Texas Press, Austin 1964.
- Svava Jakobsdóttir, *Gunnlöð and the Precious Mead*, in *The Poetic Edda: Essays on Norse Mythology*, Acker & Larrington, New York/London 2002.
- Carl Gustav Jung, *Analytical Psychology*, London 1976.
- Maria Kvilhaug, *The Maiden with the Mead*, Oslo 2004.
- Maria Kvilhaug, *The Seed of Yggdrasil*, Whyte Tracks, Helsinge 2013.
- Charles Webster Leadbeater, *Science of the Sacraments*, The St. Alban Press, Los Angeles/London/Sydney 1920.00
- Heinrich Luden, *Geschichte des Teutschen Volkes*, Volume 10, Gotha, 1835.
- James MacKillop, *Oxford Dictionary of Celtic Mythology*, Oxford University Press, Oxford 1998.
- Lucillo Merci, *Volkssagen aus Südtirol*, Manfrini Editori, Calliano 1989.
- Harry Mountain, *The Celtic Encyclopedia*, Universal Publishers, 1998.
- Britt-Mari Näsström, *Freyja, the Great Goddess of the North*, University of Lund, Lund 1995.
- Laurence Newey, *The Conscience of Love*, a talk given at *Esoteric Perspectives on a Science of Consciousness*, Lucis Trust, London 2003.
- Vincent Ongkowidjojo, *De Horizon in het Licht van het Mesopotamische Wereldbeeld*, Leuven 2002.
- Vincent Ongkowidjojo, *Secrets of Asgard*, Mandrake, Oxford, 2011.
- Vincent Ongkowidjojo, *Toverspreuken en runen*, Deel 1, in De Ravenbanier 43, Viking Genootschap, Turnhout 2013.
- Marcel Otten, *Edda*, Ambo, Amsterdam 1994.
- Simo Parpola, *The Assyrian Tree of Life: Tracing the Origins of Jewish Monotheism and Greek Philosophy*, in Journal of Near Eastern Studies, vol.52 no.3 pp.161-208, The University of Chicago Press, Chicago 1993.

- Stephen Pollington, *The Mead Hall*, Anglo-Saxon Books, Hockwold-cum-Wilton 2003.
- Arthur E. Powell, *The Solar System*, The Theosophical Publishing House, London 1930.
- George E.J. Powell & Eiríkur Magnússon, *Icelandic Legends*, London 1866.
- B. Raptschinsky, *Russische Heldensagen en Legenden*, W.J. Thieme & Cie., Zutphen 1924.
- Graham Robb, *The Ancient Paths, Discovering the Lost Map of Celtic Europe*, Pan Macmillan, 2013.
- Rudolf Simek, *Dictionary of Northern Mythology*, D.S. Brewer, Cambridge 1993.
- Gro Steinsland, *Det Hellige Bryllup og Norrøn Kongeideologi*, Solum Forlag, Larvik 1991.
- Elsa-Brita Titchenell, *The Masks of Odin*, Theosophical University Press, Pasadena 1998.
- Gabriel Turville-Petre, *Myth and Religion of the North*, Holt, Rinehart & Winston, New York 1964.
- Herman Vanstiphout, *Het epos van Gilgameš*, Roularta Books, Roeselare 2002.
- Felice Vinci, *The Baltic Origins of Homer's Epic Tales*, Inner Traditions, Vermont 2006
- Alice Woutersen-van Weerden, *Tussen Wodan en Widar*, Uitgeverij Vrij Geestesleven, Zeist 1997.

Afterword

Divine love and wisdom take innumerable forms. A religious fact I am deeply aware of as a (Gnostic) priest of the Goddess Nerthus, and partially explaining the resurgence of Northern Mysteries within twenty first century Britain. After all, the relentless pressures generated by a global market seem to demand both a re-examination of our essential values, as well as a necessary recovery of perennialist inquiry. In other words, a reactivation of Traditionalism at its Heathen best.

Yet, this type of Asatru revival in itself begs unprecedented questions. Why not, for example, simply embrace Christianity once again? Indeed, should one not return to the spiritual customs of our recent kindred? Attempting, perhaps, to recapture their sense of communal stability? However, even a cursory investigation of these conjectures quickly produces a feeling that something is badly wrong. A disjunction associated with organized Christendom that demands we retrace our steps back to where this ethical error occurred. To the exact point wherein our tribal confusions started. Exacerbated, as they were, by this doctrinaire foreign faith as it repudiated inherited Norse lore. With all due respect to other Pagan paths, our ageless (earth-based) metaphysic alone goes back into the hallowed mists of antiquity. Founding, as it did, the basic structures of society as they were lived by our forebears. Nowadays, this noted, although only the barest fragments of our ancestral conventions endure, they nevertheless continue to impress our collective psyche - through place-names, historic villages, ancient monuments, half-forgotten shrines, folklore, rural lifestyles, and enduring socio-biological "echoes".

As such, I find Ludwig Wittgenstein (1889-1951) of the utmost importance to Asatru. At the end of the day, any man who can write "Not how the world is, is the mystical, but that it is" seems to be a nascent Heathen. Certainly, Wittgenstein appears to have put his finger on the underlying pulse of spiritual experience: along with its area of origin.

Of course, Wittgenstein never committed himself to any formal religious tradition. Allied to that, his countless remarks on morality suggest a "conservative" nature – despite being at ease with radical, dynamic - not to mention evocative - expositions of "right-minded" human interaction. A stance, or attitude, that runs as a theme throughout his writings on ethics and religion. An outlook, dare one say, upholding the paramount importance of goodness, meaning, and value in one's affairs, even though in the final analysis they are beyond our human sphere. For Wittgenstein, living in a "pure" way involves an acceptance of our rapport with the World: or God's will, or Life, or Fate. Insisting, as he consistently does, that anyone who lives this way must come to see our Earth as a miracle. So, answering those who seek a solution to the so-called "problem of life", Wittgenstein replies resolution dawns with the disappearance of the issue. Itself, by origin, a mistaken mental concoction. All giving proponents of the view that Wittgenstein openly advocated mystical truths (that, confessedly, cannot be expressed by any usual means) - a firm foundation upon which to stand their ground.

Plainly, there is little to say about such an attitude short of commending it, while admitting, unfortunately, that in a world of contingency one cannot demonstrate any position as the correct one to take. Superficially, this sounds like relativism, although it must be recalled, relativism is just one more viewpoint: albeit one without accumulated wisdom, or a rich tradition, to support it. Undeniably, our contemporary crude relativism - succinctly phrased as the universal judgement that one cannot make universal judgements ... is self-contradictory. Whether Wittgenstein's opinions suggest a more sophisticated form of relativism is another matter: notwithstanding the spirit of relativism seeming very far from his inbuilt conservatism; coupled with Wittgenstein's absolute intolerance towards his own moral shortcomings. Compare, as a case in point, so-called contemporary "tolerance", or worded differently, the thinly disguised "anything goes" attitude that apparently motivates relativism with Wittgenstein's declaration to Bertrand Russell (1872-1970), that he would prefer "by far" an "organization dedicated to war and slavery to one committed to peace and freedom". A comment, obviously, which should not be taken literally, but rather revealing a number of stark truths regarding liberal modernity. From his side, Wittgenstein was no warmonger and even advocated letting oneself be massacred instead of taking part in hand-to-hand combat. Nevertheless, it was the complacency, or more likely the unadulterated self-righteousness, of Russell's "liberal" cause that Wittgenstein objected to with such passion.

With regard to Heathenry, I continually find that my personal gratitude to Wittgenstein's inspirational writings can never be repaid. Intellectually, he set me free to explore my native Tradition: or at least the remnants of it, following centuries of Christian dogmatism. Moreover, my own opposition to interpretations of religion that emphasize doctrine or philosophical arguments, at the expense of archetypal religious rituals and elative symbols, evolved directly from Wittgenstein's corpus. It comes back to mind, fascinatingly, that he likened the ritual of religion to a great gesture, as when one kisses a photograph. An action of this type is by no means trivial, nor is it based on the false faith that the person in the photograph will feel the kiss, let alone return it, or for that matter become grounded in any other adjacent viewpoint. It is what it is! Nothing more, but manifestly nothing less. Neither is such a kiss simply a substitute for a heartfelt phrase, like "I love you." Contrarily, this kiss is akin to religious activity in expressing a fundamental stance: an attitude wherein no substitute would suffice. All gifting me with clues relating to our native Goddesses and Gods. An intellectual intimation that Asatru will never yield to the type of deconstructive processes interpreting these indigenous Divinities as mere personifications, historical confusions, or the projected hopes of suppressed workers. No, by divergence, Wittgenstein's latter masterwork (Philosophical Investigations), whispers in my ears that somewhere, just somewhere, between the raw, primitive, spiritually energised, potent, and ragged antecedents of Myth and Hieroglyph, they eternally hold Court. That our sacred British Traditions arose from the living environment around us and openly await our return to the true faith of these abiding lands. Our Heathen theologies, when all said and done, developed from rituals linked with the rocks and trees of Albion, not from alien and abstract words and pictures. Our Heathen ceremonies honouring the fertile soils we stand on as a meeting place for real religious pilgrims - not far away locations made holy by their distance. In which case, the language-games we play defiantly acknowledge these analyses, while grasping those Inscrutable Sources continually bringing them forth. Putting us in a robust and sturdy position to recover our tribal treasures.

Hence, avant-garde Skalds like Vincent Ongkowidjojo feel the time has come to climb Heimdall's esoteric Bridge anew by reinvestigating poetic fable, diverse occult authors, runic meditation, galdr singing, and the entire Western philosophical enterprise, in order to shed a rainbow light on long lost sorcerous sciences. Overall, an audacious undertaking even though one pursued with equal precision and flair. Undoubtedly, therefore, his excellent book *Doors of Valhalla: An Esoteric Interpretation of Norse Mythology* demands our attention, while clearly setting fresh standards for this sort of scholarship. All allowing me, in turn, to say I wholeheartedly recommend this book to the Pagan community at large, and at the same time fully endorse Vincent's groundbreaking explorations in rarefied fields of human spirituality.

© David Parry
London 2016

VOLUSPA

1.
Hljóðs bið ek allar helgar kindir,

meiri ok minni mögu Heimdallar.

Viltu at ek, Valföðr, vel fyr telja

forn spjöll fira, þau er fremst um man.

2.
Ek man jötna ár um borna,

þá er forðum mik fædda höfðu.
Níu man ek heima, níu íviðjur,

mjötvið mæran fyr mold neðan.

3.
Ár var alda, þar er ymir bygði,

var-a sandr né sær né svalar unnir;

jörð fannsk æva né upphiminn,

gap var ginnunga en gras hvergi.

4.
Áðr Burs synir bjöðum um ypptu,

þeir er Miðgarð mæran skópu;
sól skein sunnan á salar steina,

þá var grund gróin grænum lauki.

1.
Hearing I bid from all the holy kin,
The greater and lesser families of Heimdal.
You, Father of the Slain, want that I tell well
Of the ancient stories of the world, those I first remember

2.
I remember Jotun giants born of yore
Who furthered me, fed my head
Nine worlds I remember, nine Ividjur,
The famed Mjotvid, beneath the earth

3.
In ages of yore when Ymir settled there was
No sand nor sea nor the cold waves
Jord was not found yet nor the raised heaven
The gap was full of Ginn, but grass nowhere

4.
Soon the sons of Bur lifted the bottom
They shaped the famous Midgard
Sól shone from the south on halls of stone
Then there was the ground grown with green leek

5.
Sól varp sunnan, sinni mána,

hendi inni hægri um himinjöður;

sól þat né vissi hvar hon sali átti,

stjörnur þat né vissu hvar þær staði áttu.
máni þat né vissi hvat hann megins átti

6.
Þá gengu regin öll á rökstóla,

ginnheilög goð, ok um þat gættusk;
nótt ok niðjum nöfn um gáfu,

morgin hétu ok miðjan dag,

undorn ok aftan, árum at telja.

7.
Hittusk æsir á Iðavelli,

þeir er hörg ok hof hátimbruðu;

afla lögðu, auð smíðuðu,
tangir skópu ok tól gerðu.

8.
Tefldu í túni, teitir váru,

var þeim vettergis vant ór gulli,

uns þrjár kvámu þursa meyjar

ámáttkar mjök ór Jötunheimum.

5.
From the south Sól, in the company of Máni, cast
Her dexterous hand about the edge of heaven.
Sól did not know where she had her hall.
The stars did not know where they had their positions.
Máni did not know what might he had.

6.
Then all the Regin went to the Seats of Destiny
The Ginn-Holy gods, and over this deliberated:
Nótt and the new moon they gave names
They named the morning and the middle of the day,
Tea and evening, to count the years.

7.
The Aesir gathered together on the Idavoll Plain.
They wrought altar and temple, built high.
Hearths they laid, forged riches,
Shaped tongs and made tools.

8.
They played *tafl* in the garden and were happy
There was for them no want for gold
Until three came, the daughters of Thurses,
Very much mighty, from Jotunheim

9.
Þá gengu regin öll á rökstóla,

ginnheilög goð, ok um þat gættusk,
hver skyldi dverga dróttir skepja

ór Brimis blóði ok ór Bláins leggjum.

10.
Þar var Móðsognir mæztr um orðinn
dverga allra, en Durinn annarr;

þeir mannlíkun mörg um gerðu

dvergar ór jörðu, sem Durinn sagði.

11.
Nýi, Niði, Norðri, Suðri,
Austri, Vestri, Alþjófr, Dvalinn,
Bívurr, Bávurr, Bömburr, Nóri,
Án ok Ánarr, Ái, Mjöðvitnir.

12.
Veigr ok Gandálfr, Vindálfr, Þráinn,
Þekkr ok Þorinn, Þrór, Vitr ok Litr
Nár ok Nýráðr, nú hefi ek dverga,

Reginn ok Ráðsviðr, rétt um talda.

13.
Fíli, Kíli, Fundinn, Náli,
Hefti, Víli, Hannar, Svíurr,
Frár, Hornbori, Frægr ok Lóni,

9.
Then all the Regin went to the Seats of Destiny
The Ginn-Holy gods, and over this deliberated:
Who would shape the leader of the dwarves
From Brimir's blood and Blain's legs?

10.
There was Modsognir. He became a master
Of all the dwarves, but Durin was second.
They shaped many in the likeness of man,
Dwarves out of Jord. The same as Durin said:

11.
Nyi, Nidi, Nordri, Sudri
Austri, Vestri, Althjof, Dvalin
Bivur, Bavur, Bombur, Nori
An and Anar, Ai, Mjodvitnir

12.
Veig and Gandalf, Vindalf, Thrain
Thekk and Thorin, Thror, Vit and Lit
Nar and Nyrad. Now have I the dwarves,
Regin and Radsvid, rightly counted.

13.
Fili, Kili, Fundin, Nali
Hefti, Vili, Hannar, Sviur
Frar, Hornbori, Fraeg and Loni

Aurvangr, Jari, Eikinskjaldi.

Aurvang, Jari, Eikinskjaldi

14.
Mál er dverga í Dvalins liði

ljóna kindum til Lofars telja,

þeir er sóttu frá salar steini

Aurvanga sjöt til Jöruvalla.

14.
I speak of the dwarves in Dvalin's host
To human kind, counting up to Lofar.
They sought, away from the halls of stone,
Aurvang's settlers, Joruvellir.

15.
Þar var Draupnir ok Dolgþrasir,

Hár, Haugspori, Hlévangr, Glói, Skirvir, Virfir, Skáfiðr, Ái.

15.
There was Draupnir and Dolgthrasir
Har, Haugspori, Hlevang, Gloi Skirvir, Virfir, Skafid, Ai

16.
Álfr ok Yngvi, Eikinskjaldi,
Fjalarr ok Frosti, Finnr ok Ginnarr;
þat mun æ uppi meðan öld lifir,
langniðja tal Lofars hafat.

16.
Alf and Yngvi, Eikinskjaldi
Fjalar and Frosti, Finn and Ginnar

This will, while people live above,
Have been the descendants counted up to Lofar

17.
Unz þrír kvámu ór því liði
öflgir ok ástkir æsir at húsi,

fundu á landi lítt megandi

Ask ok Emblu örlöglausa.

17.
Until three came from that host,
Strong and affectionate, Aesir, to a house.
They found on the land with little main
Ask and Embla without Orlog.

18.
Önd þau né áttu, óð þau né höfðu,
lá né læti né litu góða;

önd gaf Óðinn, óð gaf Hænir,

18.
Breath they owned not. Mind they had not;
Vitality nor personality nor a good hue.
Breath gave Odin. Mind gave Hoenir.

lá gaf Lóðurr ok litu góða.	Vitality gave Lodur and a good hue.

19.
Ask veit ek standa, heitir Yggdrasill,
hár batmr, ausinn hvíta auri;
þaðan koma döggvar þærs í dala falla,
stendur æ yfir grænn Urðarbrunni.

19.
I know where Ask stands. He is called Yggdrasil.
High tree. Sprinkled with white mud.
Thence comes the dew which runs in the valleys.
Stands ever over the green Well of Urd.

20.
Þaðan koma meyjar margs vitandi
þrjár ór þeim sæ, er und þolli stendr;
Urð hétu eina, aðra Verðandi,
- skáru á skíði,- Skuld ina þriðju.
Þær lög lögðu, þær líf kuru
alda börnum, örlög seggja.

20.
Thence come the maidens, conscious of many things
Three, out of this sea which stands under the thole
Urd is called one, the other Verdandi.
They score the wood. Skuld is the third.
They laid down the laws. They chose the lives
Of the children of the Age, said Orlog.

21.
Þat man hon fólkvíg fyrst í heimi,
er Gullveigu geirum studdu
ok í höll Hárs hana brenndu,
þrisvar brenndu, þrisvar borna,
oft, ósjaldan; þó hon enn lifir.

21.
This she remembers: the first folk fight in the world,
When they steadied Gullveig with spears
And in the hall of Havi burnt her.
Three times burnt her. Three times she was born,
Often, not seldom, though she still lives.

22.
Heiði hana hétu hvars til húsa kom,

22.
Heidi she is called. Wherever she comes to a house,

völu velspáa, vitti hon ganda;

seið hon, hvars hon kunni, seið hon leikinn,
æ var hon angan illrar brúðar.

Of the well done Volva visions, she charms the artifacts.

Sorcery she can. She charmed the possessed.
Aye she was the perfume of evil brides.

23.
Þá gengu regin öll á rökstóla,

ginnheilög goð, ok um þat gættusk
hvárt skyldu æsir afráð gjalda

eða skyldu goðin öll gildi eiga.

23.
Then all the Regin went to the Seats of Destiny

The Ginn-Holy gods, and over this deliberated:
Whether the Aesir should pay the tribute,

Or should all of the gods own the payment of debt?

24.
Fleygði Óðinn ok í folk um skaut,

þat var enn folkvíg fyrst í heimi;

brotinn var borðveggr borgar ása,

knáttu vanir vígspá völlu sporna.

24.
Flung Odin (his spear) and in battle shot about.

That was the first folk fight in the world.

Broken was the plank-wall of the fortress of the Aesir.

The Vanir knew how to trample the fight vision of the field.

25.
Þá gengu regin öll á rökstóla,

ginnheilög goð, ok um þat gættusk
hverjir hefði loft allt lævi blandit

eða ætt jötuns Óðs mey gefna.

25.
Then all the Regin went to the Seats of Destiny

The Ginn-Holy gods, and over this deliberated:
Who had all the air with treason blended?

Or to the Jotun tribe had Od's girl given?

26.
Þórr einn þar vá þrunginn móði,

26.
Thor alone fought there, in a pressing mood.

hann sjaldan sitr - er hann slíkt um fregn.	He seldom sits, when he is informed of such things.
Á gengusk eiðar, orð ok særi,	To and fro went oaths, words and swearing.
mál öll meginlig er á meðal fóru.	Speech all mainly middling fared.

27.	27.
Veit hon Heimdallar hljóð um folgit	She knows Heimdal's hearing to be hidden
und heiðvönum helgum baðmi;	Under the bright wonted holy beam
á sér hon ausask aurgum fossi	Water she sees sprinkling from the clay waterfall
af veði Valföðrs . Vituð ér enn - eða hvat?	From Slain-Father's wage. Do you know yet, or what?

28.	28.
Ein sat hon úti þá er inn aldni kom	Alone she sat outside. Then that Old One came,
yggjungr ása ok í augu leit:	The Terrible One of the Aesir, and seeks the eye.
Hvers fregnið mik? Hví freistið mín?	"What do you ask of me? Why do you challenge me?"
Allt veit ek, Óðinn, hvar þú auga falt,	I know everything, Odin, about where your eye is hidden
í inum mæra Mímisbrunni.	In that famous Well of Mimir
Drekkr mjöð Mímir morgun hverjan	Mimir drinks mead every morning
af veði Valföðrs . Vituð ér enn - eða hvat?	From the Slain-Father's wage. Do you know yet, or what?

29.	29.
Valði henni Herföðr hringa ok men,	Host-Father chose for her rings and necklaces
fekk spjöll spaklig ok spá ganda,	He caught my stoic spells and vision artifacts
sá hon vítt ok um vítt of veröld hverja.	She saw wide and wide about in every world

30.	30.
Sá hon valkyrjur vítt um komnar,	She saw Valkyries come from

görvar at ríða til Goðþjóðar;
Skuld helt skildi, en Skögul önnur,

Gunnr, Hildr, Göndul ok Geirskögul.
Nú eru taldar nönnur Herjans,

görvar at ríða grund valkyrjur.

wide away
Ready to ride to the god people
Skuld held the shield, but Skogul is the other

Gunn, Hild, Gondul and Geirskogul
Now are counted the Nannas of Herjan

Ready to ride over the earth the Valkyries are

31.
Ek sá Baldri, blóðgum tívur,

Óðins barni, örlög fólgin;
stóð um vaxinn völlum hæri
mjór ok mjög fagr mistilteinn.

31.
I saw Balder's, the bloody war god,

Odin's child, Orlog hidden
It stood waxed higher on the field
Slim and very fair, the mistletoe.

32.
Varð af þeim meiði, er mær sýndisk,
harmflaug hættlig, Höðr nam skjóta.
Baldrs bróðir var of borinn snemma,
sá nam Óðins sonr einnættr vega.

32.
That beam became, which seemed slim,
A harm-flight, dangerous. Hoder took to shooting.
Balder's brother was quickly born.
He, Odin's son, one night, took to fighting.

33.
Þó hann æva hendr né höfuð kembði,
áðr á bál um bar Baldrs andskota;

en Frigg um grét í Fensölum
vá Valhallar. Vituð ér enn - eða hvat?

33.
Though he never (washed) hands nor head combed
Soon to the pyre he bore Balder's adversary
But Frigg grieved in Fensalir,
The woe of Valhalla. Do you know yet, or what?

34.
Haft sá hon liggja undir Hveralundi,

34.
A bound one she saw lying under Hveralund,

lægjarns líki Loka áþekkjan.
Þar sitr Sigyn þeygi um sínum

ver vel glýjuð. Vituð ér enn - eða hvat?

35.
Á fellur austan um eitrdala

söxum ok sverðum, Slíðr heitir sú.

36.
Stóð fyr norðan á Niðavöllum
salr ór gulli Sindra ættar;

en annarr stóð á Ókólni
bjórsalr jötuns, en sá Brimir heitir.

37.
Sal sá hon standa sólu fjarri

Náströndu á, norðr horfa dyrr.
Falla eitrdropar inn um ljóra,

sá er undinn salr orma hryggjum.

38.
Sá hon þar vaða þunga strauma

menn meinsvara ok morðvarga

ok þann er annars glepr eyrarúnu.

Þar saug Niðhöggr nái framgengna,
sleit vargr vera. Vituð ér enn - eða hvat?

Treason hungry, Loki's body alike.
There sits Sigyn, though not about her

Husband very happy. Do you know yet, or what?

35.
A river runs from the East about the poison valleys
Of knives and swords. Slid is called this one.

36.
At the North stood on Nidavöll
A hall of gold of the family of Sindri

But another stood at Okolnir
The beer hall of a Jotun, but he is called Brimir

37.
A hall she sees standing further from Sól

At Nastrand, north faces the door
Drops of poison run in from the vent

The hall is wound with snake spines

38.
There she sees wade through heavy streams

Men of oath breaking and murdering Varg wolves

And those who others confuse with ear-secrets

There Nidhogg sucks corpses of those who passed away
The Varg wolf slits men. Do you know yet, or what?

39.
Austr sat in aldna í Járnviði

ok fæddi þar Fenris kindir.
Verðr af þeim öllum einna nokkurr
tungls tjúgari í trölls hami.

39.
In the East sat that old one from Jarnvid Wood
And fed Fenrir's kind there
Of them all, one will become someone
He will pierce the moon in troll shape

40.
Fyllisk fjörvi feigra manna,

rýðr ragna sjöt rauðum dreyra.

Svört verða sólskin um sumur eftir,
veðr öll válynd. Vituð ér enn - eða hvat?

40.
He fills himself with the lives of fey men
Reddens the Regin host with red blood
Black becomes the sunshine (Sól) in the summers after
The weather is all woe-tempered. Do you know yet, or what?

41.
Sat þar á haugi ok sló hörpu

gýgjar hirðir, glaðr Eggþér;
gól um honum í galgviði

fagrrauður hani, sá er Fjalar heitir.

41.
There sat on a mound and struck the harp
A Gygja shepherd, glad Eggther.
Sung to him from the gallow's wood
A fair red rooster, which is called Fjalar.

42.
Gól um ásum Gullinkambi,

sá vekr hölða at Herjaföðrs;

en annarr gelr fyr jörð neðan
sótrauðr hani at sölum Heljar.

42.
Sang among the Aesir, Gullinkambi,
He wakes the heroes, at Host-Father's
Another sings beneath Jord
A soot red rooster in the halls of Hel

43.
Geyr nú Garmr mjök fyr Gnipahelli,

43.
Now Garm barks much in front of Gnipahellir

festr mun slitna en freki renna.

Fjölð veit hon fræða, fram sé ek lengra
um ragna rök römm sigtíva.

The leash shall be slit, but Freki will run

A lot of lore she knows – I see from a long way off
Bitter Ragnarok of the war gods of victory.

44.
Bræðr munu berjask ok at bönum verðask,
munu systrungar sifjum spilla;
hart er í heimi, hórdómr mikill,

skeggöld, skálmöld, skildir ro klofnir,
vindöld, vargöld, áðr veröld steypisk,
mun engi maðr öðrum þyrma.

44.
Brothers will beat each other and become each other's slayer
Sisters shall spoil their siblings.
Hard it is in the world, much whoredom.

An Age of Axes, an age of short swords, shields are cloven.
An Age of Wind, an Age of Varg Wolves, ere the world stoops
Shall no man the other respect.

45.
Leika Míms synir, en mjötuðr kyndisk
at inu galla Gjallarhorni.
Hátt blæss Heimdallr, horn er á lofti,
mælir Óðinn við Míms höfuð.
ymr it aldna tré, en jötunn losnar.

Skelfr Yggdrasils askr standandi

45.
Mim's sons lick while Mjotud is kindled
At the call of Gjallarhorn
High blows Heimdal, the horn aloft
Odin speaks with Mim's head.
The old tree howls, but the Jotun giant gets loose
The trembling ash Yggdrasil is standing.

46.
Geyr nú Garmr mjök fyr Gnipahelli,
festr mun slitna en freki renna.

Fjölð veit ek fræða, fram sé ek lengra
um ragna rök römm sigtíva.

46.
Now Garm barks much in front of Gnipahellir
The leash shall be slit but Freki will run

A lot of lore I know – I see from a long way off
Bitter Ragnarok of the war gods of victory.

47.
Hrymr ekr austan, hefisk lind fyrir,
snýsk Jörmungandr í jötunmóði.

Ormr knýr unnir, en ari hlakkar,

slítr nái nef fölr, Naglfar losnar.

48.
Kjóll ferr austan, koma munu Múspells
um lög lýðir, en Loki stýrir.

Fara fíflmegir með freka allir,

þeim er bróðir Býleists í för.

49.
Hvat er með ásum? Hvat er með álfum?
Gnýr allur Jötunheimr, æsir ro á þingi,
stynja dvergar fyr steindurum,

veggbergs vísir. Vituð ér enn - eða hvat?

50.
Surtr ferr sunnan með sviga lævi,

skínn af sverði sól valtíva,

grjótbjörg gnata, en gífr rata,
troða halir helveg en himinn klofnar.

47.
Hrym drives from the east, bears the linden (shield) in front
Jormungand coils in a Jotun mood

The snake knocks the waves, but the eagle screeches
The pale beak slits corpses. Naglfar gets loose.

48.
A keel fares from the east. Of Muspell shall come
Over the sea his people. But Loki steers.
All the kin of monsters fare with Freki
The brother of Byleist is with them on the journey

49.
What's with the Aesir? What's with the Elves?
All Jotunheim resounds. The Aesir are at Thing.
The dwarves groan before their stone doors,
Guides of the rock wall. Do you know yet, or what?

50.
Surt fares from the south with the treason of the bough
Sól of the slain war gods shines from the sword
Gravel grinds but fiends reel
The heroes tread the way of Hel but heaven is cloven

51.
Þá kemr Hlínar harmr annarr fram,
er Óðinn ferr við úlf vega,

en bani Belja bjartr at Surti;

þá mun Friggjar falla angan.

51.
Then appears to Hlin another harm
When Odin fares to fight with the wolf

But the bane of Beli (fights) against bright Surt

Then shall Frigg's sweetheart fall

52.
Þá kemr inn mikli mögr Sigföður,

Víðarr, vega at valdýri.

Lætr hann megi Hveðrungs mundum standa
hjör til hjarta, þá er hefnt föður.

52.
Then comes the powerful kin of Victory-Father,

Vidar, to fight against the beast of death

He stands with his hands the kin of Hvedrung
The sword into the heart. Then he avenged the Father.

53.
Þá kemr inn mæri mögr Hlóðynjar,
gengr Óðins sonr við orm vega,

drepr af móði Miðgarðs véurr,

munu halir allir heimstöð ryðja;

gengr fet níu Fjörgynjar burr
neppr frá naðri níðs ókvíðnum.

53.
Then comes the famous kin of Hlodyn
Odin's son goes to fight with the snake

He hits in a mood, Midgard's templar

All the heroes will clear their home stead

He goes nine feet, Fjörgyn's child, Chilled from the viper, by humility unconcerned

54.
Sól tér sortna, sígr fold í mar,

hverfa af himni heiðar stjörnur.
Geisar eimi ok aldrnara,

leikr hár hiti við himin sjálfan.

54.
Sól looks like turning black. The field sinks into the sea.

Clear stars are cast from heaven
Smoke and life's sustenance (fire) chafe.

The heat licks high against heaven itself

55.
Geyr nú Garmr mjök fyr Gnipahelli,
festr mun slitna en freki renna,

fjölð veit ek fræða fram sé ek lengra
um ragna rök römm sigtíva

56.
Sér hon upp koma öðru sinni
jörð ór ægi iðjagræna.
Falla fossar, flýgr örn yfir,

sá er á fjalli fiska veiðir.

57.
Finnask æsir á Iðavelli

ok um moldþinur máttkan dæma

ok minnask þar á megindóma

ok á Fimbultýs fornar rúnir.

58.
Þar munu eftir undursamligar

gullnar töflur í grasi finnask,

þærs í árdaga áttar höfðu.

59.
Munu ósánir akrar vaxa,
böls mun alls batna, Baldr mun koma,
búa þeir Höðr ok Baldr Hrofts

55.
Now Garm barks much in front of Gnipahellir
The leash shall be slit but Freki will run

A lot of lore I know – I see from a long way off
Bitter Ragnarok of the war gods of victory.

56.
She sees come up a second time
Jord out of Aegir, very green.
The waterfalls run. The eagle flies over it,
Who catches fish at the fell.

57.
The Aesir gather together at Idavoll Plain

And about the mighty earth-hoop they deem

And they each remember the mighty doom there

And the ancient runes of Fimbultyr.

58.
There shall afterwards the wondrous

Gold *tafl* pieces be found in the grass

Those of the clan they had in the early days

59.
Unsown the acres will wax
All misfortune will get better.
Balder will come
They dwell, Hoder and Balder, in

sigtóftir
vé valtívar. Vituð ér enn - eða hvat?

60.
Þá kná Hænir hlautvið kjósa

ok burir byggja bræðra tveggja

vindheim víðan. Vituð ér enn - eða hvat?

61.
Sal sér hon standa sólu fegra,

gulli þakðan á Gimléi.
Þar skulu dyggvar dróttir byggja

ok um aldrdaga yndis njóta.

62.
Þar kemr inn dimmi dreki fljúgandi,
naðr fránn, neðan frá Niðafjöllum;
berr sér í fjöðrum, - flýgr völl yfir, -
Niðhöggr nái. Nú mun hon sökkvask.

Hropt's Sigtoftir
The sacred space of the slain war gods. Do you know yet, or what?

60.
Then Hoenir knows how to choose the lot-wood
And the sons settle, the two brothers,
In wide Vindheim. Do you know yet, or what?

61.
A hall she sees stand, fairer than Sól
Gold roofed at Gimlé
There the doughty lords shall settle
And make use of joy for all days.

62.
There comes the dim dragon a-flying,
The glistening viper, from beneath Nidafjöll.
He bears in his feathers – he flies over the planes –
Corpses, Nidhogg does. Now will she sink back.

LOKASENNA

Loki kvaddi hann:
1.
"Segðu þat, Eldir, svá at þú einugi

feti gangir framar,
hvat hér inni hafa at ölmálum

sigtíva synir."

Eldir kvað:
2.
"Of vápn sín dæma ok um vígrisni sína
sigtíva synir;
ása ok alfa er hér inni eru,

manngi er þér í orði vinr."

Loki kvað:
3.
"Inn skal ganga Ægis hallir í
á þat sumbl at sjá;
jöll ok áfu færi ek ása sonum,

ok blend ek þeim svá meini mjöð."

Eldir kvað:
4.
"Veiztu, ef þú inn gengr Ægis hallir í
á þat sumbl at sjá,
hrópi ok rógi ef þú eyss á holl regin,
á þér munu þau þerra þat."

Loki said to him:
1.
"Tell me this, Eldir, before you go one more
Foot from here
What kind of beer-speech have here
The sons of the gods of victory?"

Eldir said:
2.
"Of their weapons they deem and about their feats of arms
The sons of the gods of victory,
Of Aesir and Alfar, who are in here,
No-one has for you a friendly word."

Loki said:
3.
"I shall go in into Aegir's halls
To see that symbel
Beer and milk I bring to the sons of the Aesir
And so blend harm with their mead."

Eldir said:
4.
"You know, if you enter Aegir's halls
To see that symbel
If with noise and insult you sprinkle the Regin in the hall,
Then at you will it be wiped."

Loki kvað:
5.
"Veiztu þat, Eldir, ef vit einir skulum
sáryrðum sakask,
auðigr verða mun ek í andsvörum,
ef þú mælir til margt."

Loki kvað:
6.
"Þyrstr ek kom þessar hallar til,
Loftr, um langan veg
ásu at biðja, at mér einn gefi
mæran drykk mjaðar.

7.
Hví þegið ér svá, þrungin goð,

at þér mæla né meguð?
Sessa ok staði velið mér sumbli at

eða heitið mik heðan."

Bragi kvað:
8.
"Sessa ok staði velja þér sumbli at
æsir aldregi,

því at æsir vitu, hveim þeir alda skulu
gambansumbl of geta."

Loki kvað:
9.
"Mantu þat, Óðinn, er vit í árdaga

blendum blóði saman?
Ölvi bergja lézktu eigi mundu,
nema okkr væri báðum borit."

Loki said:
5.
"You know, Eldir, if we one another shall
Hurt with sore words
Rich will I become in answers
If you speak too much."

Loki said:
6.
"Thirsty I come to these halls
Loptr, from a long way away
The Aesir I bid to give me one
More drink of the mead.

7.
Why are you so silent, anxious gods?
That you might not speak?
A seat and a position choose for me at the symbel
Or tell me leave hence."

Bragi said:
8.
"Choose seat and position for you at the symbel
The Aesir will never
Because the Aesir know who of all people they should
Invite at the great symbel."

Loki said:
9.
"Do you remember this, Odin, that in the days of yore we
Blended our blood together
Beer would you not taste
Unless to us both it was born."

Óðinn kvað:
10.
"Rístu þá, Viðarr, ok lát ulfs föður

sitja sumbli at,
síðr oss Loki kveði lastastöfum

Ægis höllu í."

11.
"Heilir æsir, heilar ásynjur
ok öll ginnheilög goð –
nema sá einn áss er innar sitr,

Bragi, bekkjum á."

Bragi kvað:
12.
"Mar ok mæki gef ek þér míns féar,
ok bætir þér svá baugi Bragi,

síðr þú ásum öfund of gjaldir,
grem þú eigi goð at þér."

Loki kvað:
13.
"Jós ok armbauga mundu æ vera
beggja vanr, Bragi;
ása ok alfa, er hér inni eru,

þú ert við víg varastr

ok skjarrastr við skot."

Bragi kvað:
14.
"Veit ek, ef fyr útan værak, svá

Odin said:
10.
"Rise you then, Vidar, and let the Wolf's father
Sit at the symbel.
Lest to us, Loki, you utter your slander-staves

In Aegir's halls."

(Loki said)
11.
"Hail Aesir, hail Asynjur
And all the Ginn-Holy gods
Except this one of the Aesir, who sits in the centre,
Bragi, on the bench."

Bragi said:
12.
"A mare and a sword I give to you, my riches,
And I compensate you, thus Bragi's oath-ring

Lest you pay the Aesir envy
The anger of the gods you call on you."

Loki said:
13.
"Horse and arm-ring will ever
Both be a want, Bragi.
Of the Aesir and Alfar, who are in here,
You are with fighting the most wary
And the most shy with shooting."

Bragi said:
14.
"I know, if I was outside, just like

sem fyr innan emk,
Ægis höll of kominn,
höfuð þitt bæra ek í hendi mér;

lykak þér þat fyr lygi."

Loki kvað:
15.
"Snjallr ertu í sessi, skal-at-tu svá gera,
Bragi bekkskrautuðr;
vega þú gakk, ef þú vreiðr séir;
hyggsk vætr hvatr fyrir."

Iðunn kvað:
16.
"Bið ek þik, Bragi, barna sifjar duga
ok allra óskmaga,
at þú Loka kveðir-a lastastöfum

Ægis höllu í."

Loki kvað:
17.
"Þegi þú, Iðunn, þik kveð ek allra kvenna
vergjarnasta vera,
síztu arma þína lagðir ítrþvegna

um þinn bróðurbana."

Iðunn kvað:
18.
"Loka ek kveðk-a lastastöfum
Ægis höllu í:
Braga ek kyrri bjórreifan;
vilk-at ek, at it vreiðir vegizk."

I am now inside
Having come to Aegir's halls
Your head I would bear in my hands
I would lock you for your lies."

Loki said:
15.
"Quick you are in the seat, (but) you shall not do so,
Bragi, bragger of the bench.
Go fighting, if you are so wroth.
The bold minds naught in advance."

Idun said:
16.
"I bid you, Bragi, help the children of our tribe (Sif)
And all our adopted kin.
That you not utter slander-staves at Loki
In Aegir's halls."

Loki said:
17.
"Shut up, Idun, you, I say, of all women
Yearn most after men.
Back then you laid your arms, white-washed,
About your brother's bane."

Idun said:
18.
"At Loki I utter no slander-staves
In Aegir's halls
Bragi I calm, beer-happy
I can't have it that you two fight wroth."

Gefjun kvað:
19.
"Hví it æsir tveir skuluð inni hér
sáryrðum sakask?
Loftki þat veit, at hann leikinn er

ok hann fjörg öll fía."

Loki kvað:
20.
"Þegi þú, Gefjun, þess mun ek nú geta,
er þik glapði at geði
sveinn inn hvíti, er þér sigli gaf

ok þú lagðir lær yfir."

Óðinn kvað:
21.
"Ærr ertu, Loki, ok örviti,

er þú fær þér Gefjun at gremi,

því at aldar örlög hygg ek, at hon öll of viti
jafngörla sem ek."

Loki kvað:
22.
"Þegi þú, Óðinn, þú kunnir aldregi
deila víg með verum;
oft þú gaft, þeim er þú gefa

skyldir-a, inum slævurum sigr."

Óðinn kvað:
23.
"Veiztu, ef ek gaf, þeim er ek gefa né skylda,

Gefjun said:
19.
"Why should two Aesir in here
Hurt each other with sore words?
Of Loptr it is known that he plays around
And he deeply hates all."

Loki said:
20.
"Shut up, Gefjun, this I will now get to:
Who fooled your mind?
That white boy, who gave you a trinket
And you laid your thigh on him."

Odin said:
21.
"Crazy are you, Loki, and out of your mind
That you bring on you Gefjun's anger
Because of people's Orlog, methinks, she knows all
Even quite the same as I."

Loki said:
22.
"Shut up, Odin, you could never

Deal a fight among men
Often you gave it to them who you should not give,
To those slow ones, victory."

Odin said:
23.
"You know, if I gave it to them who I should not give,

inum slævurum, sigr,	To those slow ones, victory.
átta vetr vartu fyr jörð neðan,	Eight winters you were beneath the earth (Jord)
kýr mólkandi ok kona,	A dairy cow and a woman
ok hefr þú þar börn borit,	And there you have born children
ok hugða ek þat args aðal."	And I think that is the mark of *ergi*."

Loki kvað:	Loki said:
24.	24.
"En þik síða kóðu Sámseyu í,	"But you witched, they say, on Samsø
ok draptu á vétt sem völur;	And beat the lid like a Volva
vitka líki fórtu verþjóð yfir,	A Vitki alike did you fare among the men folk
ok hugða ek þat args aðal."	And I think that is the mark of *ergi*."

Frigg kvað:	Frigg said:
25.	25.
"Örlögum ykkrum skylið aldregi	"Of your Orlog should you two never
segja seggjum frá,	Tell a poet
hvat it æsir tveir drýgðuð í árdaga;	What two Aesir committed in the days of yore
firrisk æ forn rök firar."	Shun ever that old destiny."

Loki kvað:	Loki said:
26.	26.
"Þegi þú, Frigg, þú ert Fjörgyns mær	"Shut up, Frigg, you are Fjorgyn's girl
ok hefr æ vergjörn verit,	And have ever been yearning after men
er þá Véa ok Vilja léztu þér, Viðris kvæn,	There was when you, the wife of Vidrir, let Vé and Vili
báða i baðm of tekit."	Both take you in your tree."

Frigg kvað:	Frigg said:
27.	27.
"Veiztu, ef ek inni ættak Ægis	"You know, if I had one in Aegir's

höllum i	halls
Baldri líkan bur,	A son like Balder
út þú né kvæmir frá ása sonum,	You would not come away with the sons of the Aesir
ok væri þá at þér vreiðum vegit."	And were he, he would fight you wroth"

Loki kvað:
28.
"Enn vill þú, Frigg, at ek fleiri telja
mína meinstafi:
ek því réð, er þú ríða sér-at

síðan Baldr at sölum."

Loki said:
28.
"But do you want, Frigg, that I tell more
Of my harm-staves?
That time I contrived that you would ride never to see
Balder at the halls."

Freyja kvað:
29.
"Ærr ertu, Loki, er þú yðra telr

ljóta leiðstafi;
örlög Frigg, hygg ek, at öll viti,
þótt hon sjalfgi segi."

Freyja said:
29.
"Crazy you are, Loki, that you tell yourself
Ugly suffer-staves:
Orlog Frigg, methinks, knows all
Though she says nothing herself."

Loki kvað:
30.
"Þegi þú, Freyja, þik kann ek fullgörva,
er-a þér vamma vant:
ása ok alfa, er hér inni eru,

hverr hefir þinn hór verit."

Loki said:
30.
"Shut up, Freyja, of you I know quite fully
That a flaw is not wanting
The Aesir and Alfar, who are in here,
To each you have been a whore."

Freyja kvað:
31.
"Flá er þér tunga, hygg ek, at þér fremr myni
ógótt of gala;
reiðir ro þér æsir ok ásynjur,

Freyja said:
31.
"Loose is your tongue, I think that for you it will
Sing no good
Wroth are with you the Aesir and Asynjur

hryggr muntu heim fara." | Rueful will you fare home."

Loki kvað:
32.
"Þegi þú, Freyja, þú ert fordæða

ok meini blandin mjök,
síz þik at bræðr þínum stóðu blíð regin
ok myndir þú þá, Freyja, frata."

Loki said:
32.
"Shut up, Freyja, you are a sorceress
And blend much harm
Since the gentle Regin caught you with your brother
And you would then, Freyja, fart."

Njörðr kvað:
33.
"Þat er válítit, þótt sér varðir

vers fái, hós eða hvárs;
hitt er undr, er áss ragr er hér inn of kominn
ok hefir sá börn of borit."

Njord said:
33.
"That is very little, though she is liable for
Catching a partner, here or there.
One among us is the god of *ergi*, he has come in here
And he has born children."

Loki kvað:
34.
"Þegi þú, Njörðr, þú vart austr heðan
gíls of sendr at goðum;
Hymis meyjar höfðu þik at hlandtrogi
ok þér í munn migu."

Loki said:
34.
"Shut up, Njord, you came here from the East
As a hostage sent to the gods
Hymir's girls use your head as a piss-trough
And pee in your mouth."

Njörðr kvað:
35.
"Sú erumk líkn, er ek vark langt heðan
gísl of sendr at goðum,
þá ek mög gat, þann er mangi fíár,

ok þykkir sá ása jaðarr."

Njord said:
35.
"For this I am soothed, who have long been hence
A hostage sent to the gods
Then I begot kin, who is hated by no-one
And is thought to be the best of the Aesir."

Loki kvað:
36.
"Hættu nú, Njörðr, haf þú á hófi þik,
munk-a ek því leyna lengr:
við systur þinni gaztu slíkan mög,
ok er-a þó vánu verr."

Týr kvað:
37.
"Freyr er beztr allra ballriða
ása görðum í;
mey hann né grætir né manns konu
ok leysir ór höftum hvern."

Loki kvað:
38.
"Þegi þú, Týr, þú kunnir aldregi
bera tilt með tveim;
handar innar hægri mun ek hinnar geta,
er þér sleit Fenrir frá."

Týr kvað:
39.
"Handar em ek vanr, en þú hróðrsvitnis,
böl er beggja þrá;
ulfgi hefir ok vel, er í böndum skal
bíða ragnarökrs."

Loki kvað:
40.
"Þegi þú, Týr, þat varð þinni

Loki said:
36.
"Cease now, Njord, know you your measure
I will conceal this no longer
With your sister did you beget such kin
And he is not yet the hoped man."

Tyr said:
37.
"Frey is the best of all the bold knights
In the gardens of the Aesir.
A girl he does not grieve nor a man's wife
And loosens everyone from cuffs."

Loki said:
38.
"Shut up, Tyr, you could never
Bring a charge between two.
That right hand, shall I get to that?
Which Fenrir slit off you?"

Tyr said:
39.
"A hand I am wanting but you Hrodvitnir
A misfortune it is to us both.
The Wolf has it no better, who shall in bonds
Bide till Ragnarok."

Loki said:
40.
"Shut up, Tyr, this becomes of

konu, at hon átti mög við mér; öln né penning hafðir þú þess aldregi vanréttis, vesall."	your wife That she owns kin with me Ell nor penny have you got for this Idle claim, poor one."
Freyr kvað: 41. "Ulfr sé ek liggja árósi fyrir, unz rjúfask regin; því mundu næst, nema þú nú þegir, bundinn, bölvasmiðr."	Frey said: 41. "The Wolf I see lying in front of the river mouth Until the Regin are annihilated. You will be next, unless you shut up, In bounds, Smith of Misfortune."
Loki kvað: 42. "Gulli keypta léztu Gymis dóttur ok seldir þitt svá sverð; en er Múspells synir ríða Myrkvið yfir, veizt-a þú þá, vesall, hvé þú vegr."	Loki said: 42. "With gold you bought Gymir's daughter And sold your sword But when the sons of Muspel ride through Myrkvid Wood You know not then, poor one, how to fight."
Byggvir kvað: 43. "Veiztu, ef ek eðli ættak sem Ingunar-Freyr ok svá sælligt setr, mergi smæra mölða ek þá meinkráku ok lemða alla í liðu."	Byggvir said: 43. "You know, if I had the same ancestry as Ingunar-Frey And so blessed a seat Then the marrow to butter I'd grind of that harm-crow And lame all his limbs."
Loki kvað: 44. "Hvat er þat it litla er ek þat löggra sék ok snapvíst snapir? At eyrum Freys mundu æ vera ok und kvernum klaka."	Loki said: 44. "What is this little thing which I see begging (like a dog) And snuffle for a crumb? At Frey's ears you will always be And twitter under the mill."

Byggvir kvað:
45.
"Byggvir ek heiti, en mik bráðan kveða
goð öll ok gumar;
því em ek hér hróðugr, at drekka Hrofts megir
allir öl saman."

Loki kvað:
46.
"Þegi þú, Byggvir, þú kunnir aldregi
deila með mönnum mat,
ok þik í flets strái finna né máttu,

þá er vágu verar."

Heimdallr kvað:
47.
"Ölr ertu, Loki, svá at þú ert örviti,
- hví né lezk-a-ðu, Loki? -
því at ofdrykkja veldr alda hveim,

er sína mælgi né man-at."

Loki kvað:
48.
"Þegi þú, Heimdallr, þér var í árdaga
it ljóta líf of lagit;
örgu baki þú munt æ vera
ok vaka vörðr goða."

Skaði kvað:
49.
"Létt er þér, Loki; mun-at-tu lengi

Byggvir said:
45.
"Byggvir I am called, but they call me impatient
All the gods and younglings do.
For this I am here praised, to drink with the kin of Hroptr
All together ale."

Loki said:
46.
"Shut up, Byggvir, you could never
Deal meat among men
And you in the flat's straw aren't found nor might they
When men are fighting."

Heimdal said:
47.
"Drunken are you, Loki, so that you are out of your mind
Why not let go, Loki?
Because too much drink will heat any
Who will not remember his babbling."

Loki said:
48.
"Shut up, Heimdal, on you was in the days of yore
An ugly life laid
With a wet back you will always be
And watch as the guardian of the gods."

Skadi said:
49.
"Light do you speak, Loki. You

svá
leika lausum hala,
því at þik á hjörvi skulu ins
hrímkalda magar
görnum binda goð."

Loki kvað:
50.
"Veiztu, ef mik á hjörvi skulu ins
hrímkalda magar
görnum binda goð,
fyrstr ok efstr var ek at fjörlagi,

þars vér á Þjaza þrifum."

Skaði kvað:
51.
"Veiztu, ef fyrstr ok efstr vartu at fjörlagi,
þá er ér á Þjaza þrifuð,
frá mínum véum ok vöngum skulu
þér æ köld ráð koma."

Loki kvað:
52.
"Léttari í málum vartu við
Laufeyjar son,
þá er þú létz mér á beð þinn
boðit;
getit verðr oss slíks, ef vér görva skulum
telja vömmin vár."

53.
"Heill ver þú nú, Loki, ok tak við
hrímkálki
fullum forns mjaðar,

will not long be thus
Playing loosely with your tail
Because you at a sword with the
rime-cold's kin's
Yarns the gods will bind."

Loki said:
50.
"You know, if me at a sword with
the rime-cold's kin's
Yarns the gods will bind,
Then I was the first and chief at
the homicide
There where we seized Thjazi."

Skadi said:
51.
"You know, if you were the first
and chief at the homicide
Then when you seized Thjazi,
Then from my sacred places and
my fields shall I
At you ever come with cold
plans."

Loki said:
52.
"Lighter in speech you were with
Laufey's son
When you summoned me to your
bed
You get us such to happen, if we
shall quite
Tell our flaws."

(Sif said)
53.
"We hail you now, Loki, and take
the rime-cold chalice
Full of ancient mead

heldr þú hana eina látir með ása sonum
vammalausa vera."

54.
"Ein þú værir, ef þú svá værir,

vör ok gröm at veri;
einn ek veit, svá at ek vita þykkjumk,
hór ok af Hlórriða,
ok var þat sá inn lævísi Loki."

Beyla kvað:
55.
"Fjöll öll skjalfa; hygg ek á för vera
heiman Hlórriða;
han ræðr ró, þeim er rægir hér

goð öll ok guma."

Loki kvað:
56.
"Þegi þú, Beyla, þú ert Byggvis kvæn
ok meini blandinn mjök,
ókynjan meira kom-a með ása sonum;
öll ertu, deigja, dritin."

Þá kom Þórr at ok kvað:
57.
"Þegi þú, rög vættr, þér skal minn þrúðhamarr,
Mjöllnir, mál fyrnema;
Herða klett drep ek þér halsi af,

Because her only you let off
among the sons of the Aesir
Without flaw."

(Loki said)
54.
"One you are, if you are such a one,
Wary and angry at the husband.
One I know, such a one I know, methinks,
A whore, and Hlorridi's,
And was that not to that treacherous Loki?"

Beyla said:
55.
"The fells are all shaking. I think, from his journey he is
Home, Hlorridi
He punishes him who defames here
All the gods and younglings."

Loki said:
56.
"Shut up, Beyla, you are Byggvir's wife
And blend much harm
More wonderless comes none among the sons of the Aesir
You are, dairy-maid, all dirty."

Then Thor arrived and he said:
57.
"Shut up, offensive wight, from you shall my power-hammer,
Mjollnir, take away the speech.
Your hard rock I beat from your neck

ok verðr þá þínu fjörvi of farit."	And then your life will be taken away."
Loki kvað: 58. "Jarðar burr er hér nú inn kominn, hví þrasir þú svá, Þórr? En þá þorir þú ekki, er þú skalt við ulfinn vega, ok svelgr hann allan Sigföður."	Loki said: 58. "Jord's child, who has come in here now Why do you quarrel so, Thor? But you will not quarrel when you fight with the Wolf And he will swallow all of Victory-Father."
Þórr kvað: 59. "Þegi þú, rög vættr, þér skal minn þrúðhamarr, Mjöllnir, mál fyrnema; upp ek þér verp ok á austrvega, síðan þik manngi sér."	Thor said: 59. "Shut up, offensive wight, from you shall my power-hammer, Mjollnir, take away the speech. Up I cast you and into the Ways of the East. Ever since no-one sees you."
Loki kvað: 60. "Austrförum þínum skaltu aldregi segja seggjum frá, síz í hanska þumlungi hnúkðir þú einheri, ok þóttisk-a þú þá Þórr vera."	Loki said: 60. "Your journeys of the East shall you never Tell a poet Since when you crouched in a glove's thumb, Einheri, And thought not yourself to be Thor then."
Þórr kvað: 61. "Þegi þú, rög vættr, þér skal minn þrúðhamarr, Mjöllnir, mál fyrnema; hendi inni hægri drep ek þik Hrungnis bana, svá at þér brotnar beina hvat."	Thor said: 61. "Shut up, offensive wight, from you shall my power-hammer, Mjollnir, take away the speech. With that right hand I beat you with Hrungnir's bane So that your every bone be broken."

Loki kvað:
62.
"Lifa ætla ek mér langan aldr,

þóttú hætir hamri mér;

skarpar álar þóttu þér Skrýmis vera,
ok máttir-a þú þá nesti ná,

ok svalzt þú þá hungri heill."

Þórr kvað:
63.
"Þegi þú, rög vættr, þér skal minn þrúðhamarr,
Mjöllnir, mál fyrnema;
Hrungnis bani mun þér í hel koma
fyr nágrindr neðan."

Loki kvað:
64.
"Kvað ek fyr ásum, kvað ek fyr ása sonum,
þats mik hvatti hugr,
en fyr þér einum mun ek út ganga,
því at ek veit, at þú vegr.

65.
Öl gerðir þú, Ægir, en þú aldri munt
síðan sumbl of gera;

eiga þín öll, er hér inni er,

leiki yfir logi,
ok brenni þér á baki."

Loki said:
62.
"Life, I suppose, (will last) a long time for me

Though you threaten me with the hammer

Sharp, you thought, were Skrymir's straps
And no might had you when approaching the victuals

And you starved from hunger, healthy."

Thor said:
63.
"Shut up, offensive wight, from you shall my power-hammer,
Mjollnir, take away the speech.
By Hrungnir's bane will you come into Hel
Beneath Nagrind."

Loki said:
64.
"I spoke to the Aesir. I spoke to the sons of the Aesir,
That which my mind urged me
But for you alone will I go away
Because I know that you fight.

65.
Ale you made, Aegir, but you will never
Since (today) make another symbel

All of your possessions, which are in here,
The fire will lick
And burn you on the back."

Cabinet de Curiosités

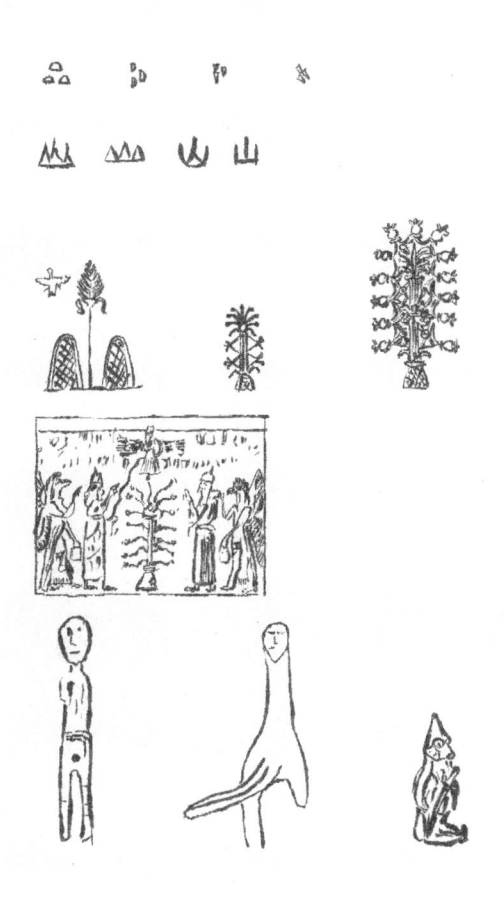

1. KUR *'mountain', evolution from pictograph to cuneiform sign*
2. shan *'mountain', evolution from pictograph to Chinese character*
3. *Sumerian Tree of Life, detail from a tablet from Shulgi period*
4. *Late Assyrian Tree of Life*
5. *Late Assyrian Tree of Life*
6. *Neo-Assyrian cylinder seal, depicting Tree of Life*
7. *Dagenham idol, 2250BCE, Dagenham, Britain*
8. *Broddenbjerg idol, 535-520BCE, Viborg, Denmark*
9. *Frey figurine, 11th century CE, Rällinge, Sweden*

1. *Tyr initiate flanked by two shapeshifters, Öland die, 7th century, Torslunda Denmark*
2. *Odin initiate and shapeshifter, Öland die, 7th century, Torslunda Denmark*
3. *Boar crest, 7th century, Benty Grange, Britain*
4. *Boar crest, Öland die, 7th century, Torslunda, Denmark*
5. *Raven crest, 7th century, Vendel, Sweden*
6. *Raven crest, 9th century, Vendel, Sweden*
7. *Darum bracteate,* **frohila laþu***, 5th-7th century, Darum, Denmark*

DOORS OF VALHALLA 341

1. Odin, Icelandic manuscript SÁM 66, 18th century
2. Thor, Icelandic manuscript, 1760
3. Trojaburg, Visburg, Sweden
4. Windelburg, Stolp, Pommern, Germany

1. *Matronae Aufaniae, votive altar, 150-250CE, Nettersheim, Germany*
2. *Matronae Aufaniae, votive altar, 164CE, Bonn, Germany*
3. Die drei Beten Ambeth, Wilbeth, Worbeth, *1420CE, Worms, Germany*
4. Die drei Beten Ainpet, Gberpet, Firpet, *1643CE, Starnberg, Germany*

DOORS OF VALHALLA

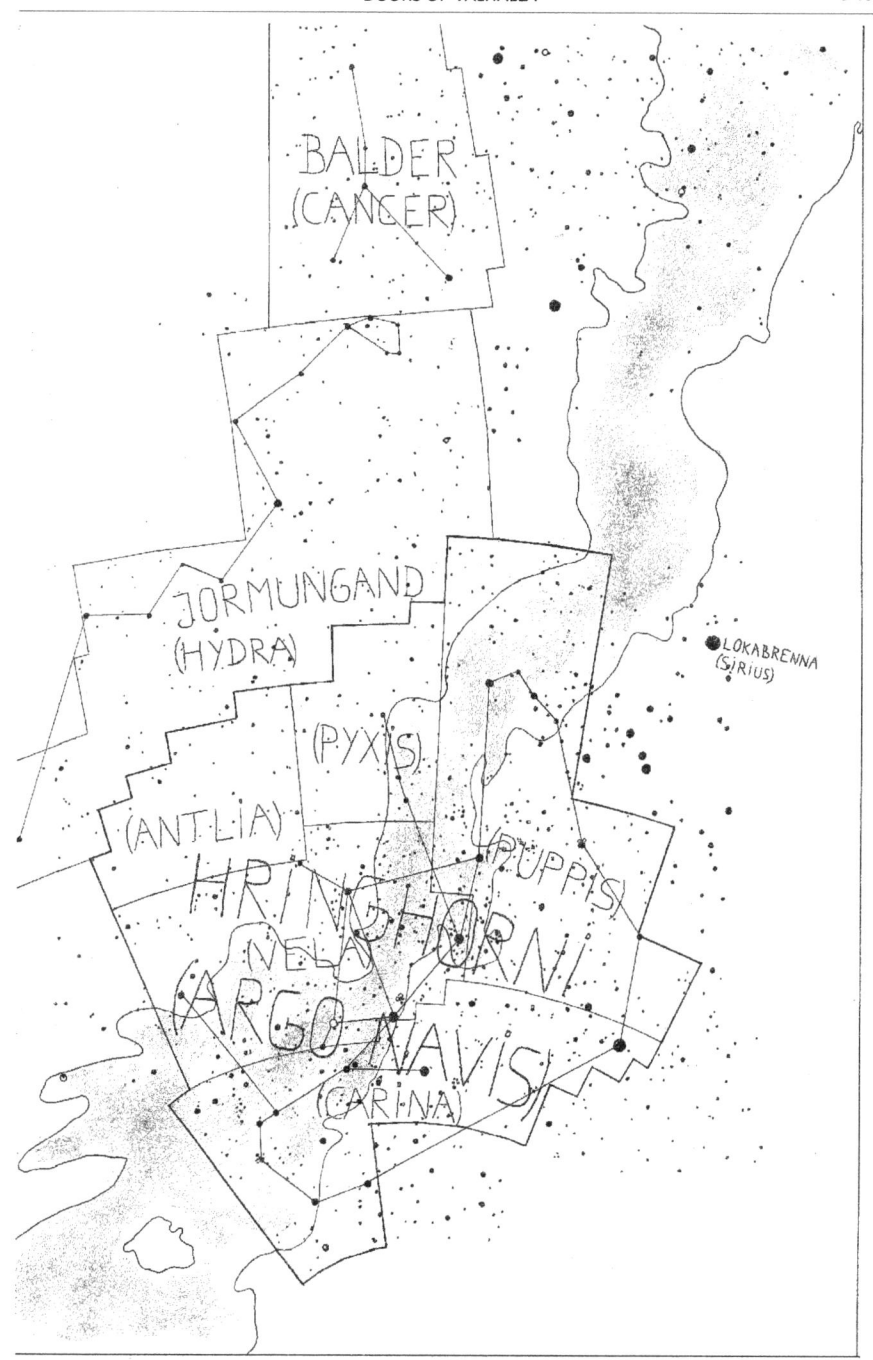

BALDER
(CANCER)

JORMUNGAND
(HYDRA)

●LOKABRENNA
(SIRIUS)

(PYXIS)

(ANTLIA)   (PUPPIS)

HRINGHORNI
(VELA)
(ARGO NAVIS)
(CARINA)

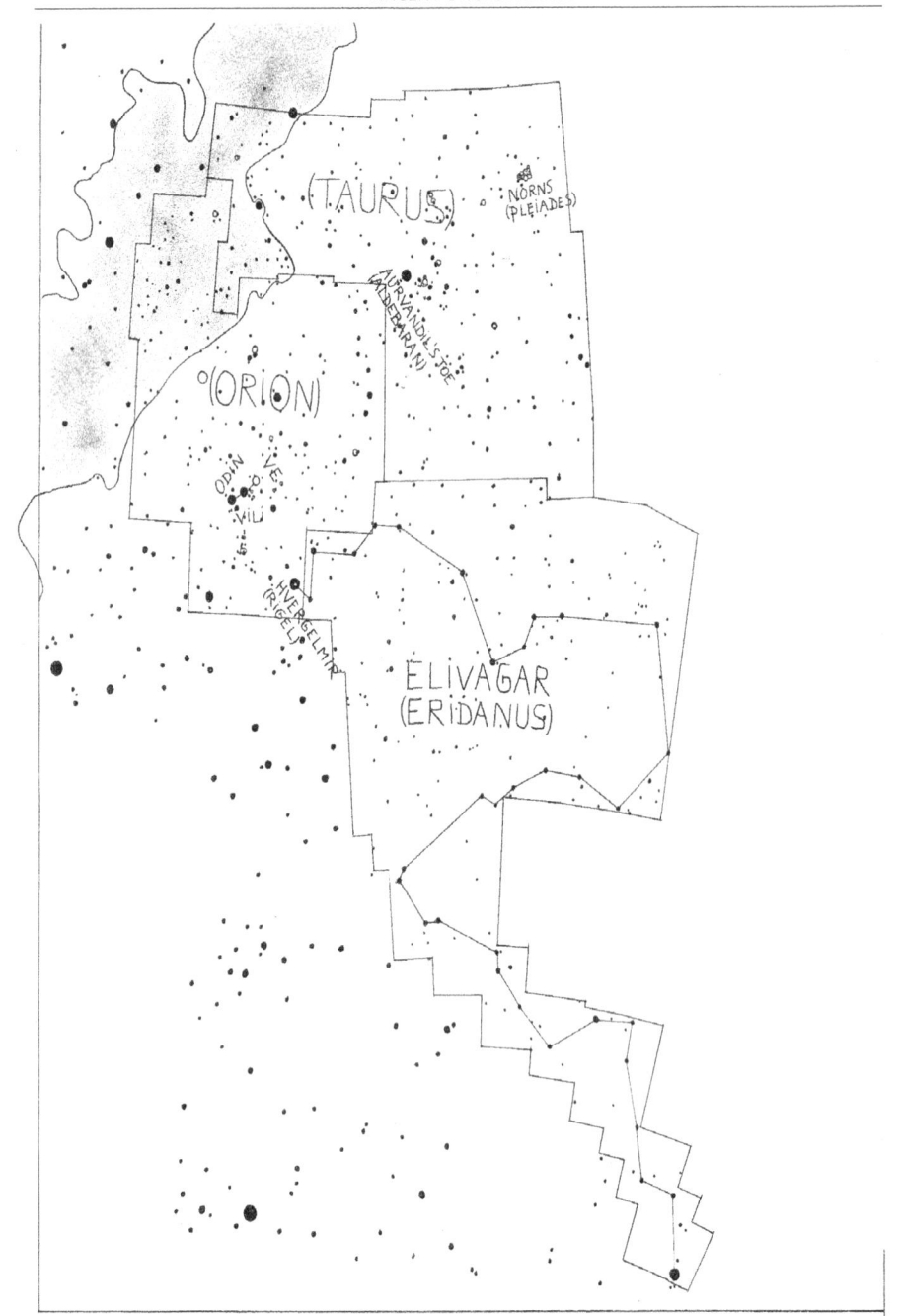

Index

Symbols

1/One 79, 207
2/Two 67, 56, 58, 79, 109, 119, 132, 140, 217, 225, 226, 229, 233, 257, 258
3/Three 22, 25, 31, 37, 38, 44, 49, 59, 60, 61, 62, 63, 64, 65, 75, 76, 77, 78, 79, 80, 87, 91, 92, 93, 98, 105, 107, 110, 111, 114, 119, 121, 123, 124, 125, 131, 140, 141, 143, 148, 149, 151, 155, 159, 160, 163, 167, 176, 180, 182, 183, 193, 199, 209, 211, 213, 216, 217, 220, 230, 238, 239, 247, 248, 258, 262, 282
4/Four 22, 31, 229, 269, 284
6/Six 195
7/Seven 22, 25, 31, 82, 221, 246, 247
8/Eight 260, 292
9/Nine 22, 24, 25, 65, 70, 99, 133, 148, 150, 158, 166, 184, 185, 194, 229, 230, 231, 241, 262
12/Twelve 36, 59, 126, 175, 216, 221, 245, 246, 247, 249, 251, 253, 76, 120, 125, 257, 260
13/Thirteen 195, 245
14/Fourteen 245, 250
15/Fifteen 260
25/Twenty five 260
49/Forty nine 22, 31
300/Three hundred 262

A

Abzu 164, 165
Adam 64
Aegir 102, 210, 223, 228, 229, 249, 256, 257, 258, 260, 261, 262, 263, 264, 265, 276, 288, 291
Aesir (passim)
Air 29, 188, 224
Aldebaran 220
Alfar/Elves. *See* Elves
Alfheim 30, 122, 211, 244
Ali 250
Alvissmal 149, 155, 193
Amazons 227
Andi 111, 239
Angel of the Presence 98
Anima 164, 169, 173, 183
Antahkarana 109
Antaios 222, 223, 224, 230
Apsu 56
Aquarius 233
Argo 225
Argr 271, 272
Aries 219
Artemis 224, 225, 229
Asgard 26, 29, 37, 44, 78, 81, 82, 84, 89, 98, 103, 105, 122, 125, 126, 148, 149, 151, 157, 161, 174, 207, 211, 226, 234, 236, 241, 257, 261, 264, 266, 277, 291
Ask 39, 61, 62, 64, 67, 77, 224, 237
Astral plane 20, 22, 23, 25, 28, 31, 36, 39, 73, 75, 80, 85, 90, 98, 105, 107, 112, 119, 121, 134, 185, 215, 223, 243, 246, 296
Aswynn, F. 113
Asynjur 142, 194, 195, 208, 250, 253, 255, 256, 257, 279, 286, 287
Atlas 222, 223
Atma 22, 23, 25

Atmic plane 24, 246
Audumla 236, 292
Aurvandil 220, 221, 222, 232
Avesta 162, 167

B

Bailey, A.A. 20, 22, 23, 24, 25, 31, 38, 89, 97, 215, 216, 218, 220, 221, 223, 226, 230, 231, 233, 234, 236, 240, 246, 247, 281, 297, 298, 301
Balder 34, 37, 42, 47, 48, 49, 50, 51, 52, 70, 86, 87, 88, 89, 90, 91, 98, 103, 104, 117, 196, 224, 225, 233, 235, 236, 240, 249, 250, 251, 252, 253, 260, 274, 275, 279, 288, 290, 291, 294, 297
Baldrs Draumar 44, 46, 47, 93, 128, 235
Barbet 143
Baugi 148, 151, 152, 156, 158, 182
Berkana 40, 208
Besant, A. 20, 297
Beten, die 143
Beyla 258, 259, 260, 284, 285, 286, 287
Biðja 45
Bifrost 35, 37, 43, 78, 121, 149
Billing 176, 178, 179, 190, 191
Black 132, 136, 202, 248
Blavatsky, H.P. 20, 22, 23
Blóta 45
Blue 37, 135, 136, 204
Bodn 148, 155, 156
Bolthorn 166, 184, 239
Bolverk 126, 132, 139, 140, 147, 148, 150, 153, 181, 212
Bönd 149, 203, 288, 289
Bor 123
Bragi 131, 150, 250, 251, 252, 253, 256, 257, 258, 259, 260, 266, 267, 268, 272, 281, 288, 290, 293, 294
Brisingamen 35, 194, 208, 227, 269, 286, 289

Brynhild 46
Buddha 241
Buddhi 22, 25
Buddhic plane 22, 30, 168, 170, 207, 246, 263
Bur 50, 55, 58, 59, 74, 111, 123, 236, 241
Buri 123
Byggvir 258, 259, 260, 277, 278, 280, 281, 282, 284, 288, 294

C

Cancer 224, 225, 233
Capricorn 172, 224, 225, 232
Causal plane 22, 23, 24, 29, 52, 78, 109, 297
Cherubim 35
Christ 32, 235, 236, 237, 238, 240
Christianity/Christian 33, 40, 111, 135, 153, 156, 204, 206, 238, 239, 270
Cock 45, 46, 49, 87, 91, 92, 155
Conn 160
Crowley, A. 30, 297
Cup 67, 145, 158, 170, 194, 234

D

Dao 57
Dao De Jing 57
Deva evolution 61, 246, 247, 248
Diana 200
Disir 150, 196
Draupnir 34
Dream 41, 42, 43, 51, 65, 71, 232, 274, 296
Dwarves 27, 28, 35, 36, 50, 58, 60, 61, 68, 69, 76, 96, 97, 106, 140, 147, 148, 149, 154, 155, 247, 248, 269
Dweller on the Threshold 97, 98, 164, 233, 280, 291, 295

E

Eggther 46, 91
Egilssaga Einhenda ok Asmundar Berserkjabana 201
Eihwaz 39, 86

Einherjar 43, 45, 94, 185, 193, 195, 198, 199, 200, 201, 202, 203, 207, 208, 212, 285, 298
Eir 194, 195
Eldhrimnir 199
Eldir 258, 259, 260, 263, 264, 265, 288, 290
Elemental evolution 61, 246, 248
Elivagar 120, 220, 221
Elves 30, 43, 96, 106, 211, 233, 238, 239, 244, 246, 247, 258, 260, 263, 266, 279, 287, 288, 289
Embla 39, 61, 64, 67, 77, 224
Emotional plane 21, 22, 24, 25, 26, 39, 53, 75, 92, 95, 103, 112, 114, 118, 215, 229, 237, 244, 247, 248, 263, 284, 286
Enki 164, 165
Enuma Elish 56, 57
Eridanus 221
Erilaz 160, 178, 204
Etana 165
Etheric plane 22, 23, 24, 25, 26, 27, 28, 30, 61, 95, 113, 215, 243, 247
Eyrbyggjasaga 135

F

Fehu 60, 67, 278
Fenrir 36, 94, 99, 100, 121, 232, 233, 238, 256, 257, 258, 260, 280, 281, 285, 292, 294
Fensalir 44, 87
Fimafeng 258, 260, 264, 265, 288, 291
Fimbulvetr 117, 119
Fire 30, 32, 35, 37, 71, 101, 102, 120, 121, 163, 164, 215, 237, 263, 299
Fjalar 91, 92, 146, 147, 154, 155, 166
Fjolnir 126, 138, 140, 155, 210
Fjolsvin 126, 138, 159, 265
Fjolsvinnsmal 158, 164, 172, 194, 198, 200
Folkvang 208
Forseti 250, 251, 252, 253
Fortune, D. 20, 22, 24, 31, 32, 38, 39, 297
Franang 229
Fregna 46
Freista 44, 45, 46, 148, 181, 187, 189
Freki 94
Frey 30, 35, 37, 98, 100, 101, 158, 173, 187, 209, 210, 211, 212, 234, 244, 247, 249, 250, 251, 252, 253, 256, 257, 258, 259, 260, 269, 276, 277, 278, 279, 280, 281, 284, 287, 290, 292, 294, 299
Freyja 34, 37, 45, 46, 53, 67, 80, 84, 86, 108, 143, 158, 159, 165, 168, 194, 195, 196, 197, 199, 200, 207, 208, 209, 210, 212, 213, 227, 251, 252, 253, 255, 256, 257, 258, 259, 260, 269, 274, 275, 276, 286, 287, 289, 290, 292, 293, 298, 299
Frigg 30, 34, 42, 44, 53, 87, 98, 99, 125, 142, 143, 187, 194, 195, 208, 209, 212, 252, 253, 255, 256, 257, 258, 259, 260, 273, 274, 275, 276, 277, 279, 286, 287, 288, 291
Frodi 142, 166, 212
Fulla 143, 194, 195, 253, 255
Futhark 40, 185
Fylgja 135

G

Gabriel (angel) 274
Galar 147, 155
Galdr 40, 132, 135, 137, 155, 185, 197
Gambanteinn 190
Gangleri 126, 131, 140, 203, 212
Garm 49, 50, 91, 93, 94, 95, 232

Garuda 163, 165
Geð 25
Gefjun/Gefjon 194, 195, 200, 252, 253, 255, 257, 259, 260, 268, 269, 271, 287, 288, 290
Geirrod 127, 131, 133, 212, 233, 234, 235
Gemini 217, 224
Gerd 35, 163, 173, 190, 210, 253, 278, 279
Gesta Danorum 125, 196, 202, 220
Gestathattr 176, 179, 180
Gilgamesh 162, 163, 164, 165, 183, 205
Gilling 148
Gimlé 104, 105
Ginn 50, 55, 57, 59, 60, 66, 71, 120, 121, 139
Ginnungagap 30, 31, 37, 50, 55, 56, 59, 70, 71, 120, 139, 236, 299
Gjallarhorn 42, 43, 94
Gladsheim 105, 299
Glamour 73, 98, 106, 115, 168, 214, 220, 221, 223, 229, 235, 278
Gneisti 30
Gnipahellir 93
Grammaticus, S. 125, 189, 205, 220
Green 38, 55, 62, 102, 189
Grettissaga 201
Grid 196, 197, 201, 234, 285
Grimnir 126, 127, 131, 132, 135, 136, 140, 212
Grimnismal 44, 88, 125, 126, 131, 132, 133, 136, 137, 138, 164, 186, 193, 194, 195, 202, 203, 208, 210, 212, 249, 251, 252
Groa 45, 221, 232
Grogaldr 45, 158
Gullinkambi 48, 91, 92, 94, 95, 201
Gullveig 51, 53, 65, 66, 67, 68, 80, 81, 82, 83, 107, 199
Gungnir 32, 35, 196, 215
Gunnlod 139, 146, 147, 148, 150, 151, 152, 153, 155, 156, 157, 158, 160, 161, 165, 171, 176, 178, 179, 180, 181, 182, 184, 190, 193, 198, 199, 210, 212, 239, 240, 241, 270, 278
Gurdjieff, G.I. 25, 168
Gýgr 46, 91
Gylfaginning 30, 37, 42, 55, 109, 110, 123, 126, 141, 174, 195, 203, 208, 210, 212, 237, 249, 250, 251, 253, 294
Gylfi 123, 131, 181, 212
Gymir 210, 235, 257, 258, 261

H

Hades 232
Haft 129, 149, 150
Hagalaz 115
Halfdanar Thattr Svarta 201
Hamingja 161
Hamr 25, 134, 209
Haoma 162
Hapt 129, 203
Harbardsljod 137, 155, 189, 191
Haustlong 255
Havamal 45, 110, 133, 135, 136, 140, 145, 146, 149, 150, 151, 152, 153, 155, 156, 157, 159, 160, 161, 163, 166, 168, 170, 171, 175, 176, 177, 178, 179, 180, 181, 182, 183, 184, 185, 186, 190, 195, 202, 237, 239, 266, 267, 282
Heidrun 199
Heimdal 33, 34, 35, 37, 42, 49, 91, 94, 95, 98, 160, 182, 183, 213, 216, 241, 250, 251, 252, 253, 259, 260, 269, 279, 282, 288, 289, 290, 298
Heimskringla 125, 154, 211, 303
Hel (goddess) 26, 208, 237. *See also* Hella
Hel (world) 45, 46, 47, 89, 92, 233, 240, 279. *See also* Helheim

Helgakvida Hundingsbana hin fyrri 141, 194, 272
Helgakvida Hundingsbana onnur 206
Helheim 26, 27, 37
Helios 172, 173, 234
Hella 26, 93, 143, 204, 208, 212, 213
Helreid Brynhildar 46, 47
Hera 220, 227
Herakles 205, 216, 217, 218, 219, 220, 222, 223, 224, 225, 226, 227, 228, 229, 231, 232, 233, 234, 235, 241
Hermod 233, 250, 253
Hesperides 218, 222
Hippolyta 227
Hlebard 189, 217
Hlidskjalf 136, 140, 187, 188, 210
Hnitbjorg 132, 148, 153, 163, 172, 181
Hoder 86, 89, 103, 104, 196, 225, 250, 251, 253, 294
Hoenir 62, 76, 77, 104, 105, 110, 123, 124, 126, 250, 251, 253
Horus 34
Hringhorni 225
Hrolfssaga Kraka 202
Hroptr 103, 128, 129, 136
Hrungnir 200, 225, 226, 231, 284
Hrym 96, 98
Hugin 188
Hugr 25, 291
Hvergelmir (well) 222
Hymir 223, 231
Hymiskvida 36, 87, 156, 158, 223, 231, 235, 261
Hyndla 45, 46, 158
Hyndluljod 45, 46, 158, 168

I

Idavoll 58, 60, 102
Idun 124, 143, 156, 157, 209, 223, 252, 253, 255, 256, 257, 258, 259, 260, 267, 268, 278, 286
Ilias 174
Ilion 174
Illugasaga Gridarfostra 201
Illusion 28, 85, 98, 168, 219, 220, 230, 231, 233, 278
Inana 165
Indigo 38
Inguz 211
Initiation 51, 70, 71, 87, 89, 107, 145, 157, 158, 161, 169, 170, 178, 181, 182, 183, 184, 185, 204, 214, 215, 216, 235, 236, 237, 238, 240, 282, 294, 297
Islendingabok 135

J

Jesus 33, 236, 237, 238, 239, 241, 245
Jord 61, 95, 102, 113, 161, 210, 217, 246, 253, 292
Jormungand 77, 96, 99, 100, 101, 103, 121, 215, 223, 224, 229, 230, 231, 232, 238, 285
Jotunheim 26, 28, 60, 61, 68, 84, 92, 96, 148, 153, 155, 157, 172, 179, 187, 191, 209, 210, 217, 219, 227, 234, 235, 285, 293
Jötunn 39, 45, 46, 66, 71, 94, 96, 114, 127, 146, 148, 156, 158, 172, 177, 187, 189, 248
Jupiter 193

K

Kama 22, 23
Karma 64, 79, 116, 141, 233
Kerberos 218, 232
Kerlaug 149, 217
Ketilssaga Haengs 201
Kon 160, 183
Kvasir 33, 67, 90, 147, 149, 153, 154, 155, 162, 229

L

Law of Attraction 169, 192, 220
Law of Cause and Effect 19, 80
Law of Cycles 58
Law of Evolution 17

Law of Karma 17, 52
Law of Sacrifice 90, 273, 280, 282, 289
Law of Seven 25
Law of Three 25
Libra 228, 229
Ljóð 178, 185
Ljodatal 177, 178, 180, 189
Loddfafnir 176, 178, 180, 183
Loddfafnismal 176, 178, 180
Lodur 62, 76, 77, 105, 110, 112, 113, 123, 124, 126
Logoic plane 24, 246
Logos 24, 57, 246
Loka Tattur 124
Lokasenna 87, 90, 98, 123, 124, 125, 137, 214, 228, 229, 235, 244, 249, 250, 251, 252, 255, 256, 257, 258, 260, 272, 277, 279, 287, 289, 291, 292
Loki 33, 88, 89, 90, 91, 97, 98, 124, 157, 208, 209, 219, 225, 228, 229, 233, 235, 237, 245, 250, 251, 253, 256, 257, 258, 259, 260, 290, 291, 292, 293, 294, 295
Loki of Utgard 155, 219, 231
Lugh 161
Lunar Lords 97

M

Magni 217, 279
Mál 111, 112, 113, 176, 177
Manas 22, 23, 25
Mannaz 22, 34, 211
Marduk 57
Mars 218, 244
Mary 236
Masters of Wisdom 30, 63, 193, 245, 281
Matronae 140, 141, 142, 143, 200, 213
Maya 98, 106, 115. See also Illusion
Meditation 21, 26, 27, 52, 60, 65, 69, 97, 122, 124, 170, 187, 215, 242, 263, 265

Menglod 158, 159, 164, 194, 200, 201
Mental plane 18, 20, 21, 22, 24, 25, 26, 28, 29, 30, 36, 40, 41, 52, 53, 60, 72, 73, 75, 78, 80, 84, 92, 94, 95, 97, 103, 105, 107, 109, 112, 114, 116, 118, 119, 120, 121, 156, 170, 188, 189, 218, 232, 236, 237, 238, 243, 244, 246, 247, 248, 263, 288, 296
Michael (angel) 39
Midgard 26, 28, 29, 37, 50, 51, 55, 56, 57, 58, 72, 74, 78, 99, 101, 118, 119, 120, 121, 161, 174, 222, 241, 247, 284
Midsummer 49, 225
Midwinter 172, 206, 236
Milky Way 225
Mimir 18, 33, 37, 42, 45, 95, 96, 118, 130, 186, 187, 238, 239, 241
Mimir (well) 46, 186
Minnisöl 46, 158, 168, 186
Minnisveig 168
Mjolnir 32, 205, 209, 227, 231
Modi 217, 279
Monadic plane 30
Moon 48, 55, 56, 57, 72
Munin 188
Muspelheim 30, 31, 32, 37, 57, 71, 119
Mystery schools 19, 123, 142, 160, 162, 167, 170, 182, 184, 185, 201, 203, 205, 206, 207, 213, 287, 297

N

Nanna 196, 233, 253
Narfi 260, 294
Nari 260, 294
Nauthiz 142
Nereus 223, 224
Nidafjoll 106
Nidhogg 106, 107, 115
Niflheim 26, 27, 28, 31, 37, 71,

119, 121, 221
Niflhel 44
Nine Worlds 21, 22, 25, 26, 31, 41, 43, 65, 68, 136, 137, 292, 299
Ninurta 164
Njalssaga 135, 136
Njord 34, 158, 210, 249, 250, 251, 252, 253, 256, 257, 258, 259, 260, 268, 276, 277, 279, 288, 291, 292
Nornagests Thattr 141, 202
Norns 18, 33, 44, 63, 64, 65, 79, 110, 121, 122, 141, 142, 143, 153, 185, 193, 202, 209, 213, 237, 241, 269, 287, 299
Nótt 294
Nous 22, 111
Nun (god) 56

O

Od 66, 84, 123, 124, 125, 156, 207, 208, 209
Oddrunargrattr 208
Oddyseus 173
Odin 32–33, 50–51, 72, 76–77, 81, 83, 92–93, 100, 101, 103, 105, 110, 117–123, 118, 147, 148, 149, 150, 151, 152, 152–153, 153, 154, 155, 156, 157, 158, 159, 164, 165, 166, 171, 172, 177, 181, 182, 183, 184, 186, 187, 188, 189, 190, 191, 192, 193, 199, 201, 202, 203, 207, 208, 209, 210, 211, 212, 215, 216, 217, 218, 235, 236, 237, 238, 239, 240, 241, 245, 249, 250, 251, 252, 253, 256, 257, 258, 259, 260, 262, 270, 271, 272, 273, 275, 278, 279, 285, 287, 288, 290
Óðr 63, 105, 109, 110, 111, 112, 113, 124, 156, 167
Odrerir 33, 112, 146, 148, 149, 150, 153, 155, 156, 166, 167, 171, 180, 186, 207
Odysseia 173, 174
Önd 22, 109, 110, 111, 239
Ophiuchus 231
Orange 38
Orion 237
Örlög 44, 58, 61, 62, 63, 77, 79, 80, 86, 109, 114, 141, 269, 273, 274, 287, 292
Orms Thattr Storolfssonar 201
Örvar Oddssaga 201
Ottar 45, 158, 168

P

Path of Discipleship 214, 216, 218
Path of Evulotion 235
Path of Initiation 87, 89, 172, 215, 216, 231
Path of Probation 70, 87, 89, 92, 117, 214, 216
Persona 73, 76, 293
Physical plane 22, 23, 24, 25, 26, 27, 28, 33, 57, 63, 74, 78, 79, 80, 95, 97, 105, 109, 236, 243
Pisces 193, 235
Pleiades 220, 221
Pluto 263
Poison 84, 85, 100, 115, 295
Prana 23, 28
Prometheus 222, 223, 224
Purification 35, 61, 85, 101, 116, 121, 215, 233, 237, 263, 268, 291, 295, 296
Purusha 56, 57

Q

Qabbalah 25, 163, 244

R

Ragnarok 32, 42, 49, 50, 52, 55, 69, 70, 71, 87, 91, 93, 94, 97, 98, 100, 101, 103, 104, 107, 108, 116, 117, 118, 121, 128, 201, 214, 215, 231, 232, 240, 257, 279, 285

Ran 253, 258, 262
Rati 146, 148, 151
Ray 24, 31, 37, 38, 114
  Aspect 25, 31, 37, 38, 39
  Attribute 31, 39
  Celtic 39
  Seven 24, 31, 192, 247
  Norse 39
Ray I 31, 32, 36, 37, 38, 110, 111, 113, 124, 246
Ray II 31, 32, 33, 35, 37, 110, 112, 124, 193, 212, 246
Ray III 31, 33, 34, 37, 40, 110, 124, 246
Ray IV 31, 33, 34, 39, 112
Ray V 31, 34, 35
Ray VI 31, 35, 38, 112, 281
Ray VII 31, 36, 113
Red 36, 37, 48, 91, 198, 199, 204
Regin 50, 55, 58, 59, 60, 61, 66, 72, 74, 75, 76, 78, 83, 85, 94, 107, 108, 139, 244, 276, 288, 289
Regin (dwarf) 167
Reginsmal 124, 202
Rig Veda 56, 57, 163
Rigel 222
Rigsthula 35, 158, 160, 161, 182, 183, 184, 213, 282
Rind 189, 253
Ring Pass Not 77, 101, 215
Ray I 31
Rooster 48. *See also* Cock/Rooster
Runatal 177, 180
Runes 22, 40, 64, 102, 103, 129, 140, 160, 171, 177, 182, 183, 184, 185, 190, 204, 238, 299

S

Sacrifice 34, 36, 43, 45, 57, 68, 88, 89, 90, 91, 100, 101, 120, 149, 153, 171, 186, 214, 219, 220, 238, 239, 241, 261, 278, 280
Sadko 261, 262
Saga 44, 186, 194, 195, 251, 252, 253
Sagittarius 193
Samsara/Wheel of Life 216, 281
Scorpio 229, 230
Seiðr 39, 46, 67, 132, 137, 164, 185, 197, 206, 209, 271, 272
Serpens 231
Service 59, 91, 193, 215, 217, 223, 233, 238, 240, 265, 282
Sessrumnir 208
Shadow, Jungian 73, 81, 294
Shapeshifting 33, 134, 137, 138, 147, 148, 151, 157, 163, 165, 166, 167, 169, 170, 205, 209, 223, 229, 241, 286, 293, 294
Shiva 32
Sía 30
Siduri 163, 164, 183
Sif 189, 217, 252, 253, 255, 256, 257, 258, 259, 260, 283, 286, 287
Sigr 104, 128, 279, 295
Sigrdrifa 142, 164, 168, 183, 193, 197
Sigrdrifumal 164, 168, 170, 182, 183, 184, 185, 187, 201, 238
Sigtoftir 103, 104
Sigurd 142, 167, 168, 183, 184, 193
Sigyn 90, 253, 258, 260, 294, 295
Sirius 237
Skadi 90, 91, 157, 229, 251, 252, 253, 255, 256, 257, 258, 259, 260, 276, 283, 286, 287, 290, 291, 292
Skaldskaparmal 124, 142, 165, 209, 234, 249, 250, 251, 252, 253, 255, 257, 258
Skidbladnir 210
Skirnir 158, 163, 173, 190, 234, 265, 297
Skirnismal 87, 155, 156, 158, 163, 173, 210, 211
Skrymir 155, 220, 285
Skuld 18, 37, 62, 141, 142, 196, 198

Sleipnir 47, 158, 211, 292
Sóa 153
Sokkvabekk 44, 187, 194
Sól (goddess) 57, 253
Soma 162, 163, 164, 167
Són (cauldron) 148, 153, 155, 156
Són (ritual) 153, 199
Sorla Thattr 197, 208, 293
Spá 51, 67, 117, 141
Spiritual Hierarchy 30, 52, 224
Steiner, R. 24, 25
Sturluson, S. 27, 30, 42, 83, 94, 109, 111, 112, 113, 123, 124, 125, 126, 135, 141, 142, 145, 149, 150, 151, 152, 154, 156, 162, 166, 181, 194, 195, 198, 212, 221, 245, 249, 250, 251, 252, 253, 255, 257, 258, 261, 294
Sun 24, 32, 46, 48, 54, 55, 56, 57, 72, 97, 99, 101, 104, 105, 115, 120, 122, 130, 138, 139, 163, 172, 190, 222, 224, 230, 233, 236, 245, 298
Sunna 195
Surt 32, 98, 99, 101, 121, 215, 299
Sutratma 109
Suttung 129, 139, 146, 147, 148, 149, 150, 152, 153, 154, 155, 156, 157, 158, 161, 171, 179, 181, 182, 190, 191, 195, 239
Svartalfheim 26, 28
Svipdag 45, 139, 158, 297
Svipdagsmal 158, 159
Symbel 147, 149, 181, 266
Symplegades 172, 173

T

Tacitus 211
Taurus 219, 220, 222
Teiwaz 36, 128
Thelema 31
Thjalfi 219, 226
Thjazi 157, 268, 290, 291
Thor 32, 34, 36, 37, 39, 45, 75, 84, 85, 86, 90, 100, 101, 158, 161, 189, 191, 192, 201, 205, 206, 209, 215, 216, 217, 219, 220, 221, 223, 224, 225, 226, 227, 228, 229, 230, 231, 233, 234, 235, 249, 250, 251, 252, 253, 256, 257, 258, 259, 260, 284, 285, 287, 288
Thorsdrapa 201
Thought-form 29, 36, 72, 73, 79, 82, 106, 111, 119, 120, 121, 122, 218, 219, 246, 292, 297
Thrud 195, 196, 217, 253
Thrudvangar 219
Thrym 227, 228
Thrymheim 157
Thrymskvida 209, 227, 228, 231, 235, 286, 292
Þulr 133, 136, 137, 177, 181, 266
Thurisaz 60, 147, 155, 158
Tiamat 56, 57
Tivar 104, 244, 279, 288
Tree of Life 25, 64, 79, 159, 298
Troy 172, 173, 174, 175, 184, 221
Tyr 36, 94, 128, 129, 216, 223, 224, 231, 232, 249, 250, 251, 252, 253, 256, 257, 258, 259, 260, 277, 278, 279, 280, 288, 289, 292

U

Ull 125, 250, 251, 252, 253
Urd 18, 37, 44, 62, 141
Urd (well) 43, 44, 79, 177, 217, 296, 298
Utgard 28, 37, 77, 219, 230, 231, 235

V

Vafthrudnir 135, 171, 187, 212, 265
Vafthrudnismal 171, 181, 186, 187
Valgaldr 44
Valhalla 78, 87, 92, 104, 105, 123,

147, 153, 158, 174, 177, 181, 193, 199, 201, 202, 207, 208, 214, 215, 247, 266, 294, 295, 299
Vali 89, 250, 251, 252, 253, 294
Valkyrja 18, 141, 142, 143, 168, 183, 184, 185, 193, 194, 195, 196, 197, 198, 200, 201, 202, 206, 207, 209, 212, 213, 227, 268, 295, 298, 299
Valr 104, 128, 279
Vanaheim 26, 122
Vanir 30, 34, 50, 53, 66, 67, 68, 80, 81, 82, 83, 84, 96, 98, 99, 106, 147, 150, 153, 154, 196, 210, 234, 238, 244, 246, 247, 276, 278, 279, 287, 289
Vé 37, 118, 123, 124, 125, 126, 141, 213
Venus 244
Verdandi 18, 37, 62, 141
Vidar 35, 36, 37, 94, 99, 100, 215, 250, 251, 252, 253, 256, 257, 258, 259, 260, 273, 275, 279, 289
Vigrid 98
Vili 32, 37, 118, 123, 124, 125, 126, 141, 143, 174, 187, 213
Vimur 233, 234
Vindheim 104, 105
Vingolf 208
Violet 38
Virgo 227, 228, 236
Volsungasaga 184, 187, 188, 273
Volund 157, 205
Volundarkvida 156, 157, 171, 205
Voluspa 41, 42, 43, 44, 45, 46, 47, 48, 50, 51, 53, 54, 55, 57, 58, 60, 61, 63, 65, 67, 68, 70, 71, 72, 73, 74, 75, 83, 86, 87, 90, 91, 93, 94, 96, 99, 101, 102, 103, 104, 106, 107, 109, 110, 111, 112, 114, 115, 117, 119, 123, 124, 141, 147, 154,
155, 186, 188, 195, 196, 198, 199, 209, 237, 244, 289, 295
Voluspa hin Skamma 46, 292
Volva 42, 43, 44, 45, 46, 47, 48, 49, 50, 51, 52, 53, 66, 67, 117, 118, 141, 142, 187, 201, 202, 206, 213, 221, 271, 272, 287

W

War, Aesir Vanir 33, 34, 50, 51, 53, 55, 65, 66, 67, 68, 69, 70, 80, 147, 153, 173, 234
Water 28, 43, 63, 67, 71, 98, 101, 121, 229, 237
White 35, 62, 192, 202, 233, 237, 269, 298
Wilbet 143
Wild Host 132, 134, 201, 206
Wild Hunt 132, 134, 188, 201, 203, 204, 206, 207, 211, 212
World Tree 26, 47, 64, 65, 121
Wunjo 60, 104, 271
Wyrd 64

Y

Yellow 37
Yggdrasil 21, 25, 29, 43, 62, 63, 64, 79, 80, 94, 106, 133, 158, 170, 171, 172, 184, 186, 237, 239, 241, 282, 298
Ymir 27, 46, 55, 56, 57, 61, 71, 72, 78, 120, 236
Ynglingasaga 134, 137, 139, 154, 210, 212
Yule 172, 205, 206, 211, 221

Z

Zeus 188, 193, 217

Secrets of Asgard
By Vincent Ongkowidjojo
Foreword by David Beth,
Introduction Freya Aswynn
ISBN **978-1-906958-31-2**,
£12.99/$23 circa 280pp, ills.

A thesis of practical rune magic is developed which is based on the *Havamal* 144 stanza. The analysis concludes that the Runes were traditionally regarded as actual spirits. The stanza explains how to make your own set as well as other talismanic objects. The practice of *galdr*-singing is discussed in more depth to complement the *Havamal* 144 techniques. Then, a discourse is given on the most common Ancient Germanic magical formulae. They complement the practical work on talismanic objects.

A separate chapter is given on divinatory practices. Useful information on dreamwork is added and numerous other exercises used to make contact with the subconscious mind through auto-suggestion, and many other useful ritual techniques and practices. Part one centres on the meaning of the individual runes, explaining the Aettir in considerable detail. The second part centres on the application of the system, namely magic and divination and includes rituals and exercises.